Images of Modern America

Hampton and Hampton Beach

FRONT COVER: Friends set up a volleyball net on the beach next to the Seashell Complex in the early 1980s. (Hampton Historical Society; see page 14)

UPPER BACK COVER: This photograph, taken in 1998, shows a typical summer day at Hampton Beach. (Hampton Historical Society; see page 11)

LOWER BACK COVER (from left to right): This aerial view of Hampton Beach looks south, with the Hampton River and the Hampton-Seabrook Marsh visible (Hampton Beach Area Chamber of Commerce; see page 12), Glyn Eastman is delivering newspapers for Colt News (Hampton Historical Society; see page 75), veterans and servicemen are pictured at a Memorial Day ceremony in front of the New Hampshire Marine Memorial in 1997 (Hampton Historical Society; see page 63)

Images of Modern America

HAMPTON AND HAMPTON BEACH

GRACE C. LYONS

ARCADIA PUBLISHING

ISBN 978-1-4671-1663-3

Published by Arcadia Publishing
Charleston, South Carolina

Printed in the United States of America

Library of Congress Control Number: 2015955959

For all general information, please contact Arcadia Publishing:
Telephone 843-853-2070
Fax 843-853-0044
E-mail sales@arcadiapublishing.com
For customer service and orders:
Toll-Free 1-888-313-2665

Visit us on the Internet at www.arcadiapublishing.com

To Johanna, who inspires me to follow my dreams and challenges me to grow in every aspect of my life.

Contents

ACKNOWLEDGMENTS

I would like to give special thanks to Betty Moore and Candy Stellmach at the Hampton Historical Society, without whose help and guidance this book would not have been possible. I would also like to give special thanks to Johanna Lyons, who provided not only pictures and references but also day-to-day guidance. Many thanks go to the Hampton Historical Society (HHS), New Hampshire Department of Resources and Economic Development (DRED), and the Hampton Beach Area Chamber of Commerce (HCC) for the use of their images.

INTRODUCTION

Hampton Beach was one of the earliest places in New England visited solely for recreation and relaxation. New Hampshire has less than 20 miles of coastline, yet Hampton Beach became known as the "summer playground of all New England." Since its soaring popularity began over 150 years ago, the town has been a melting pot of cultures, shared histories, and collective experiences.

When Rev. Stephen Bachiler and a group of English colonists first arrived in what is now Hampton in 1638, they learned that the area had been called Winnacunnet, an Algonquian word meaning "Beautiful Place of Pines," by the Abenaki Native Americans who lived on the land. Just one year after settlement, the area was renamed Hampton. The settlers used the land and beach primarily for farming and fishing. Fishing in particular was a seasonal occupation, and many of the fishermen did not permanently live on the coast. Instead, local businessmen built living quarters along the beachfront for the fishermen to rent during the fishing season. At the beginning of the 19th century, and especially at the start of the industrial revolution, the fishing business declined, new factory jobs were in abundance, and people's leisure time increased. In response, many of the beachfront landlords transformed their lodgings into comfortable hotels for visiting tourists. There were few hotels on what would later be called Ocean Boulevard or in town; most were located on Great Boar's Head, just north of the beach. Around the turn of the 20th century, Hampton's leaders realized that the beachfront was not equipped to function as the popular tourist destination that it was rapidly becoming. In response, the town agreed to a 99-year lease that transferred rights to development of the beach to the Hampton Beach Improvement Company (HBIC) in 1898. One of the HBIC's first actions was to move the center of beach activity from Great Boar's Head to Hampton Beach proper, where the modern community is centered.

Just one year later, in 1899, a New England businessman named Wallace D. Lovell built the Hampton Beach Casino at the new center of Hampton Beach with the hope that it would become an attraction itself. The Casino received its name not because it was a house of gambling but because it was a place of social gathering, which also fit the definition of a "casino" at the time. The HBIC then built the Hampton Beach Bandstand across the street in 1901 and the boardwalk a few years later. A trolley system was also created with a stop right between the bandstand and the Casino, which allowed people from neighboring towns to easily reach Hampton Beach. It was not long before automobiles were the preferred form of transportation and parking dominated the beach side of Ocean Boulevard.

The HBIC continued in its work, but the sandy beach itself was becoming financially burdensome to Hampton. Vast development was quickly deteriorating the sand dunes that naturally protected the beach and the community just behind it. In 1933, the State of New Hampshire acquired the beach, and Hampton Beach State Park was established. The state assumed maintenance of the whole beach, which included the area just south of Great Boar's Head south to the Hampton River, which separated Hampton and Seabrook, New Hampshire. The Hampton Beach State Bathhouse was added to the southern end of the state park in 1937, and the seawall was finished in the 1950s to help protect the natural beach and the developed areas. Both of these structures allowed for further public enjoyment of the beach—the bathhouse because it included changing areas, a refreshment counter, and an observation deck, and the seawall because it became the base of the boardwalk along the beach.

Not long after the seawall was completed, one of the most well-known landmarks at the beach, the New Hampshire Marine Memorial, was installed. The memorial, which stands near the northern end of the beach, has a very interesting history. In the late 1950s, New Hampshire resident William E. Downs requested that his son's name be added to a New Hampshire memorial for sailors. The son, Capt. William D. Downs, was lost at sea during World War II. The elder Downs was told, however, that there was no existing memorial for New Hampshire sailors killed in action. Determined to create a memorial for his son and other sailors, Downs worked with the state to establish the New Hampshire Marine Memorial Commission. The commission held a competition for local artists to submit potential designs for the memorial, and Alice Cosgrove of Concord won. The memorial would include a statue of a Gold Star mother, a woman whose child was killed in the line of duty, holding a wreath and longingly looking out to sea. It would also include stone benches that would encircle the statue, with the name of every New Hampshire sailor lost at sea during every American war written on the outer side. The actual statue was created by Vermont artist Vincenzo Andreani out of New Hampshire granite. The New Hampshire Marine Memorial was finally dedicated on Memorial Day 1957.

By that time, there were so many summer visitors at the beach that loudspeakers were installed on the roof of the small bandstand so that the live music could be heard for blocks in each direction. The bandstand continued to host live local shows nearly every summer night. Just across the street, the Hampton Beach Casino hosted some of the most popular bands and shows in the country. Even though the Casino (the actual venue being called the Casino Ballroom) is quite small, its unique history and location has attracted big-name bands through the years, such as the Beach Boys, the Doors, the Who, U2, Ray Charles, and Led Zeppelin, as well as entertainers such as Jerry Seinfeld.

In the 1960s, the state decided to modernize the center of beach activity. The bandstand and the adjacent state park buildings were not enough to properly meet the needs of the thousands of visiting tourists any longer. In 1962, the bandstand was torn down to make room for the Seashell Complex, which would serve all the same functions as the previous buildings and more. The Seashell included a large stage with plenty of outdoor seating and north and south pavilions that housed the chamber of commerce and the state park offices, respectively. The Seashell stage faced Ocean Boulevard, and the back side of the structure extended onto the beach at a point, which included an observation deck and the lifeguard office. The Seashell's architecture was based on a National Park Service initiative called Mission 66. The NPS began Mission 66 in 1956 to update many of its visitor centers and buildings. According to the park service, the 10-year plan was to modernize structures' technology and architecture, but in a way that did not disturb the surrounding environment but rather blended in with it. The architectural style included geometric shapes, colors pulled from the surrounding environment, and open spaces with many windows. After the Seashell was completed, the state-owned complex became the center of beach operations and activities.

During the 1970s, a number of annual visitors began taking longer vacations, with families staying for the entire summer. Many people were no longer satisfied with long-term hotel stays and wanted places of their own to spend their summers in. In response to this, many hotel owners along the beach transformed their hotels into condominiums to accommodate people who wanted to rent or own a small beachfront space. Many hotels were even demolished to make way for new buildings. There are still several hotels left on the beach, but most of the accommodations in the area are now condominiums.

Among the biggest draws for tourists and full-summer visitors were the annual festivals and celebrations. These have always been a part of Hampton Beach's culture as a place of summer fun and recreation. Some of the festivals began nearly 100 years ago, early in the 20th century. One of the earliest ongoing traditions includes the weekly fireworks display. Originally, it was established as a way to keep people on the beach later into the night (see page 62). Another early tradition is the Miss Hampton Beach competition, which started to take shape during the annual Carnival Week when a queen of the carnival was crowned for selling the most raffle tickets. It was not until 1946 that the actual pageant began featuring young women competitors who represented Hampton Beach and its ideals. Children's Week also had early beginnings at the beach. The festival is a week of activities, games, and shows exclusively put on for the children of Hampton and all those who are visiting for the summer. The Hampton Beach Seafood Festival, on the other hand, had a much later start but is now a highly anticipated tradition. The entirety of Ocean Boulevard is closed down and local restaurants have a few days to sell some of their best seafood dishes in booths that line the street. Other annual traditions include the Christmas parade, which goes directly through downtown Hampton and is one of the town's most beloved traditions, and the Memorial Day parade, which ends at the New Hampshire Marine Memorial.

Not only are these festivals a lot of fun, but they also draw in a large amount of people who shop and eat at Hampton's many wonderful businesses. New and long-standing businesses and restaurants in town and on Ocean Boulevard perfectly capture Hampton Beach's dynamic nature. Some of the enterprises and restaurants that have evolved with generations of Hampton area visitors and residents are the Playland Arcade, Lamie's Inn (and later the Old Salt at Lamie's Inn), and Blink's Fry Doe. The Ashworth by the Sea is a hotel that has been on Hampton Beach since 1906 and has been rebuilt or remodeled several times on the same plot of land. This is also the case with many of the restaurants, hotels, and shops in the area. There have been many devastating fires throughout Hampton Beach's history, but the businesses affected have often quickly rebuilt.

In 1997, the 99-year-lease of the Hampton Beach Improvement Company expired. Its expiration resulted in the stewardship of the developed areas of Hampton Beach transferring to the town once again. To continue the development and improvement of the Hampton Beach area, a plan was drafted in 2001 called the Hampton Beach Area Master Plan. It was funded by a partnership between the New Hampshire Department of Resources and Economic Development (DRED), the Town of Hampton, and the New Hampshire Office of Energy and Planning. The plan proposed several actions that would significantly improve the area around the center of beach activity, especially around the Seashell Complex. According to DRED, the ultimate goal was to create a "more pleasant and accommodating area for visitors and residents."

By 2010, the first Seashell Complex had already hosted 48 summers of almost nightly concerts, shows, and other forms of entertainment. However, the stage was not impervious to the damaging ocean winds and weather or to changing architectural fashions. According to Patrick Cronin, writing in the *Hampton Union*, officials said that "the complex no longer met the needs of today's tourists and started to show its age." One of the first steps in the Hampton Beach Area Master Plan was to update the Seashell Complex and reorganize the surrounding area to increase efficiency. In October 2010, the Seashell was demolished to make room for a new incarnation.

The new Seashell Complex began construction in the 2010–2011 winter season. The complex is very similar to the original and includes a main stage, seating for 750 people, modern bathroom facilities, a function hall, north and south pavilions, a first aid station, and visitor information. The construction also includes two new bathhouses near the north and south ends of the main beach. The Seashell Complex was opened to the public with a ribbon-cutting ceremony on June 1, 2012.

While Hampton Beach boasts a long and unique history, an exciting future for the beach is at the forefront of people's minds.

One

Happy Hampton Beach

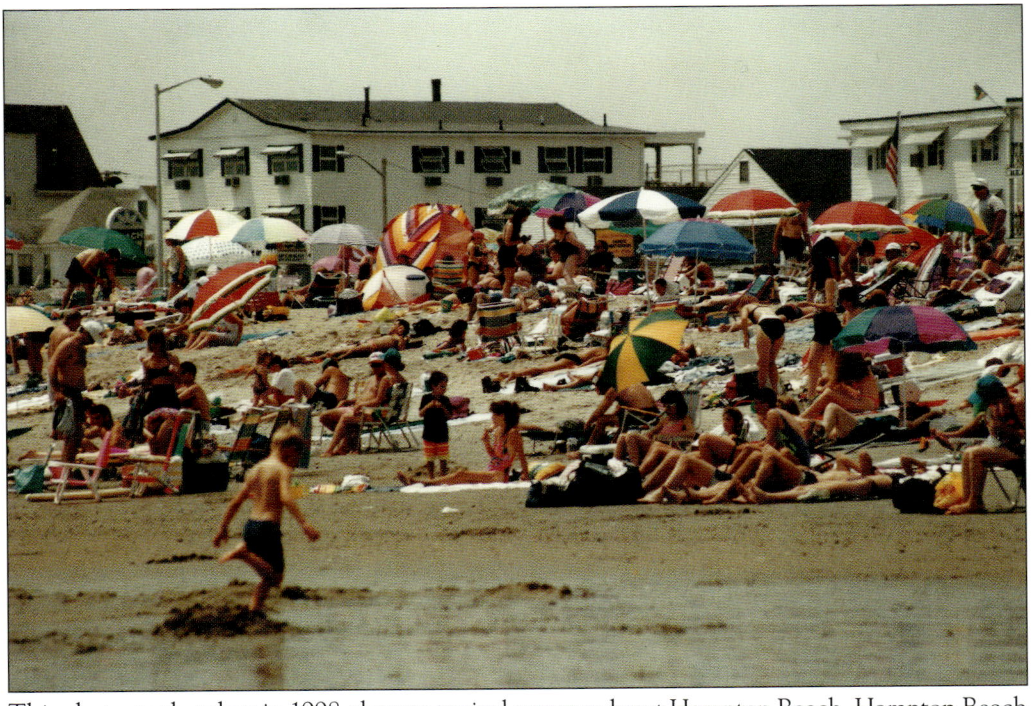

This photograph, taken in 1998, shows a typical summer day at Hampton Beach. Hampton Beach State Park is one of the most popular beaches on New Hampshire's short coastline. Locals and families from surrounding New England towns flock to the beach for a day of sunny recreation and relaxation. The many beach umbrellas, toys, and bathing suits reflect a rainbow of activity along the sandy shore. (HHS.)

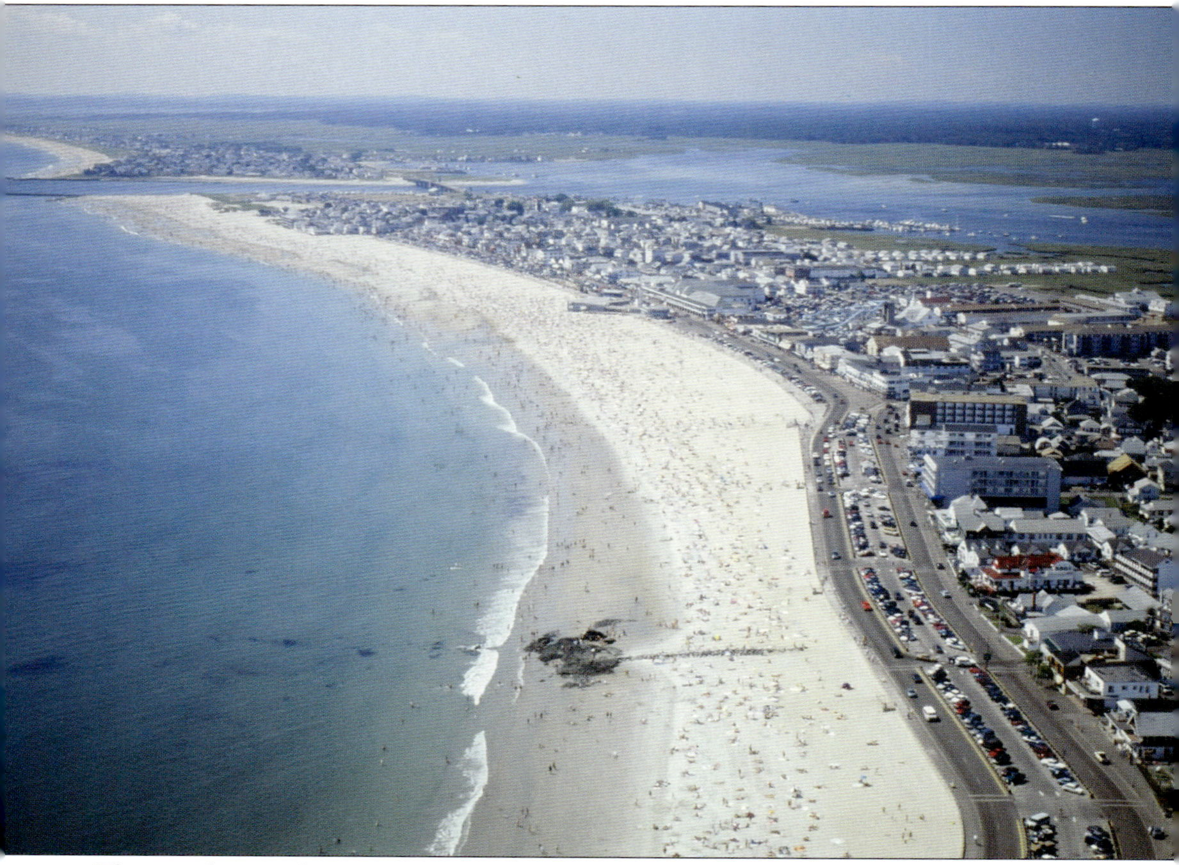

This aerial view of Hampton Beach, looking south toward Seabrook, was taken from almost directly above Great Boar's Head. Ocean Boulevard is a one-way street that follows the curvature of the beach heading north and is paralleled by Ashworth Avenue, which heads south. The two roads stay together until they split at the A Street block, just in front of the Ashworth Hotel. The roads are then only connected by the one-way streets that run back and forth through Hampton's tightly packed neighborhoods and business districts. There are 17 one-way streets that are lettered, from north to south, A through Q. The Hampton-Seabrook Marsh and the connecting Hampton Harbor can be seen at upper right. The two main roads reconnect just before the Mile Bridge, now known as the Neil R. Underwood Memorial Bridge, which spans the Hampton River and connects Hampton to Seabrook. (HCC.)

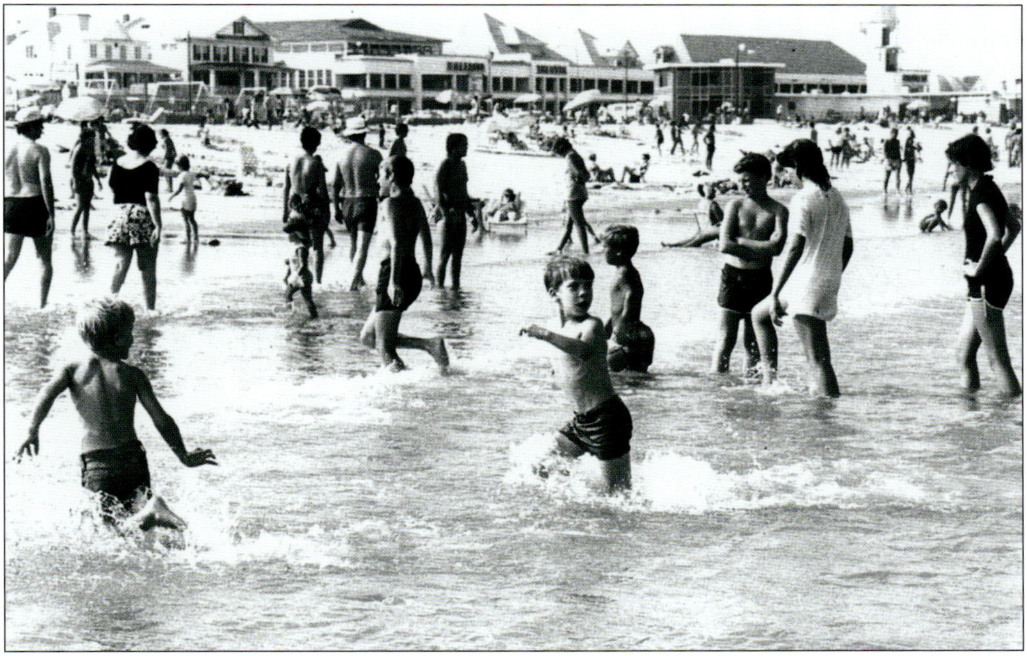

This picture, most likely taken in the 1970s, shows Hampton Beach State Park full of visiting families playing in the surf. This is at the center of beach activity, near the Seashell Complex and the Hampton Beach Casino. These young boys are brave enough to splash around in New Hampshire's chilly water, which usually only reaches a maximum temperature of around 65 degrees even during the height of summer. (DRED.)

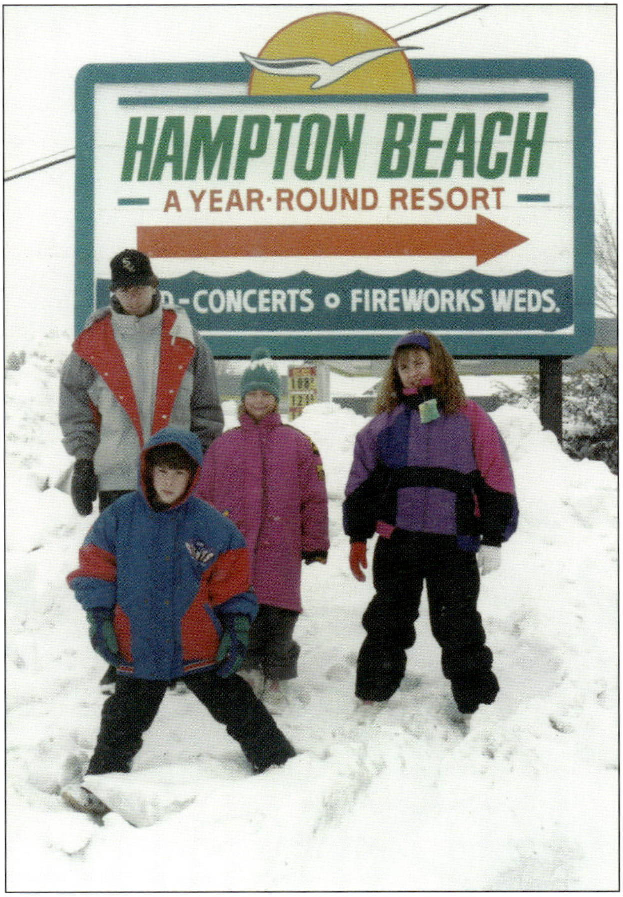

A group of children stand in front of a sign boasting that Hampton Beach is "A Year-Round Resort" during the winter of 1997. While the height of activity is in the summertime, Hampton Beach continues to have some visitors throughout the year. One activity that draws people to the beach during the winter is the Penguin Plunge, which happens annually during February. Sponsored participants bravely dive into the near-freezing ocean water to benefit New Hampshire Special Olympics. (HHS.)

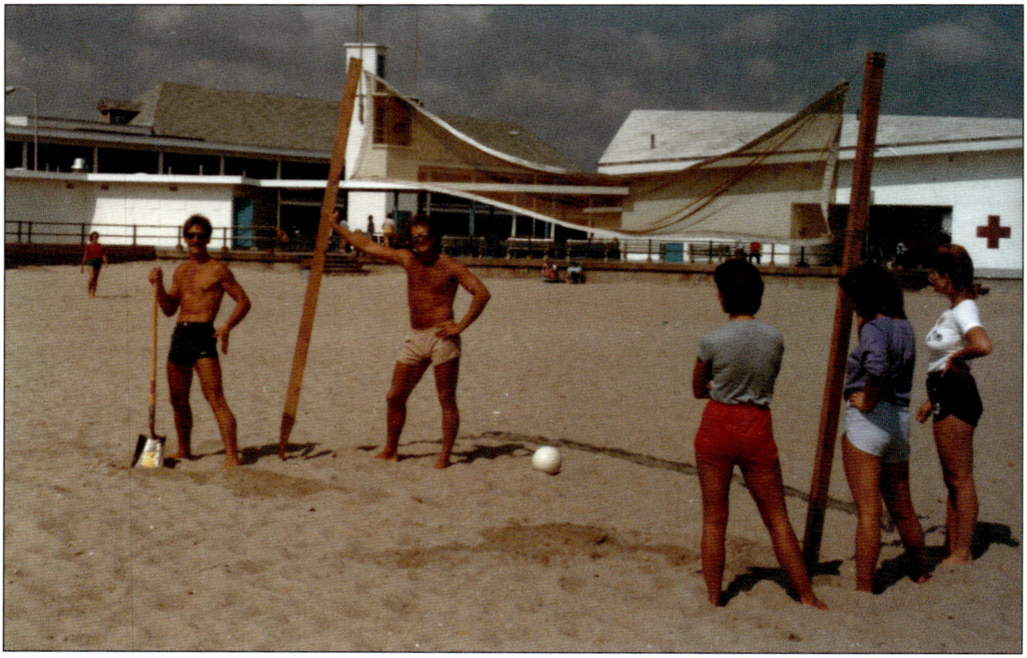

Friends set up a volleyball net on the beach in the early 1980s. Volleyball is played on Hampton Beach throughout the summer, often in large, organized tournaments put on by various organizations and groups. This particular game took place at the heart of Hampton Beach, just behind the Seashell Complex lifeguard station. (HHS.)

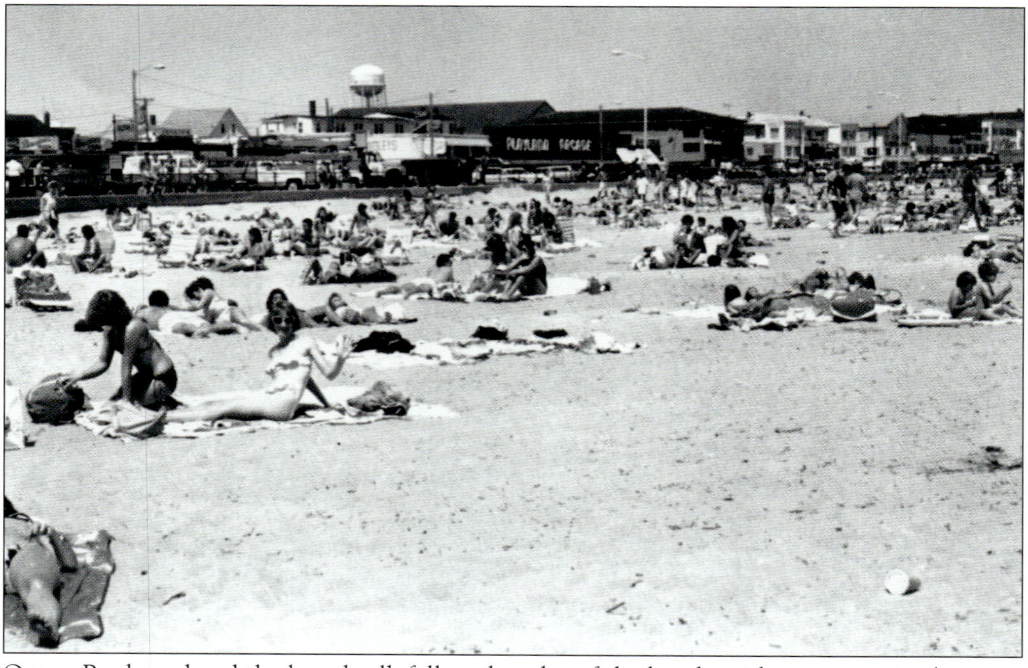

Ocean Boulevard and the boardwalk follow the edge of the beach, with no separation between them. The scene in this view from 1987 has only undergone a few changes in the last few decades. Dudley's, the Playland Arcade, Blink's Fry Doe, and the Hampton Beach water tower are just a few of the iconic landmarks that still populate the street view seen from the beach. (HHS.)

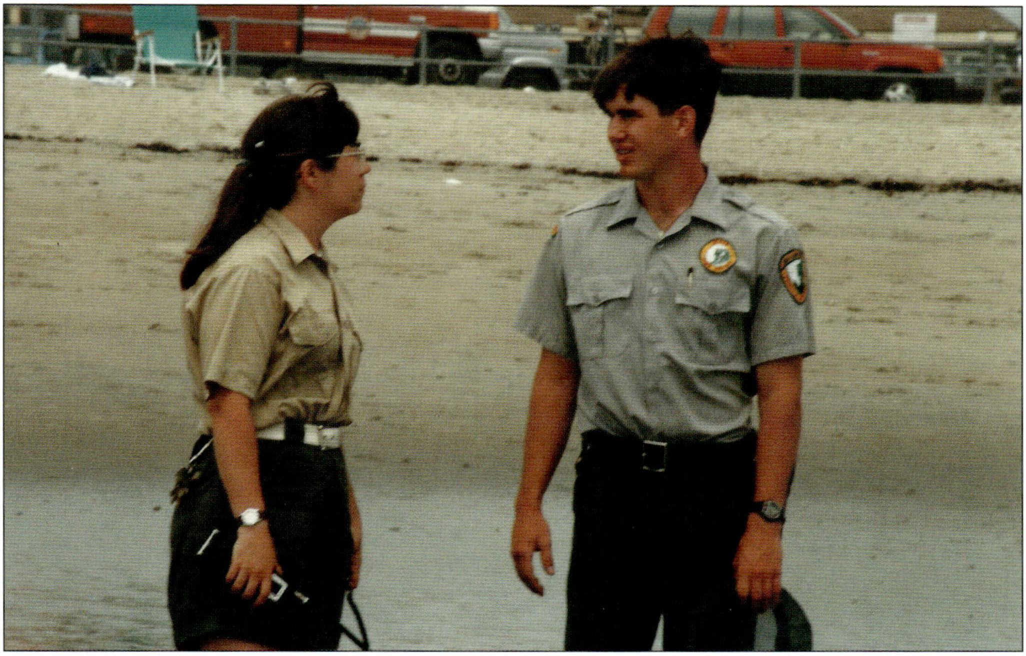

Johanna Lyons (left), now a longtime state employee, coordinates with an unidentified young state worker during the 1990 season in a search and rescue situation. Lyons is now New Hampshire's state park planning and development specialist and played a crucial role in both the lead planning team and the two-year execution of the recent Hampton Beach Redevelopment Project. (HHS.)

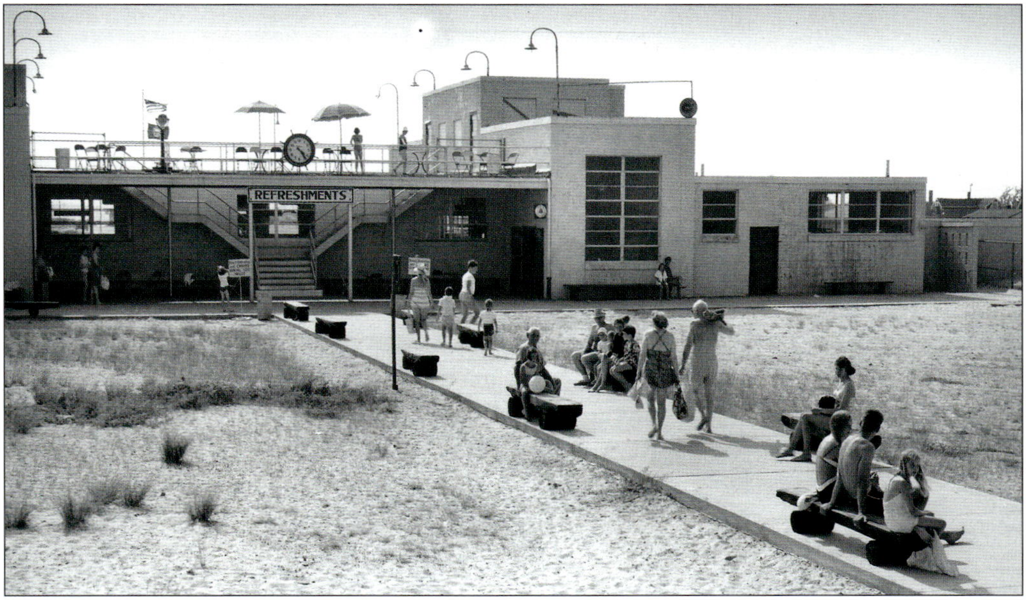

Beachgoers use the walkway to travel to and from the State Bathhouse in the 1960s. The bathhouse was built in 1938 and included showers, a refreshment counter, and a sunny observation deck on the center roof. According to *Hampton: A Century of Town and Beach*, by Peter Randall, there were plans to build extravagant additions to the bathhouse, including a swimming pool and sports fields, but the main structure was eventually torn down in 1986 without any of these improvements. (DRED.)

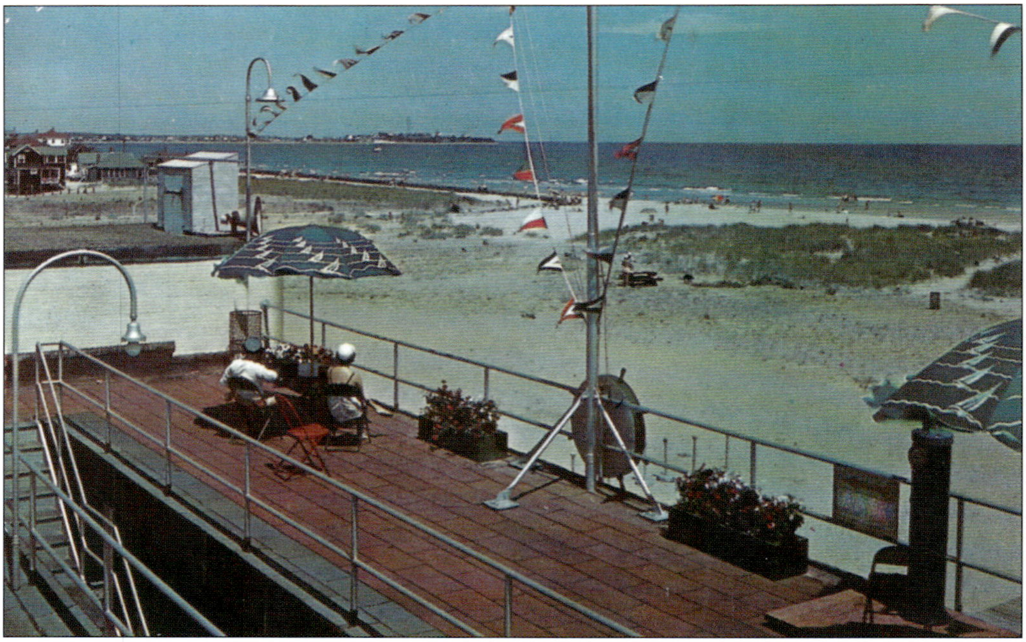

The observation deck of the State Bathhouse was located on the low center rooftop. Among the bathhouse's amenities were the refreshment counter and outdoor patio furniture for state park visitors. This 1960s photograph shows the deck's gorgeous view of Hampton Beach's sandy shore, the Atlantic Ocean, and Great Boar's Head in the distance. (DRED.)

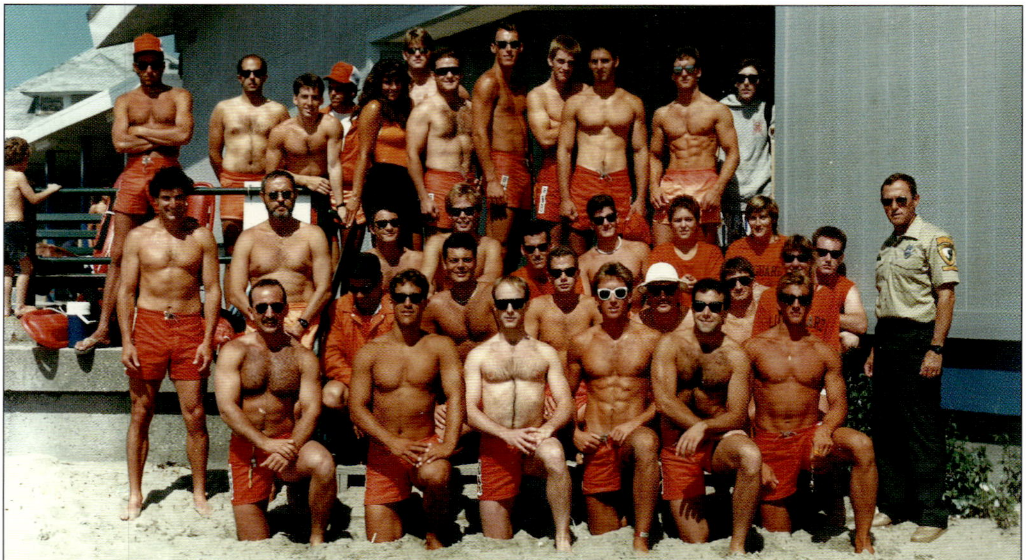

The 1988 lifeguard staff poses for a group picture next to the Seashell Complex. Jim Donahue, chief of lifeguards, stands at far right in a state park uniform. In 2009, Donahue completed his 50th year as a lifeguard for Hampton Beach State Park and has headed the lifeguard staff for many years. David Thomas (back row, second from right) was struck by lightning and killed while on duty on July 17, 1988. Some of the other lifeguards are Jim Deluca, captain (front row, far left); Chris Laganas, lieutenant (front row, second from left); Bruce Butterworth (second row, far left); and Leland Brennan, administrative lieutenant (second row, second from left). (DRED.)

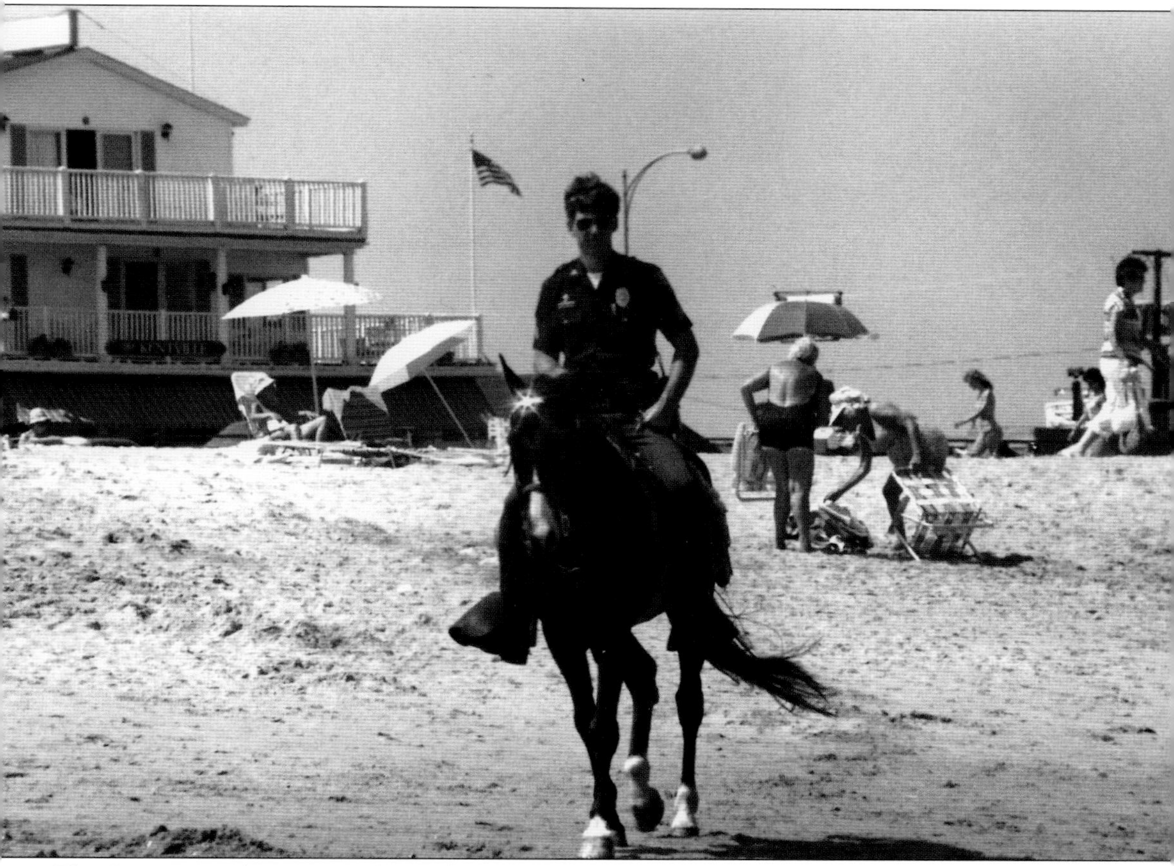

The Hampton Police Mounted Patrol Unit was created to help patrol the sandy beach, easily get through traffic-filled streets, and help manage large crowds. In this 1987 photograph, John Galvin rides one of the police department's horses along the beach. According to a 2015 *Hampton Union* article by Jack Pasi, the mounted unit has been a part of the department since 1981, the same time Galvin joined the department. Today, Galvin and his brother Joe, now both retired from the force, work part-time with the mounted unit. They help train the horses for duty alongside Dennis Pelletier, an experienced patrol horse trainer. In 2016, the unit includes two horses, Butch and Bolt. (HHS.)

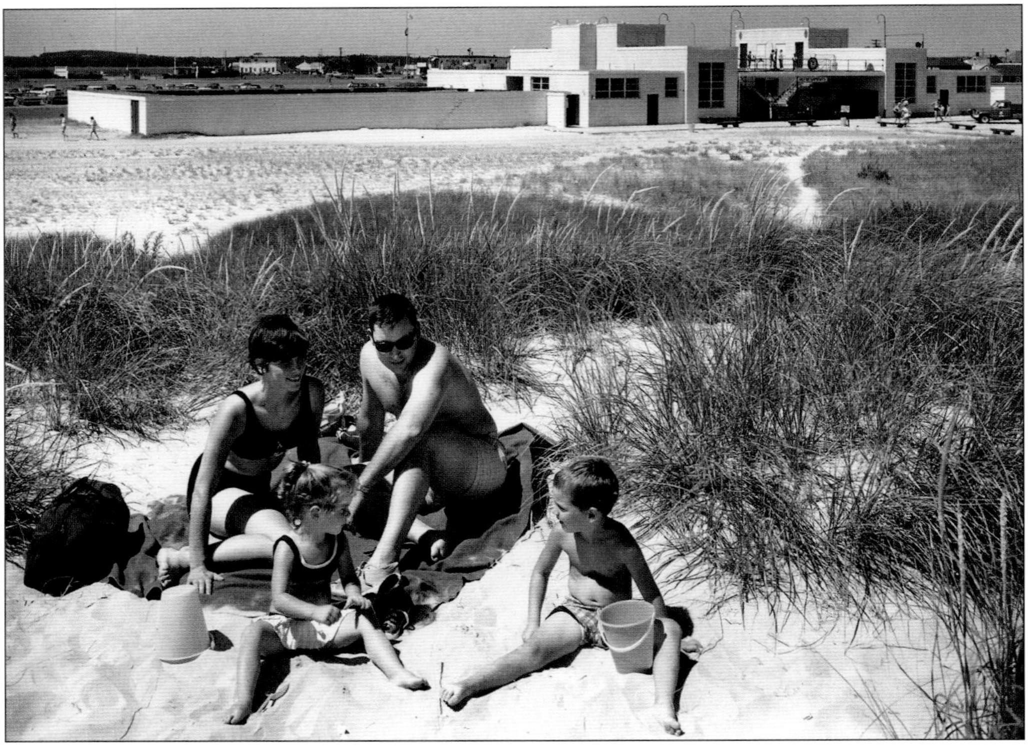

A family enjoys a sunny day at the beach near the State Bathhouse in the 1960s. This photograph and several others were taken in a state park photo shoot and were used to promote tourism and attract visitors to the beach. Robert Herbert, editor of the *Hampton Union*, said in 1988 that Hampton Beach is "the generator that runs the town's economy." (DRED.)

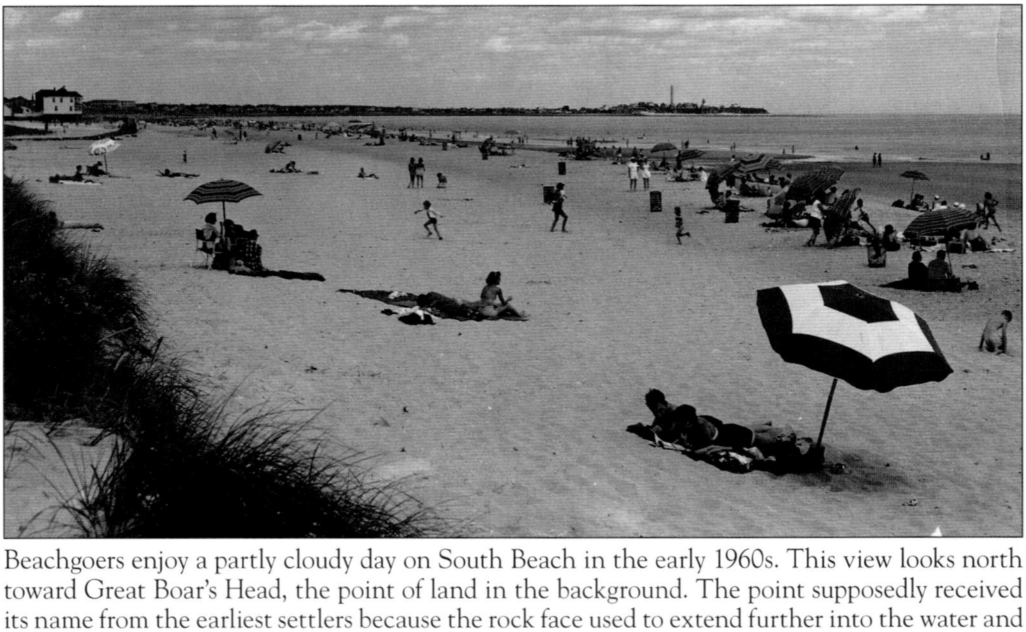

Beachgoers enjoy a partly cloudy day on South Beach in the early 1960s. This view looks north toward Great Boar's Head, the point of land in the background. The point supposedly received its name from the earliest settlers because the rock face used to extend further into the water and looked like a profile view of a boar's head. Here on south beach would have been the best place to view the rock formation. (DRED.)

Two

Along Ocean Boulevard

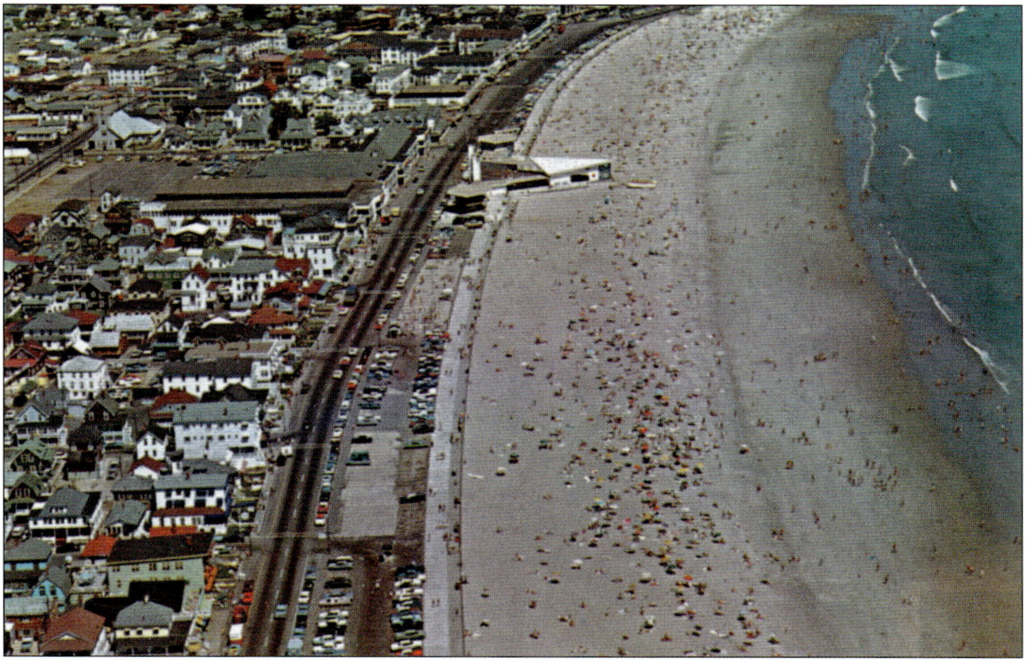

The Seashell Complex was built in 1962 and replaced the bandstand that had been at the center of the beach since 1901. Its facilities included a lifeguard station, the chamber of commerce office, public toilets, the police station, a comfort station, and ticket and popcorn stands, as well as a main stage to host concerts and shows that would have formerly been featured on the bandstand. (HHS.)

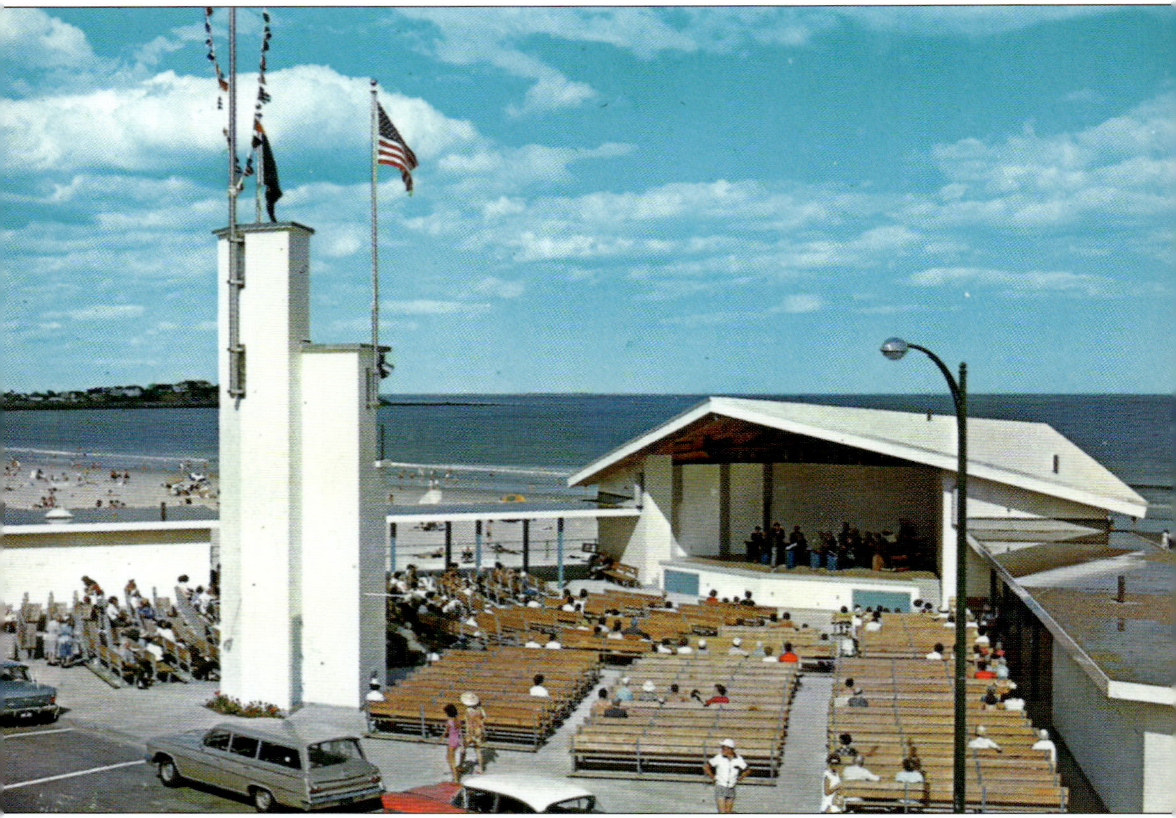

The 1962 Seashell Complex was designed to be efficient to use, easily accessible, and to limit potential impacts on the environment it was built in. The idea and the architectural design were based on a new National Park Service initiative called Mission 66, which aimed to elevate national park buildings to modern standards of comfort and efficiency while still promoting the conservation of surrounding environments. (DRED.)

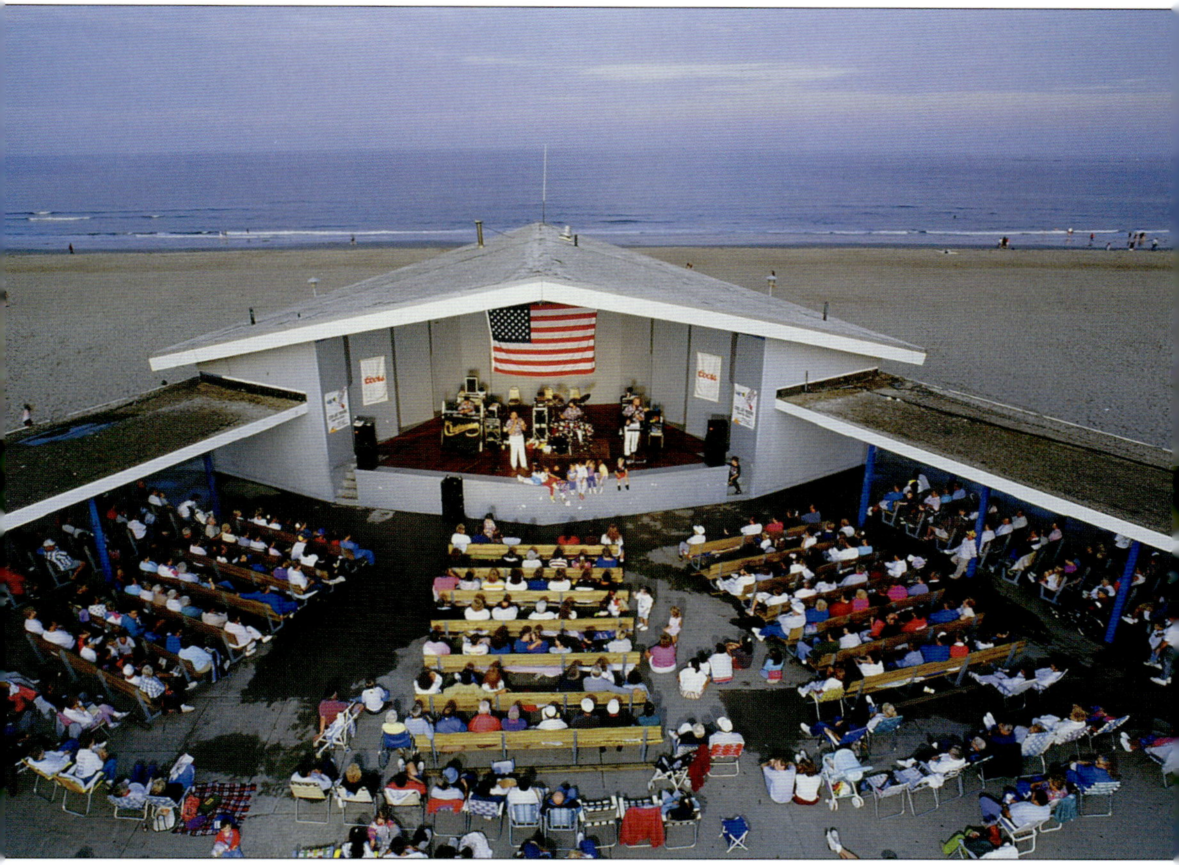

During the summer, the Seashell stage houses almost nightly shows for the public to enjoy. They include many different types of entertainment, such as well-known and local bands, magic shows, comedians, talent shows, and many others. Spectators are welcome to come and go as they please, and the stage's acoustic design projects the live music for blocks in either direction. (HCC.)

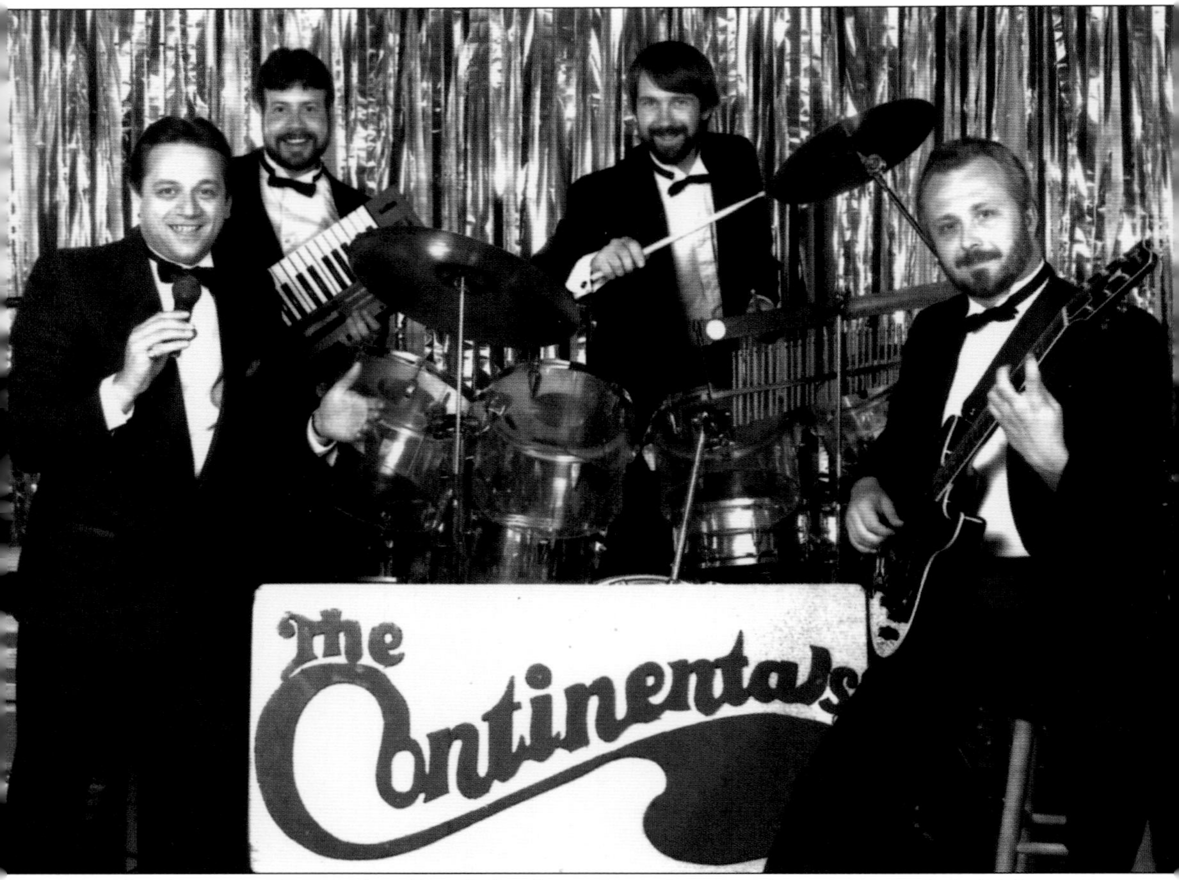

The Continentals are a local band that formed in 1971, according to an article by Melanie Gray in the *Hampton Union*. The band first performed on the Seashell stage in 1983 and now entertains every summer Wednesday night at 7:30 before the fireworks. The band's shows have become a summer tradition at Hampton, even though the lineup has changed over the years. (HHS.)

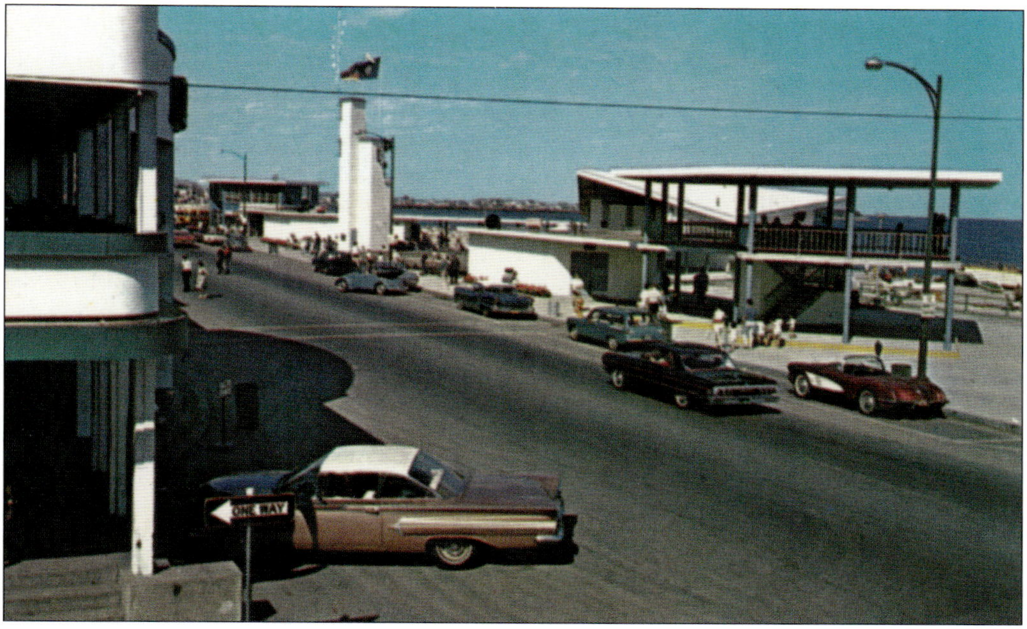

The Seashell Complex is made up of three distinct structures—the stage at the center, known to visitors as the Seashell stage, and the north and south pavilions. This picture was evidently taken very soon after the Seashell Complex was built because the southern pavilion is still open to the air as an observation deck. The pavilion was walled in only a few years after the complex was built in 1962 due to weather concerns. (HHS.)

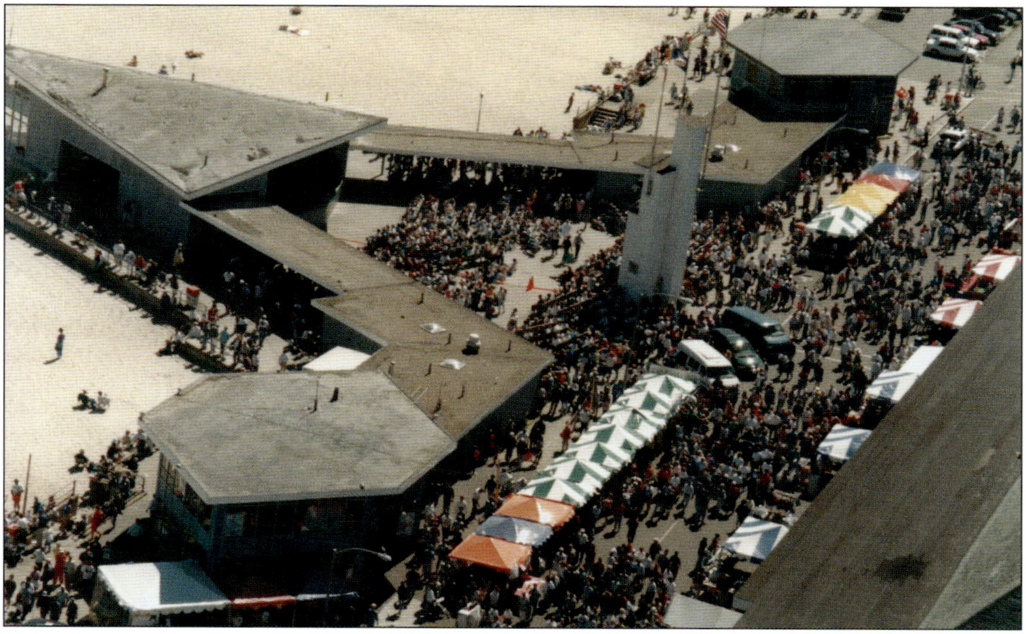

The complex was designed to be modern and efficient, and to encompass all of the needs of Hampton Beach State Park's thousands of summer visitors. Even during a busy time like the Hampton Beach Seafood Festival, the complex's open design affords plenty of space for the massive crowds. This close-up aerial view clearly shows the triangular footprint that was carried through to the 2012 Seashell Complex as well. (HHS.)

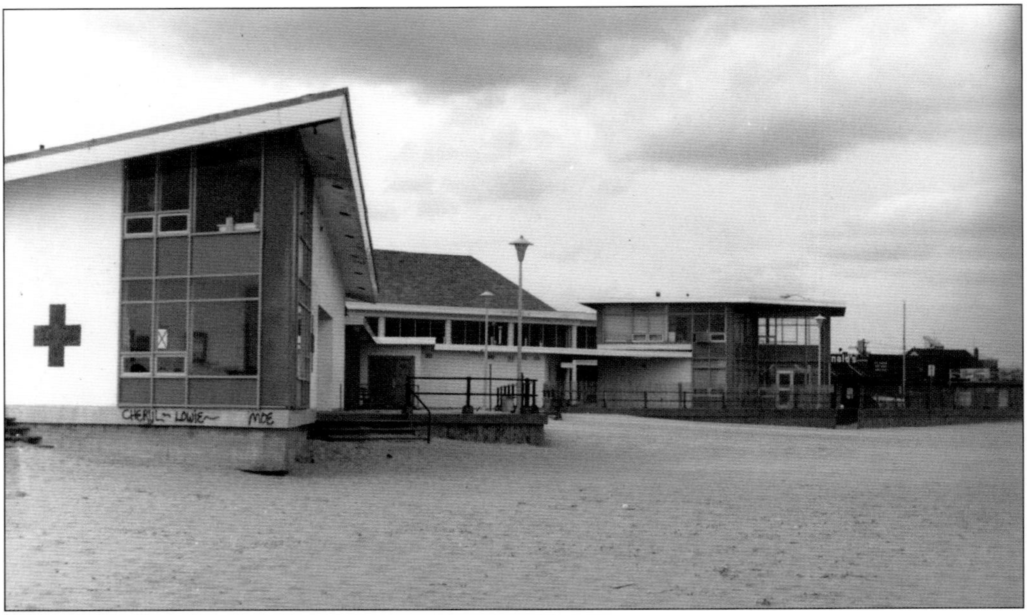

This is the Seashell from the beach side. The center of the complex, which houses the stage on the opposite side, also includes the lifeguard station, which is indicated by the red cross. The second story of this building houses the lifeguard office. The northern pavilion, connected to the stage by public facilities, housed the Hampton Beach Area Chamber of Commerce for many years. (DRED.)

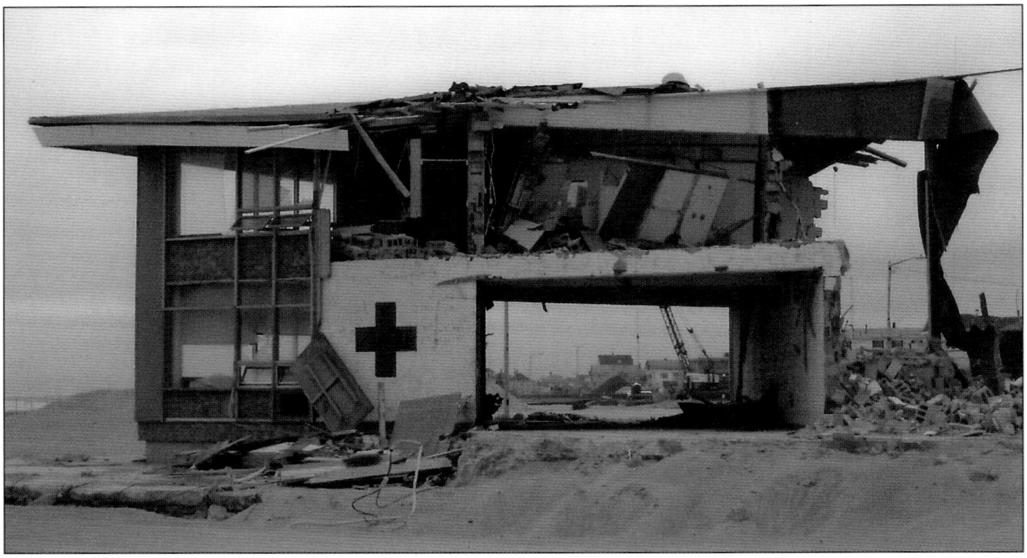

By 2010, the Seashell Complex had been on Ocean Boulevard for nearly 50 years, and it was beginning to show signs of its age. The salty sea air, rough weather, and constant use had taken a toll. The Seashell's 1960s design also looked outdated, as architectural tastes had changed much over the last 50 years. In October 2010, the Seashell Complex was demolished to make room for a modern and updated facility. According to Patrick Cronin, reporter for the *Hampton Union*, "the complex no longer met the needs of today's tourists." There was a bittersweet feeling in the community; people were sad to see the familiar Seashell go, but they were excited for a modernized version to be built. (DRED.)

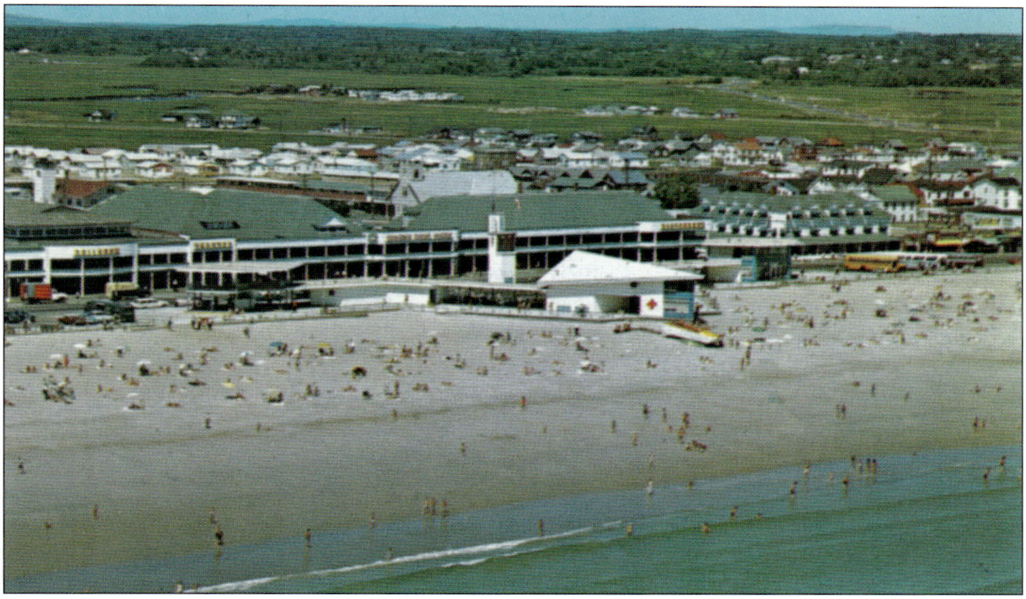

This aerial shot was taken from over the water looking west toward the beach community. It is unique because it provides a view of the beach, the Hampton-Seabrook Marsh behind it, and a section of the town—all of which have a part in the makeup of Hampton's culture. The northernmost point of the Casino (visible at far right) was the Ocean House, a hotel connected to the rest of the Casino Ballroom. (HHS.)

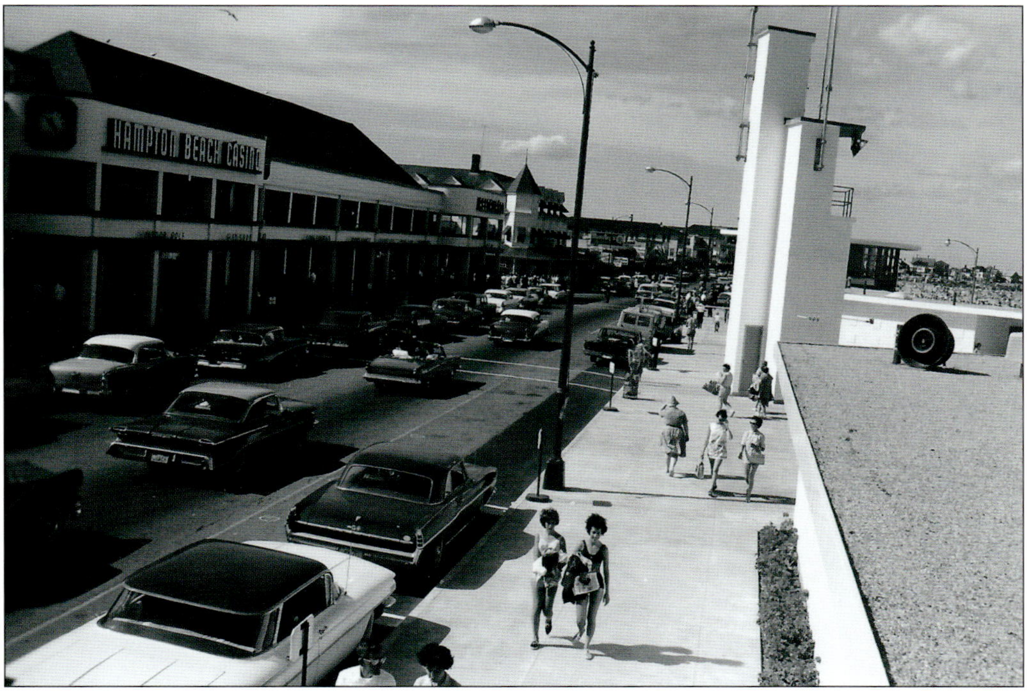

This street view from the early 1970s looks north on Ocean Boulevard, with the Seashell Complex on the right and the renovated Hampton Beach Casino on the left. During the summer, Ocean Boulevard is always quite busy, with cars going to and from the beach and people filling the sidewalks and constantly crossing from one side of the street to the other. (DRED.)

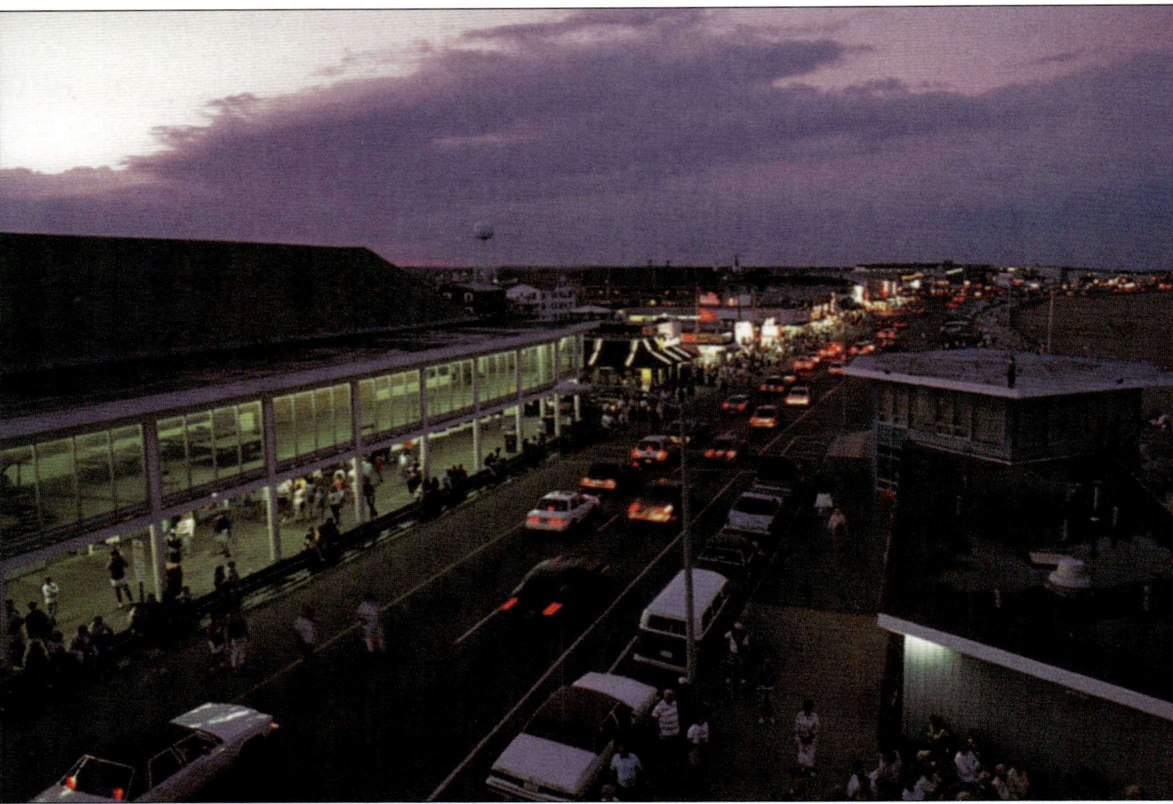

This is Ocean Boulevard, or New Hampshire Route 1A, at the center of beach activity on a busy summer night. On the right is the original Hampton Beach Seashell Complex, and on the left is the Hampton Beach Casino. As nighttime approaches, Hampton Beach's visitors move from the sandy beaches to Ocean Boulevard's many restaurants, bars, and shops and the Casino Ballroom. This is the current exterior of the Casino in 2016. (HHS.)

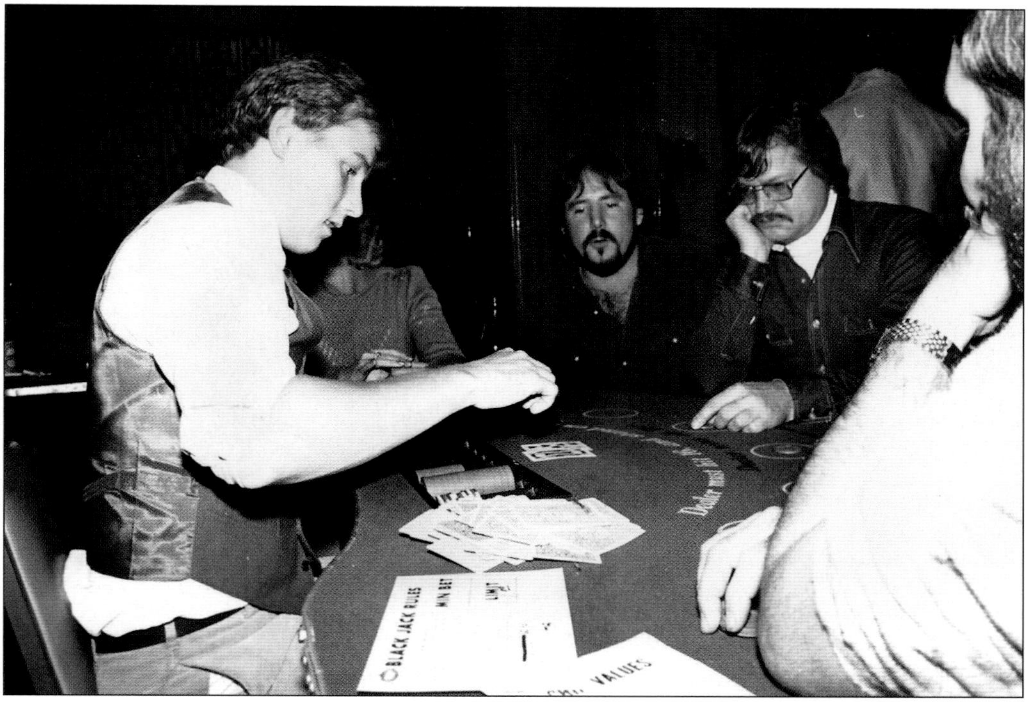

This picture was most likely taken in the Ashworth by the Sea hotel and shows what appears to be a blackjack and poker night. Although there is no gambling inside the Casino, there is a smaller casino dedicated to gambling on the main establishment's beachfront side. (HHS.)

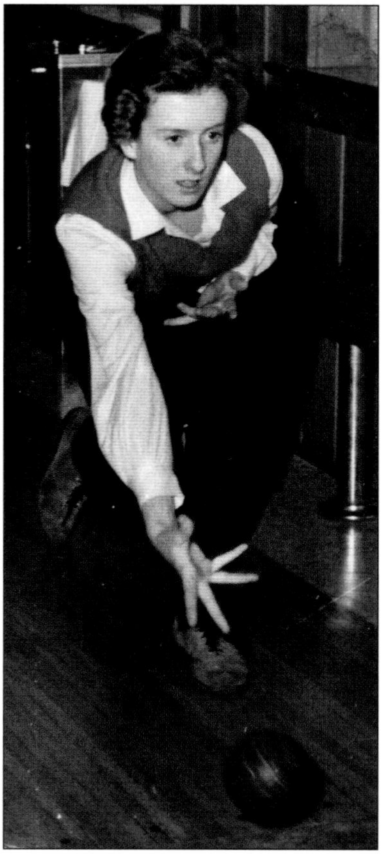

The Hampton Beach Casino has been on Ocean Boulevard for over a century. Even though it is called a casino, it has never been a place expressly dedicated to gambling, but rather a place of social gathering and entertainment. The Casino includes a concert venue called the Casino Ballroom, which is small compared to other entertainment venues, but it never ceases to draw popular bands and celebrities. This photograph, taken in 1960, shows a young man bowling at one of the Casino's two alleys, alongside its billiard and pool tables, shops, and restaurants. (HHS.)

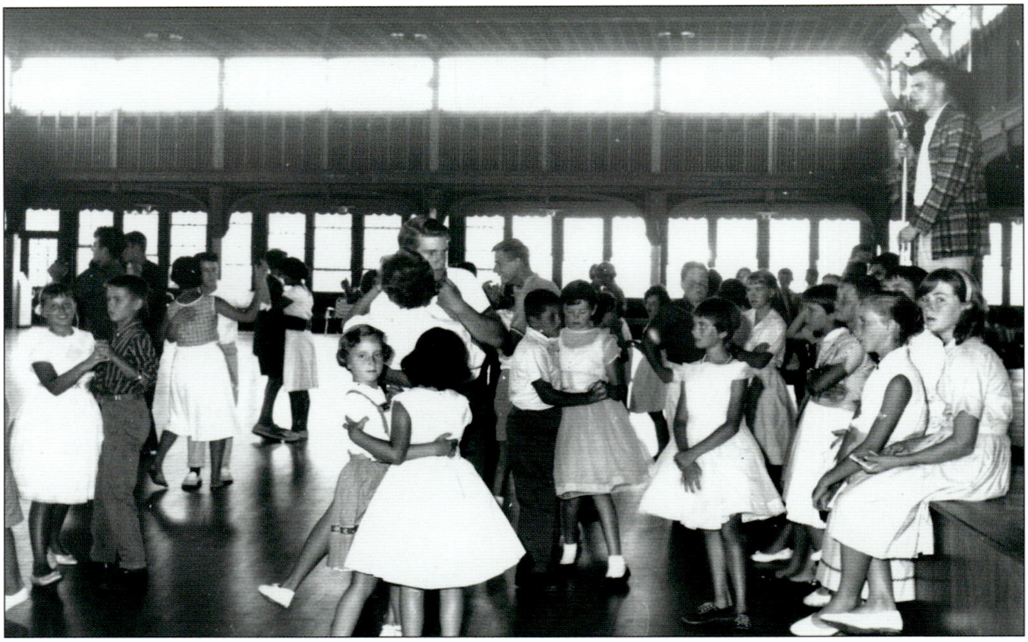

A group of children and young people enjoy a small dance in the Hampton Beach Casino Ballroom in the summer of 1960. According to the Casino's owners, today's venue can seat a maximum of 1,800 and has standing space for 2,200. The ballroom itself is a large open space with a stage on one side. In the background are two rows of windows that from the outside appear to be the first and second floors of the Casino. (HHS.)

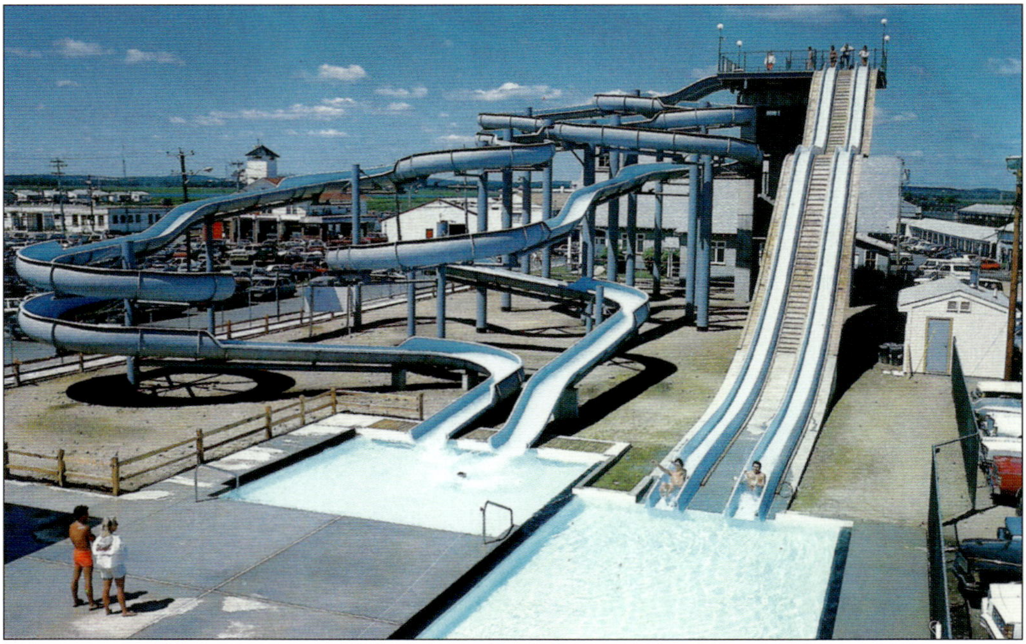

The Hampton Beach Casino Water Slide, now called the Cascade Waterslide, first opened in the summer of 1984. It is located just northwest of the Hampton Beach Casino and boasts great views of the beach from the top of the slide. The Casino encourages people to have fun on the slide and then go right next door for good food, good shopping, and great entertainment. (HHS.)

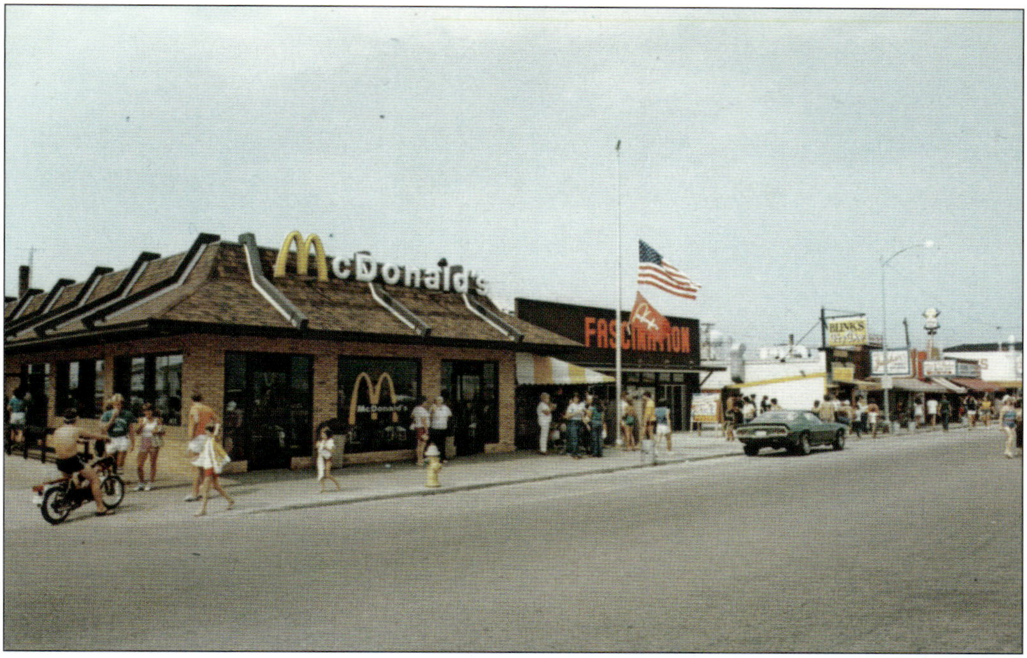

During the late 1970s and early 1980s, the Casino was going through many structural and aesthetic changes as its new owners tried to make it more appealing to younger crowds and simultaneously bring back the Casino's glory days. One of the changes was that the Ocean House, the hotel connected to the Casino's northern end, was completely demolished and replaced by a McDonald's restaurant. (HHS.)

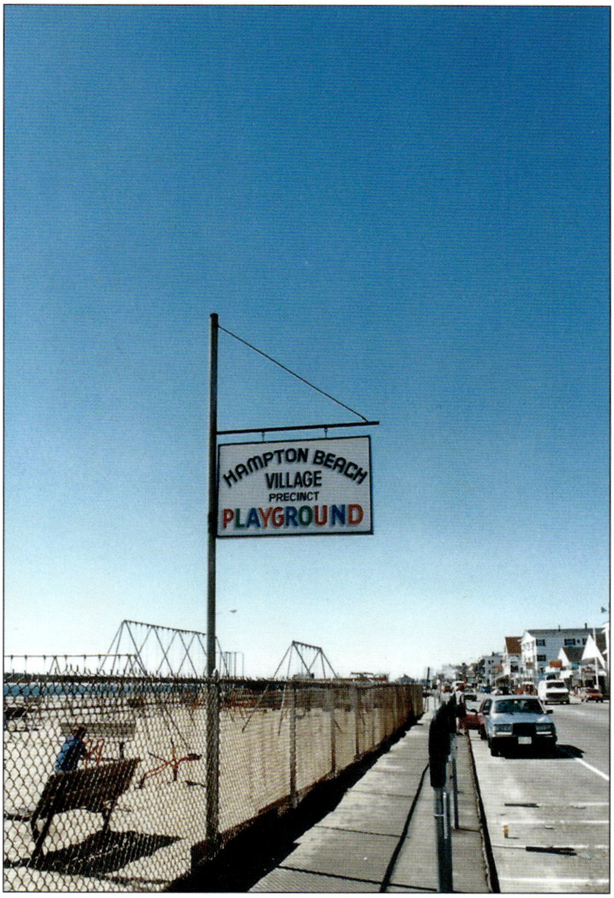

The John C. White Memorial Playground was originally opened in July 1927. As this sign reads, the playground is now called the Hampton Beach Village Precinct Playground. The playground is just south of the Seashell Complex and sits on the boardwalk next to the beach. It was originally built on the northern end of Hampton Beach but was moved farther south when the seawall was constructed in the 1950s. The playground was finally moved to its present location when the Seashell Complex was built in 1962. (HHS.)

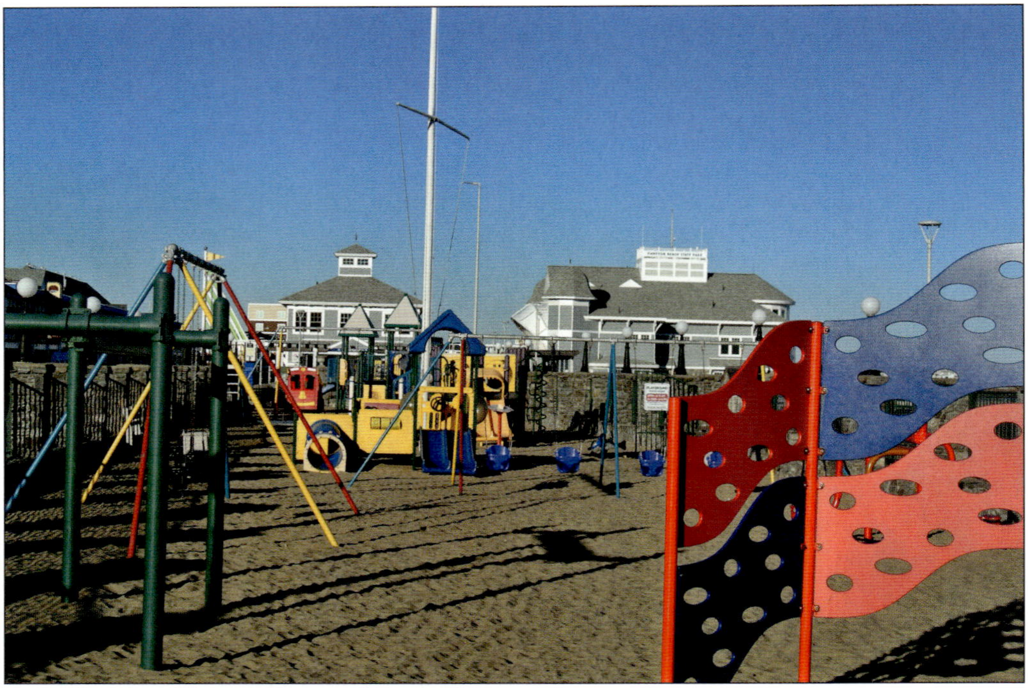

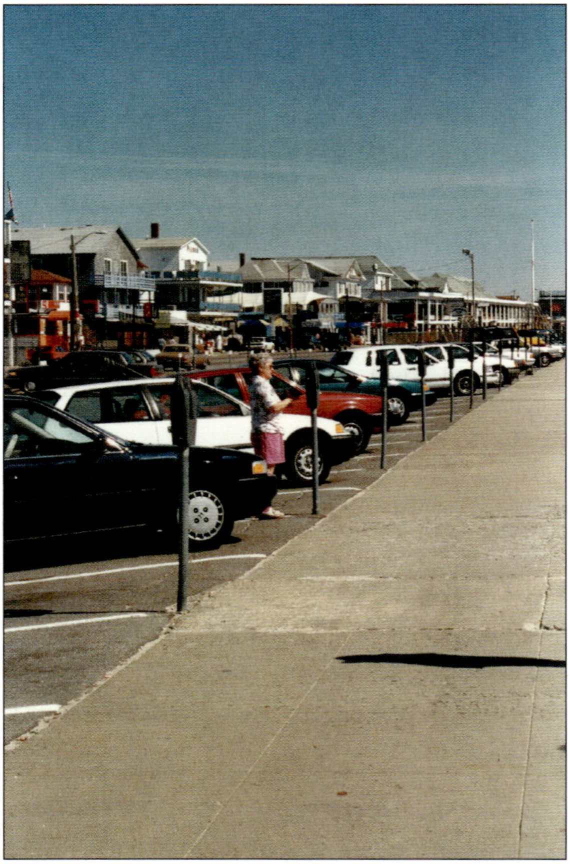

During the summer, the Hampton Beach Village Precinct Playground is filled with laughing and running children from all walks of life. The playground remained mostly untouched by the recent redevelopment, but some of the newest fish art installations stand between it and the beach. The playground remains a safe place to play while enjoying the summer days. (Author's collection.)

This 1998 photograph, with a view looking north on Ocean Boulevard toward the Casino, catches a glimpse of Hampton Beach's many parking meters along the beach. The meters were replaced with automated ticket meters during the Hampton Beach Redevelopment Project in 2013. Albert "Skip" Bellanger, a familiar face at Hampton Beach, recently celebrated his 50th year as part of the Hampton Beach Parking Patrol. (HHS.)

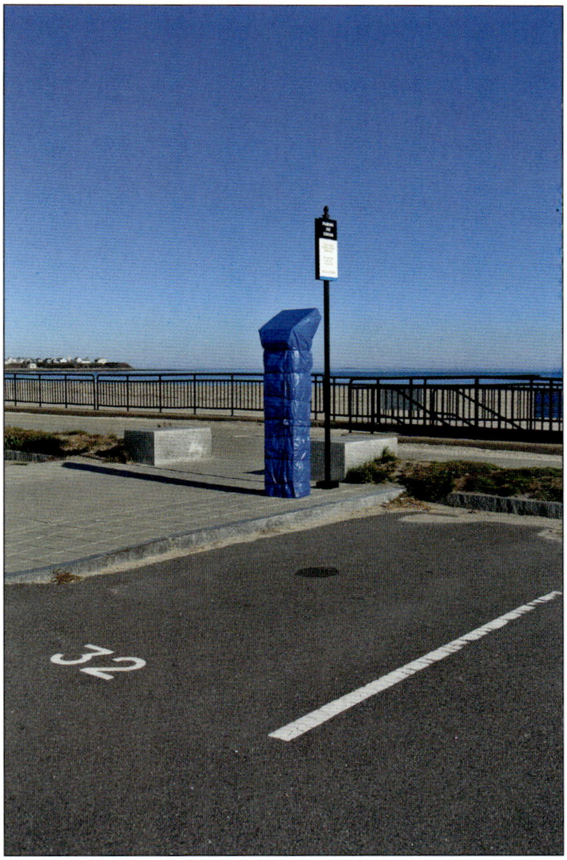

Many aspects of the beach were updated and improved during the Hampton Beach Redevelopment Project, including the parking lots and meters. The state park switched from coin-operated meters to electronic meters in order to modernize. During the summer, the lots are completely full and the parking meters bring in much of the state park's revenue. The meters are shut down for the winter season, which allows for free parking for those who want to enjoy the chilly beach. (Author's collection.)

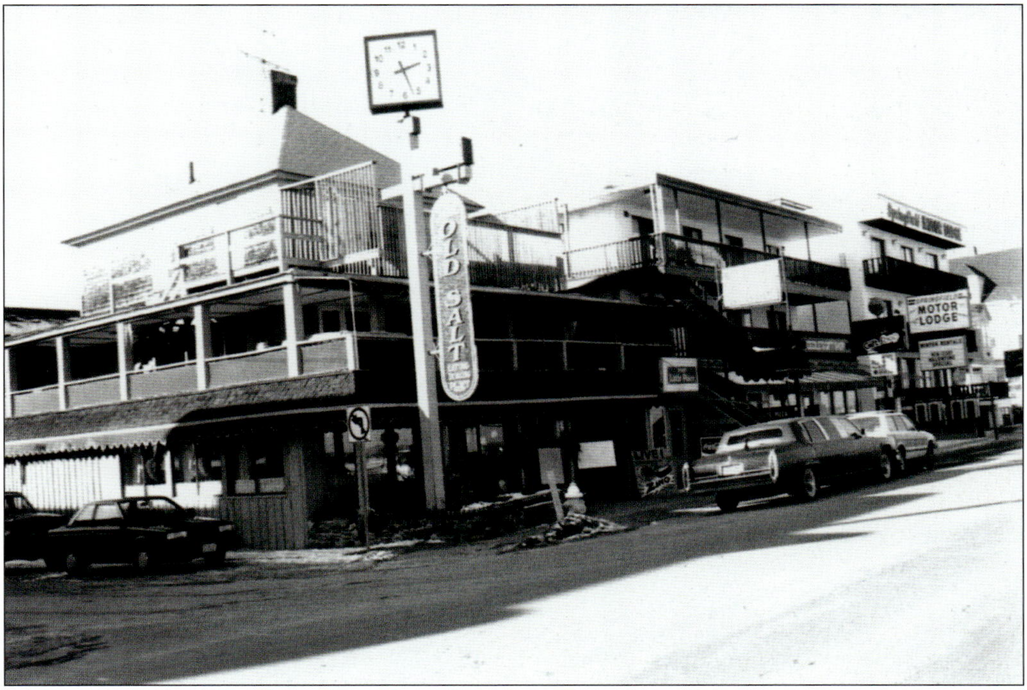

The Old Salt Eating and Drinking Place was opened by longtime Hampton Beach visitor Nancy Higgins and her family in 1986. The term "old salt" refers to an old, seasoned sailor. This picture shows the Old Salt's location at 83 Ocean Boulevard, which is several blocks south of the Seashell Complex. Longtime Hampton Beach State Park employees have fond memories of going to the Old Salt for a meal at least once a week after work. (HHS.)

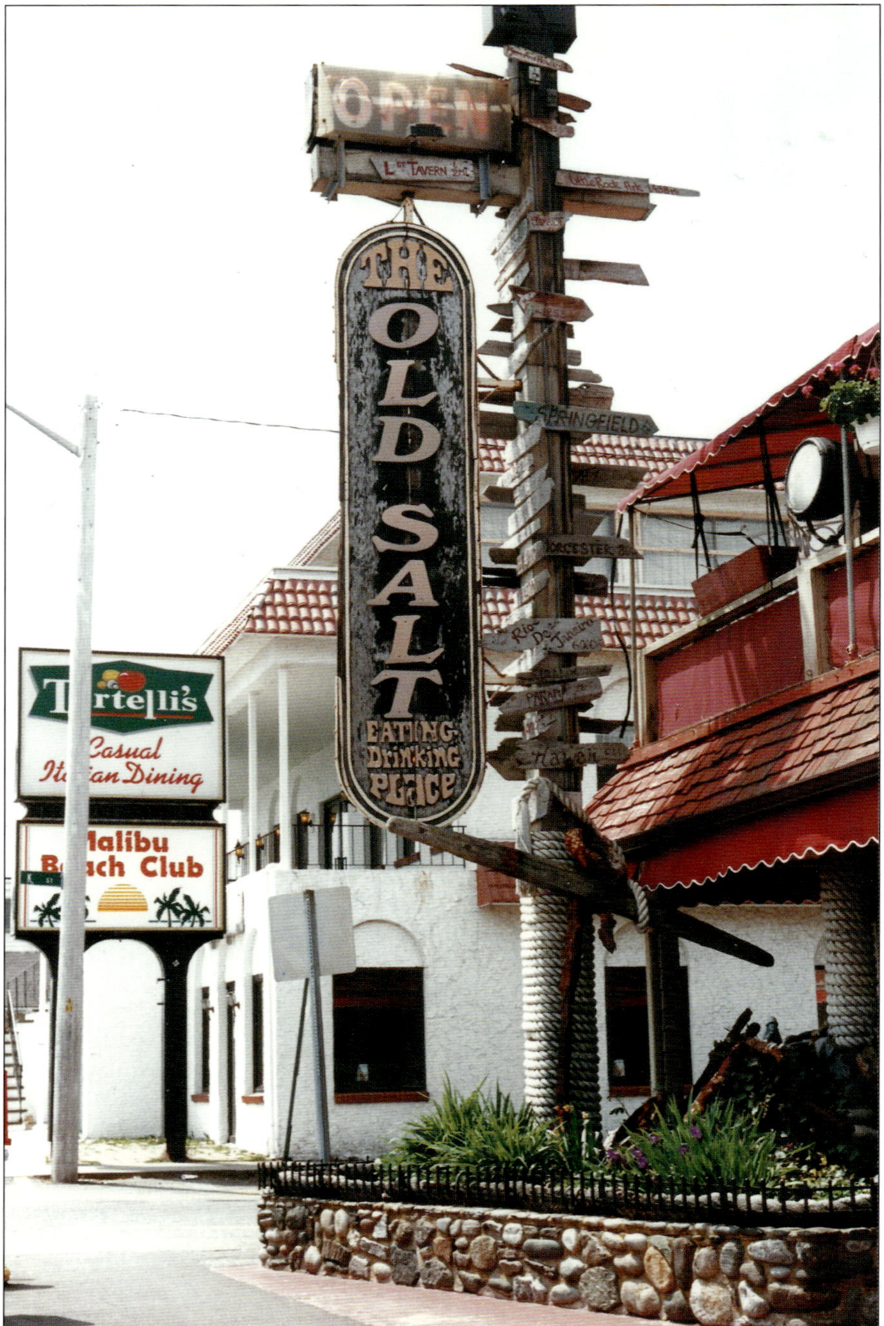

The Old Salt remained at its first location on Ocean Boulevard until tragedy struck on June 16, 1999. A fire that started at an adjacent business spread to the Old Salt and other surrounding buildings and completely destroyed the establishment. The Higgins family quickly recovered and only a few weeks later reopened the Whale's Tale Pub in the Casino complex. The business was there for a few years until the family purchased the historic Lamie's Tavern in 2001 on High Street in the middle of Hampton. The establishment is now called the Old Salt at Lamie's Inn and has successfully maintained its popularity. (HHS.)

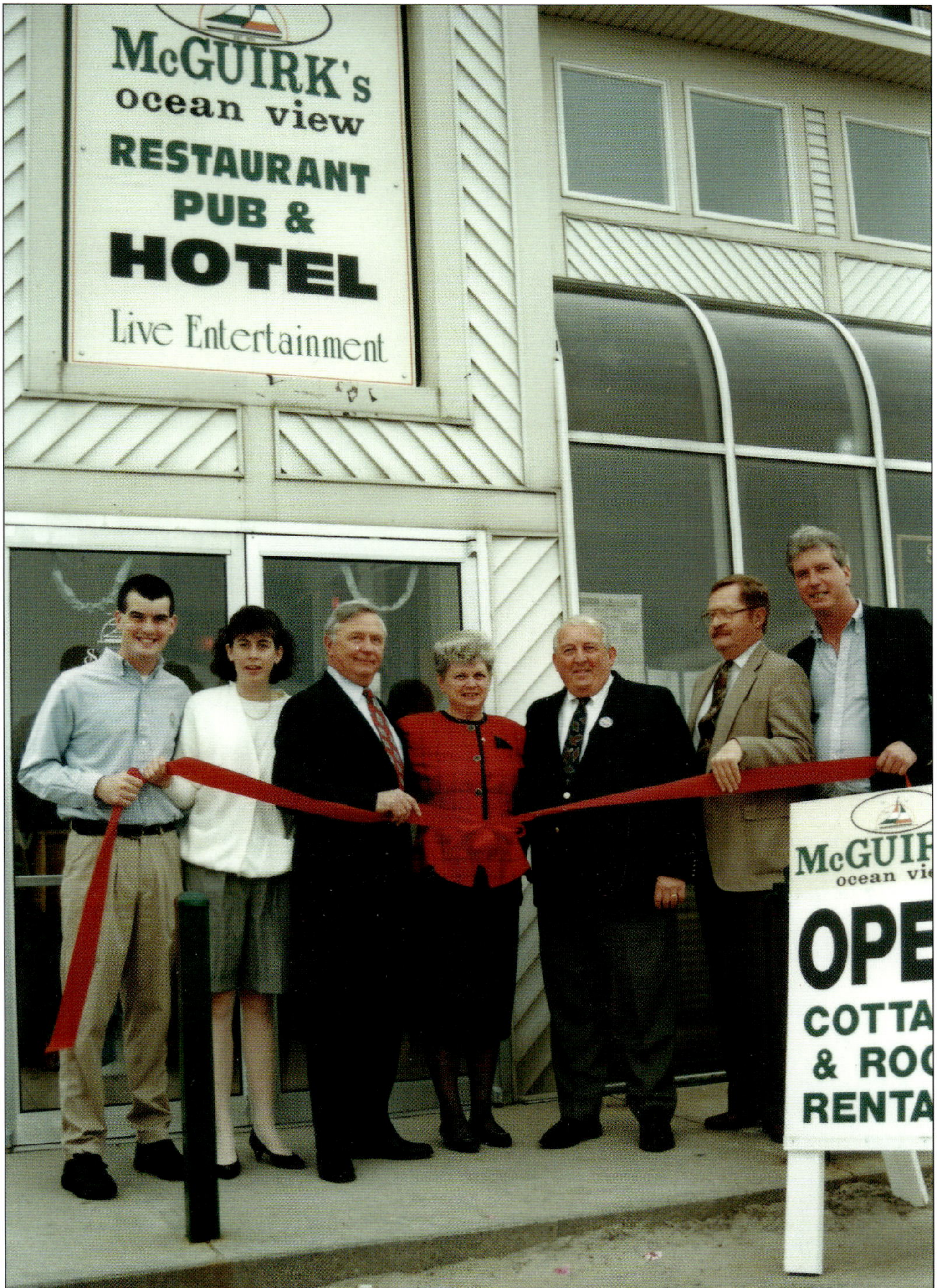

McGuirk's Ocean View Restaurant Pub and Hotel celebrated its grand opening in 1991 in the historic Lincoln House at 95 Ocean Boulevard. The McGuirk family has been summering at Hampton Beach since 1969 and opened the restaurant after Bill McGuirk retired from his job at the Worcester Fire Department in Massachusetts. (HHS.)

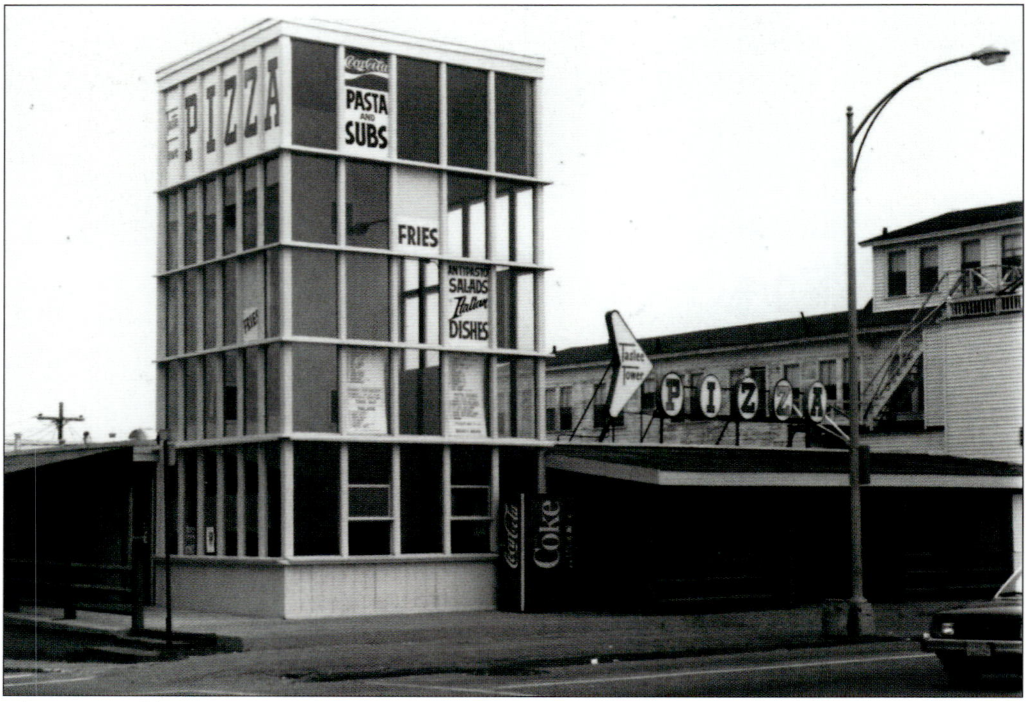

The memorable Tastee Tower of Pizza stood at 313 Ocean Boulevard at the corner of Highland Avenue, just south of the Ashworth by the Sea, from 1967 until it was demolished in the late 1990s. This 1984 photograph shows the tower, which could be seen from the beach and from several blocks in most directions. An advertisement for the restaurant in 1990 reads, "Look for the Tower at the Beach," and invites beachgoers to "Come as you are!" directly off the beach or from around town. (HHS.)

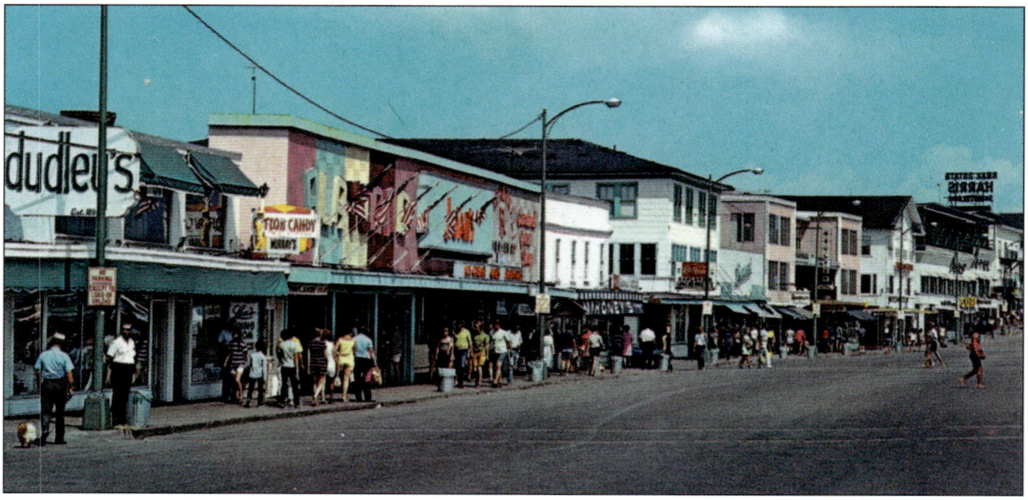

This postcard from a collection at the Hampton Beach Historical Society shows several businesses at the northern end of the beach. Dudley's Department Store, which has been at the beach since 1895, stands at 203 Ocean Boulevard at the corner of C Street. The store sold nearly everything, from small furniture to jewelry and clothing. The long-standing Playland Arcade has been on Ocean Boulevard since the 1930s. The landmark building burned down during a very destructive fire in 1950, but a new structure was erected in the same location. (HHS.)

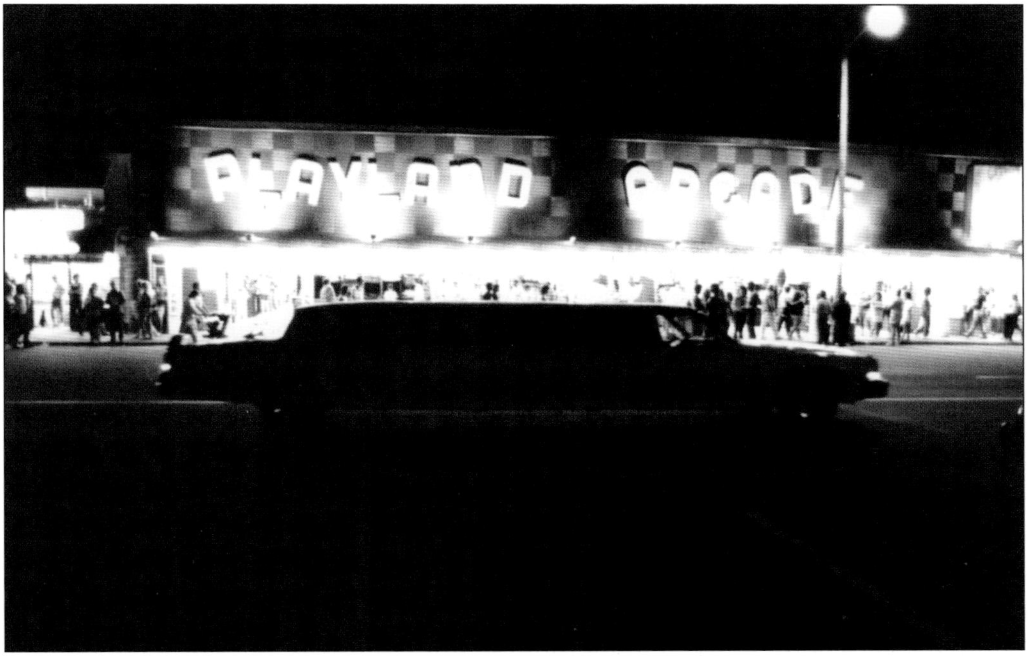

This photograph, taken in the mid-1980s, shows the Playland Arcade in the evening during the height of summer. The arcade has been popular with visiting families since the business took off in the late 1930s and has become something of a landmark at the beach. The arcade stands at 211 Ocean Boulevard, a few businesses south of the Surf Hotel. (HHS.)

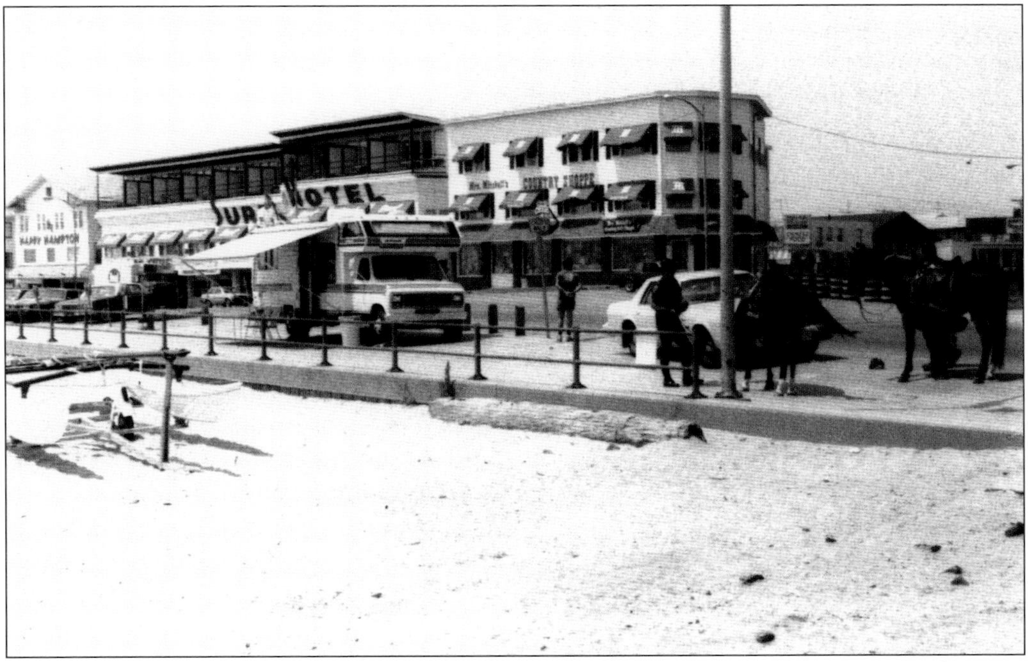

Photographed in 1986, these longtime businesses were near the corner of A Street and Ocean Boulevard. Pictured are, from left to right, the Happy Hampton Arcade, the Surf Hotel, and Mrs. Mitchell's Gifts, respectively located at 257, 263, and 279 Ocean Boulevard. The Surf Hotel and its iconic sign in particular could be seen clearly from the beach. (HHS.)

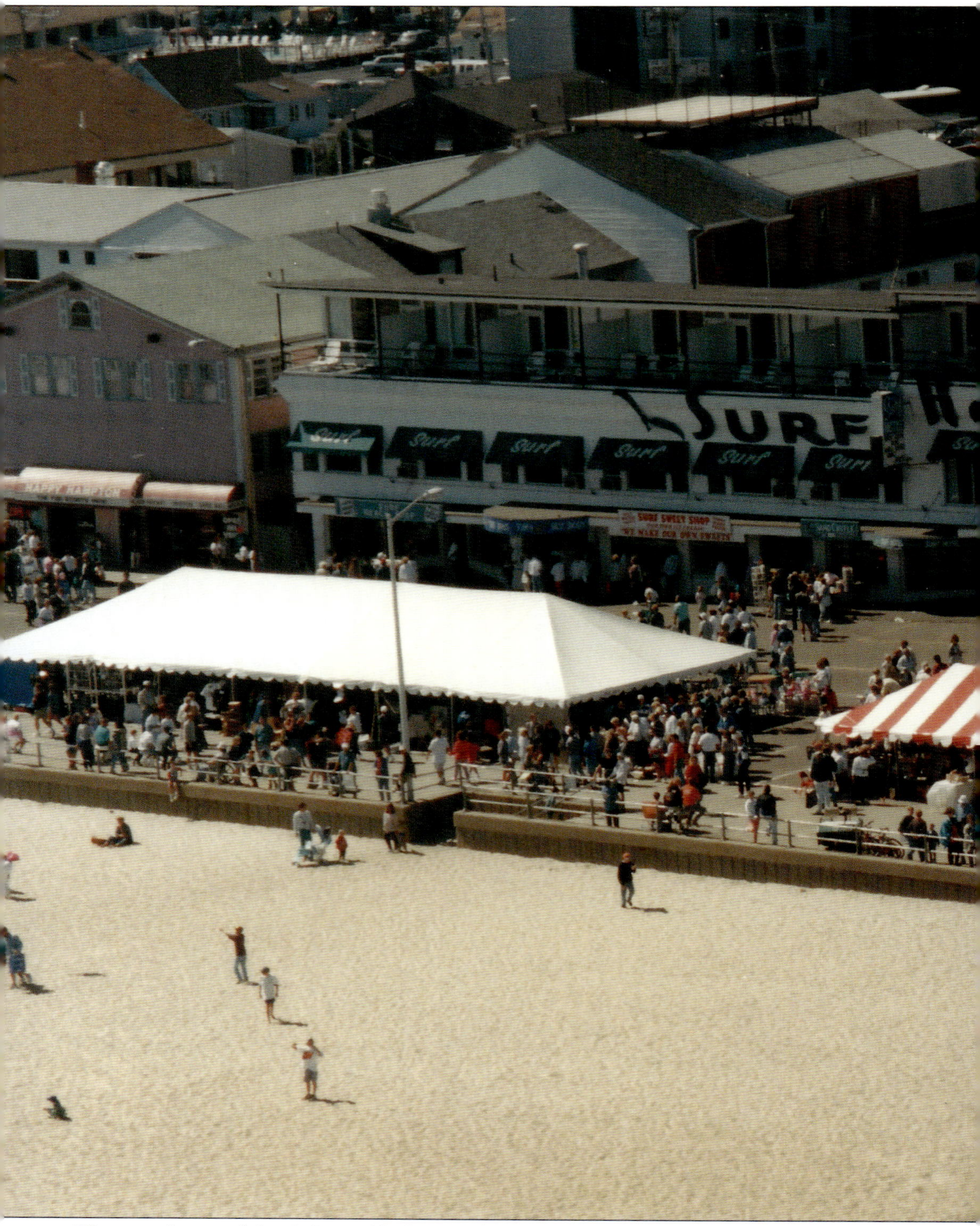

This aerial view of the A Street block was taken sometime between 1996 and 1999 during the summer Seafood Festival. The three-story hotel had remained popular even as the beach's tourist culture shifted away from hotel stays and toward condominiums. However, a condominium building

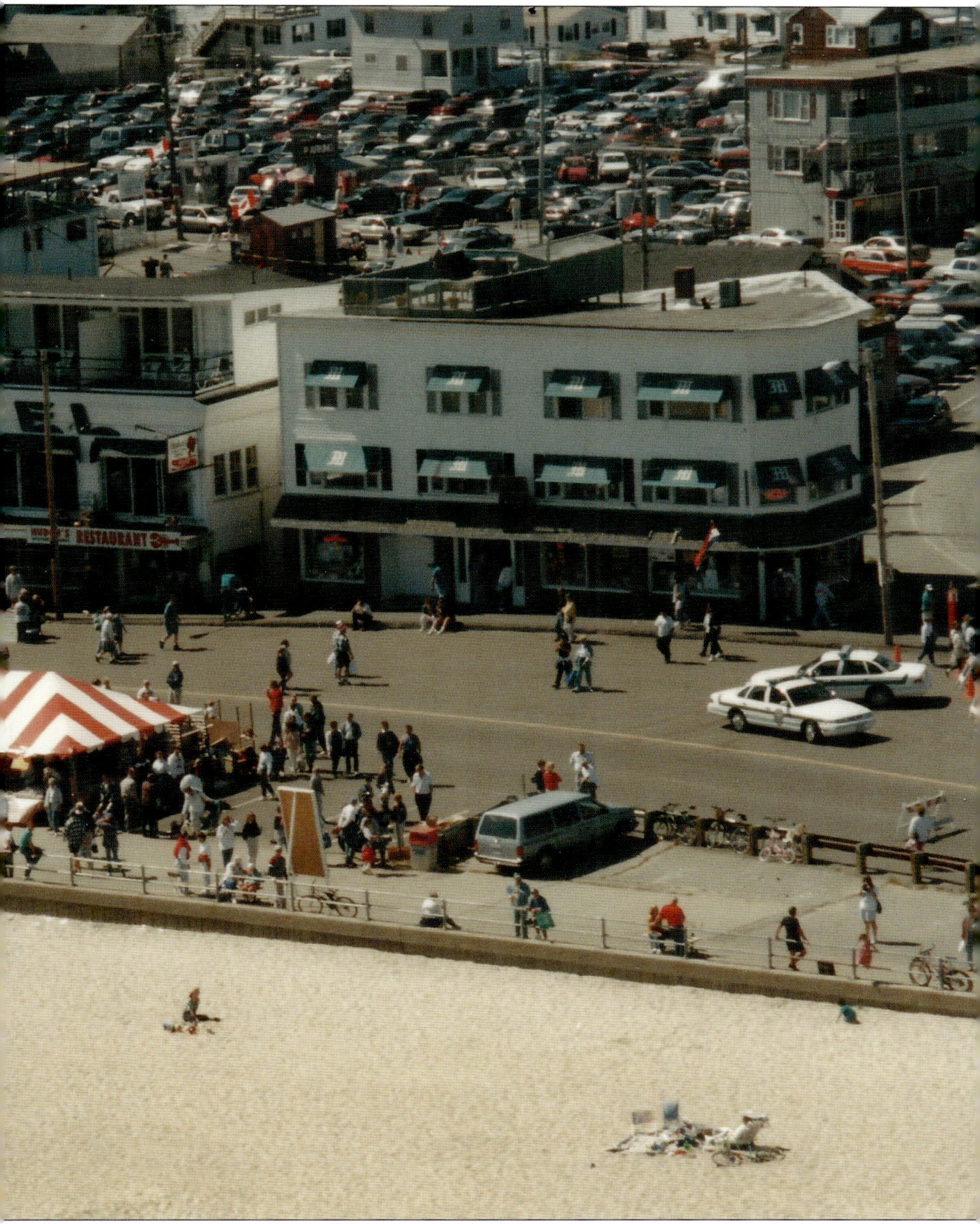

was eventually erected on the lot a few years after the block burned down during a major fire in 2010. Of the businesses lost in the fire, Mrs. Mitchell's Gifts was the only one to rebuild on the same lot. (HHS.)

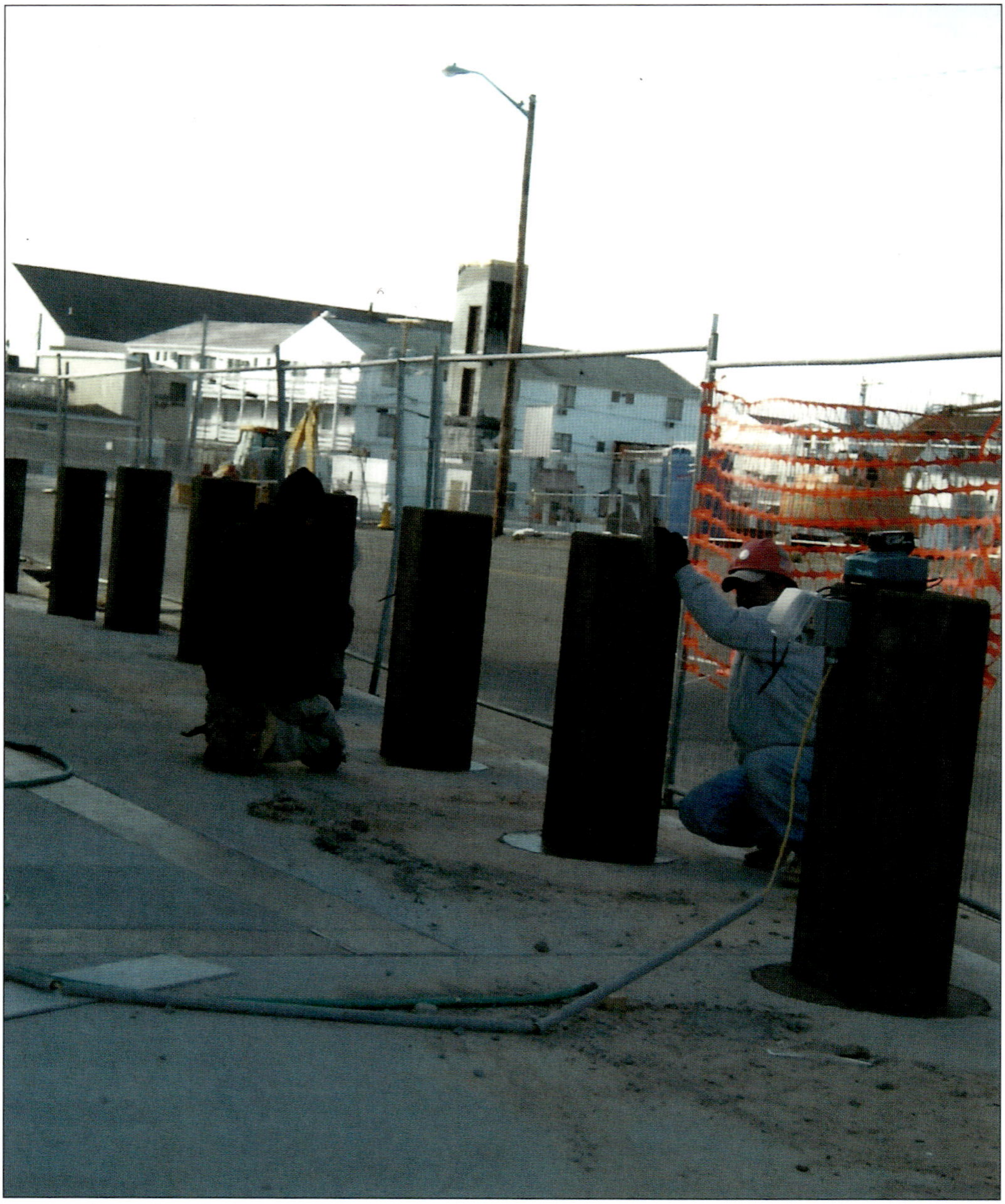

During the night of February 26, 2010, which was plagued with nearly hurricane-strength winds, a fire started in the Surf Hotel and quickly consumed the whole building. Unfortunately, it was not long before the flames spread to the other businesses on the block, including Mrs. Mitchell's Gifts, the Surf Sweet Shop, and the Happy Hampton Arcade. The flames, which could be seen from several blocks away, raged throughout the night and razed the entire block. No one was seriously injured, even though the fire was so massive that, according to an article by Patrick Cronin in the *Hampton Union*, 40 separate fire departments were on the scene. This image was captured only eight months after the fire in November and was intended to document the construction of the North Bathhouse during the Hampton Beach Redevelopment Project. The background of this picture shows all that remained of the A Street block: a charred two-story elevator shaft seen at center. (DRED.)

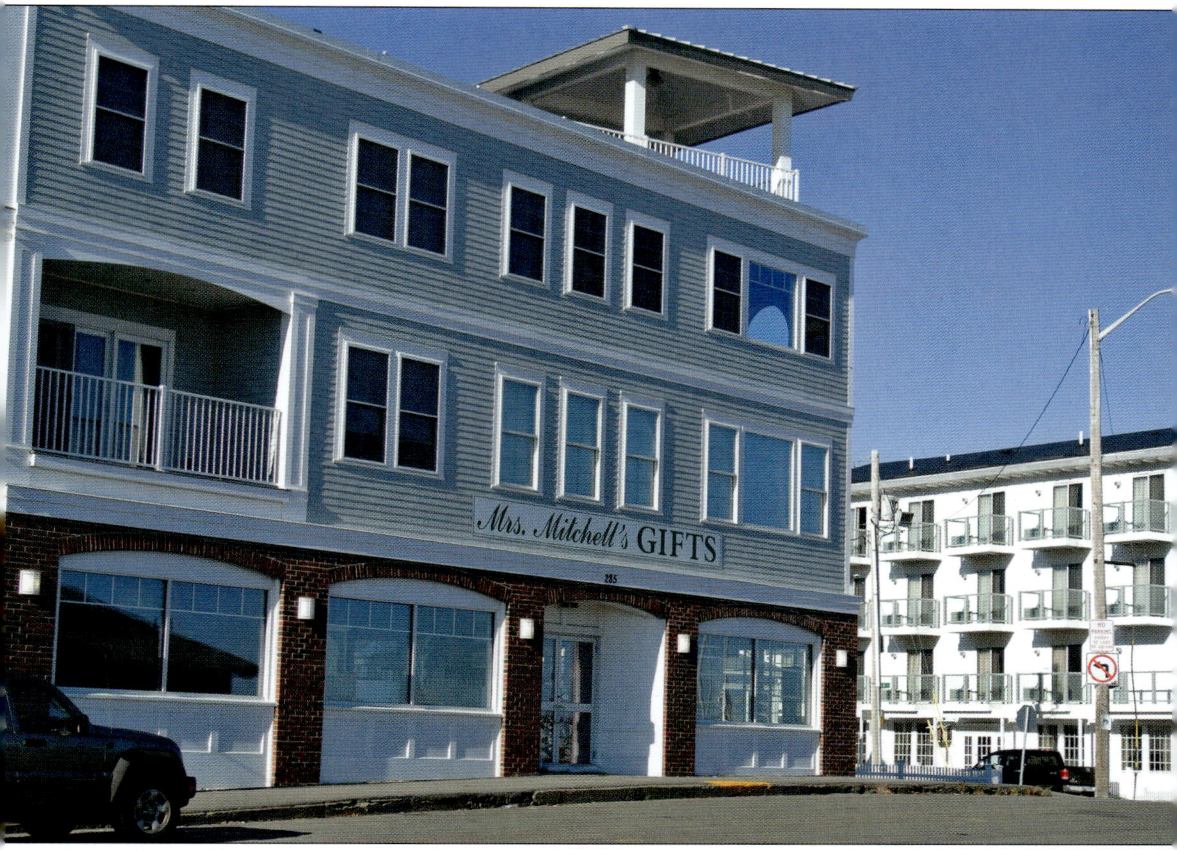

According to the current owners of Mrs. Mitchell's Gifts, Robert and Jessica Mitchell, the shop was founded by George and Freda Mitchell in 1966. Soon after the first store opened, the Mitchells included Evelyn and Frank Mitchell in their business. The first store was opened on Hampton Beach and the family has since opened stores in Hyannis and West Yarmouth in Massachusetts. Throughout its 50 year history, the business has stayed exclusively within the Mitchell family. This newly built version of the store stands on the same A Street block where the original building burned down in 2010. The Mitchells drew inspiration for their new building from the new Seashell Complex, which was being built at the same time only a few blocks away. (Author's collection.)

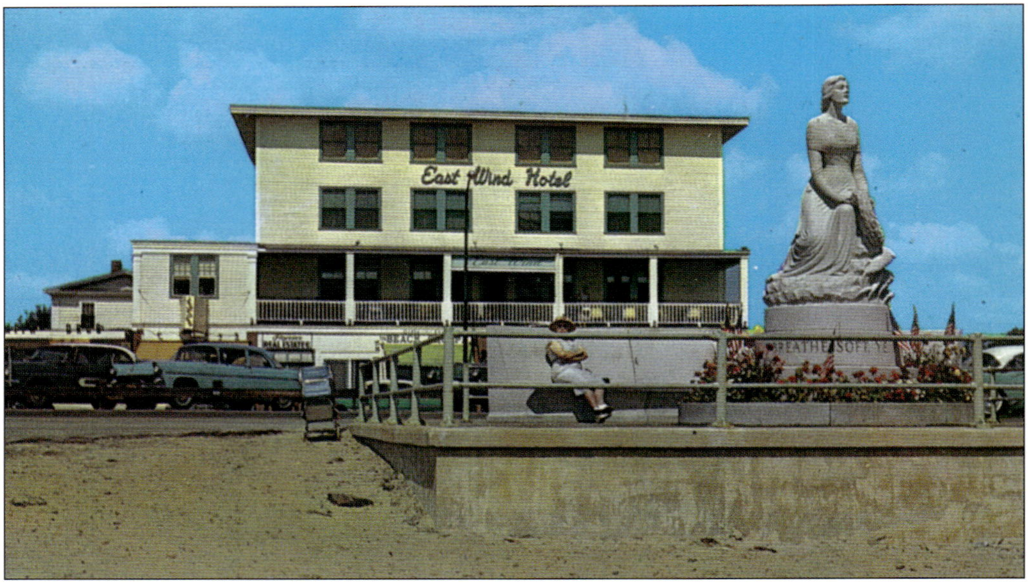

The East Wind Hotel, which was owned by Mr. and Mrs. L.T. Pease, stood on Ocean Boulevard directly across the street from the Marine Memorial. This postcard image, taken in the early 1960s, shows a woman enjoying the view of the ocean across the street from the business. In the 1970s, the hotel was bought by the owners of the Ashworth by the Sea and was demolished to make way for the brick tower of hotel rooms. (HHS.)

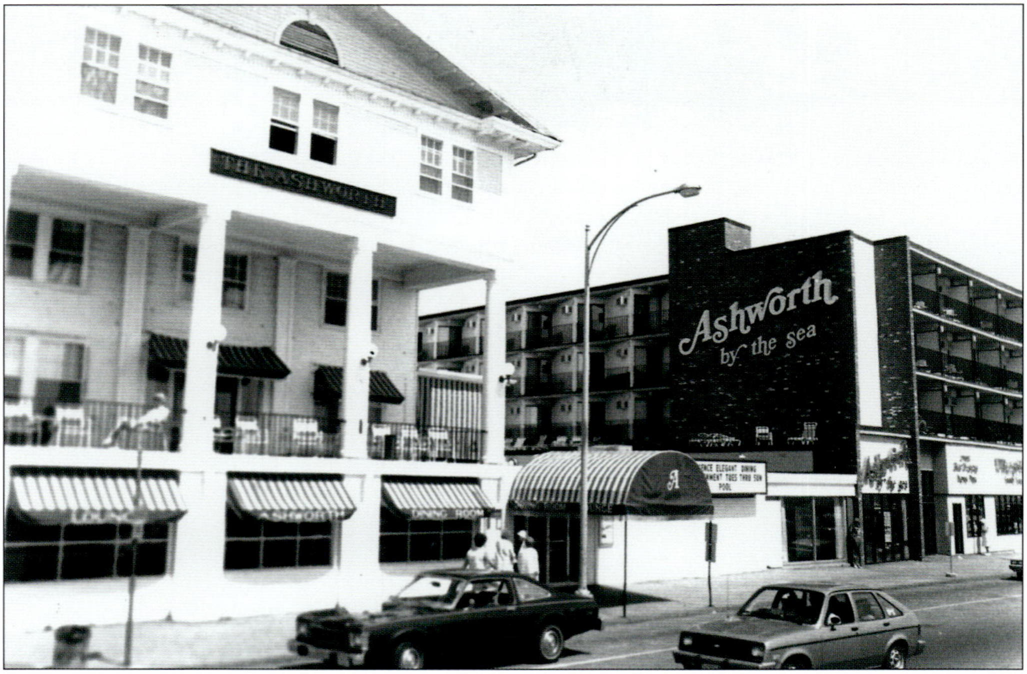

The Ashworth by the Sea hotel was originally built in 1912 by George Ashworth and has been rebuilt and renovated several times since then. This photograph, take in 1984, shows the Ashworth by the Sea only a few years after the hotel room tower replaced the East Winds Hotel. The architectural design of the main entrance, including the columns and patio, had been maintained, albeit in different forms, since it was originally built. (HHS.)

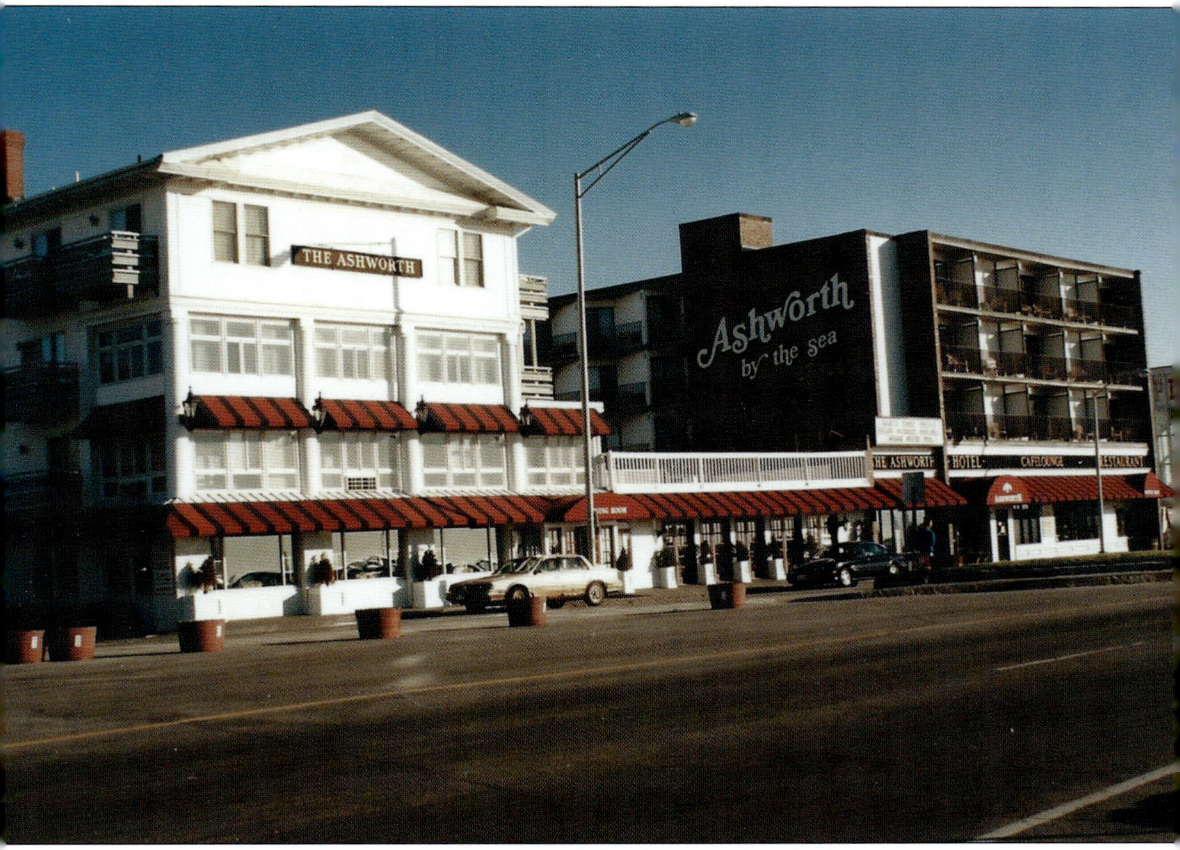

This picture, taken in 1999, shows the Ashworth by the Sea after the front entrance received its last redesign only five years earlier. The columns and patio have been closed in in favor of a smooth facade. The hotel is located at 295 Ocean Boulevard, directly across the street from the Marine Memorial, and is one of the oldest hotels still standing on Hampton Beach. (HHS.)

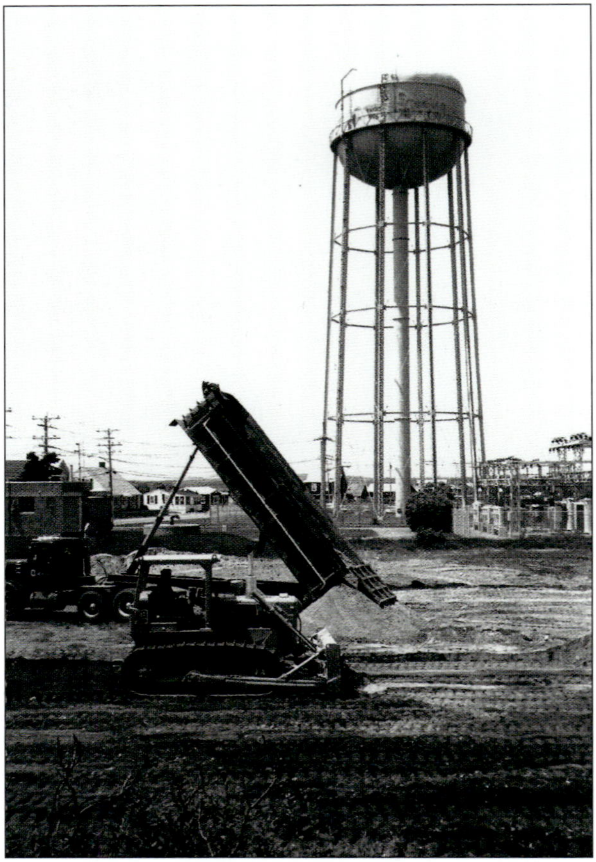

The Hampton Beach water tower stands directly next to New Hampshire Route 101, which is the main highway that crosses southern New Hampshire and continues east until it reaches the ocean. The tower is a few blocks out from the beach but has become an iconic feature of Hampton since it was built in 1953. This picture shows the construction of a parking lot for the Ashworth by the Sea in the early 1980s. (HHS.)

Dave's Garage is owned by David Lavoie and not only provides excellent service and towing but has also been a hub for locals and visitors to socialize. The garage, which is located just north of the Kentville Hotel and the Ashworth by the Sea, was one of only two gas stations on the beach section of Ocean Boulevard. A few state park employees fondly remember going to some of Dave's many parties after their workdays in the 1990s. (Author's collection.)

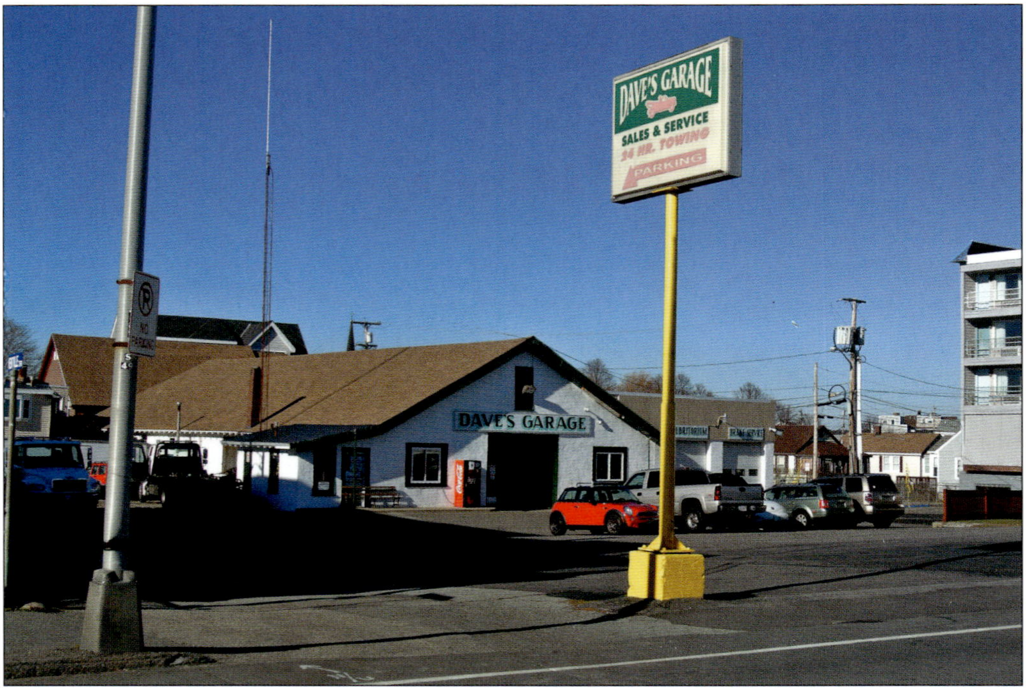

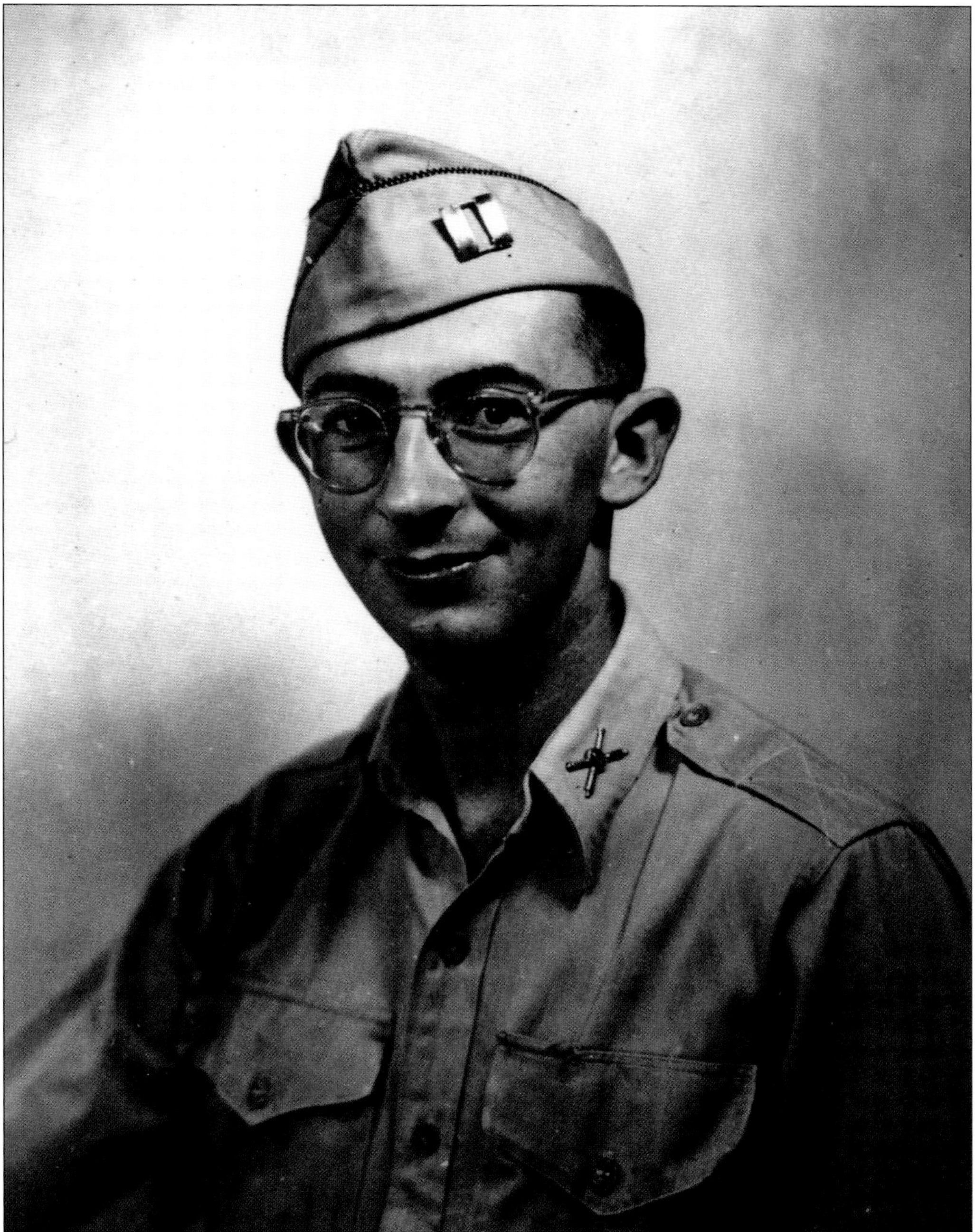

William D. Downs was born on November 24, 1919, and was a captain in the US Navy during World War II. According to Randall's *Hampton: A Century of Town and Beach*, Downs died in May 1945 after participating in the Southwest Pacific and Philippine Islands campaigns. In the 1950s, his father, William E. Downs, requested that a memorial be built after discovering that there was not one in New Hampshire to add his son's name to. (HHS.)

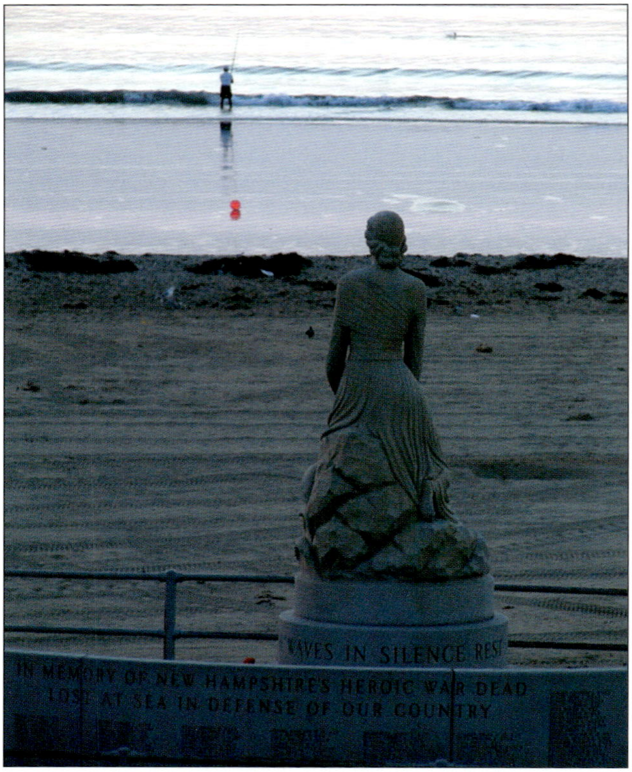

The New Hampshire Marine Memorial was created in the late 1950s in response to Downs's request. It honors New Hampshire servicemen lost at sea during all US wars and was dedicated on Memorial Day 1957. The statue, depicting a Gold Star mother, was designed by Alice Cosgrove. She says of the figure: "Reverently, she lays a wreath upon the soft waters which embrace them. As she looks across the waters, she asks that the winds and waves be gentle, as a mother who covers her sleeping child at night." Inscribed at the base of the statue are lyrics from John Gay's poem "A Letter to a Lady:" "Breathe soft, ye winds, Ye waves in silence rest." (HCC.)

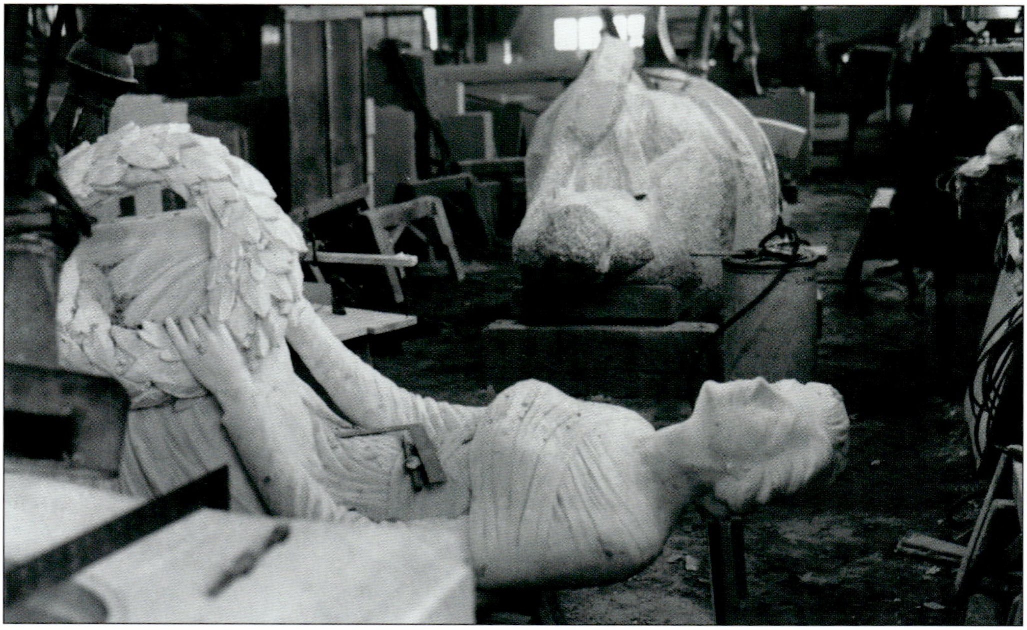

Alice Cosgrove designed the New Hampshire Marine Memorial after she won the design contest held by the New Hampshire Marine Memorial Commission. The statue itself was created by Vermont artisan Vincenzo Andreani. It is made from a solid, 24-ton block of New Hampshire granite. This picture was taken at the Marr and Gordon granite works in Barre, New Hampshire, and includes the original clay model in the background. (HHS.)

This pamphlet was made for the only fundraising event that the New Hampshire Marine Memorial Commission held. The front page asks potential donors to "Help restore the identities of more than 300 New Hampshire heroes who lost their lives at sea in all wars." The pamphlet states that there would only be one fundraiser, and that "after the memorial is erected, there will be no other solicitations." (HHS.)

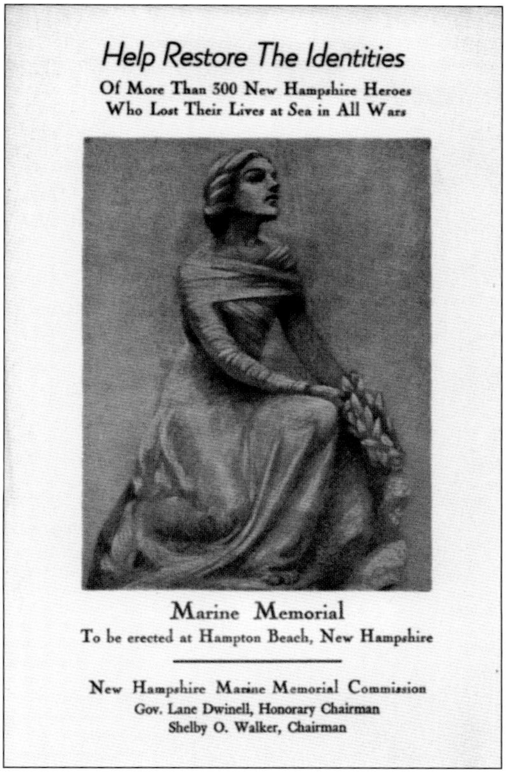
Help Restore The Identities
Of More Than 300 New Hampshire Heroes Who Lost Their Lives at Sea in All Wars

Marine Memorial
To be erected at Hampton Beach, New Hampshire

New Hampshire Marine Memorial Commission
Gov. Lane Dwinell, Honorary Chairman
Shelby O. Walker, Chairman

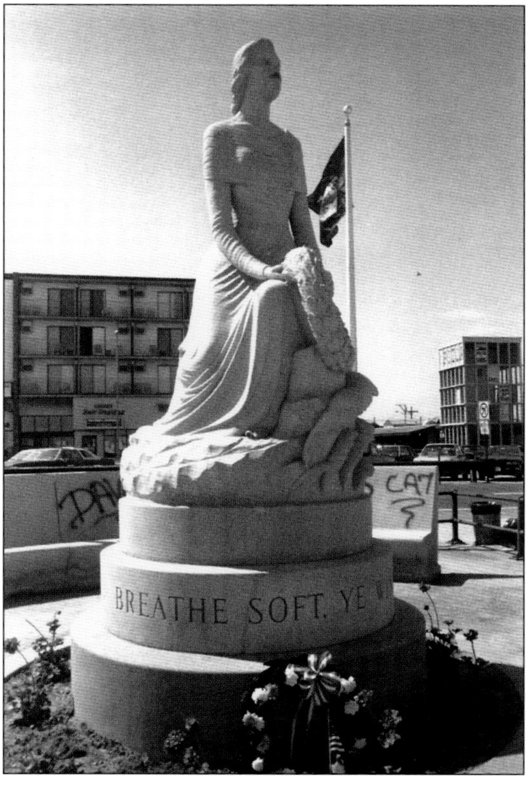

The Marine Memorial is located directly across from the Ashworth by the Sea and where the Tastee Tower of Pizza used to stand near Highland Avenue; both are seen here in the background. This 1987 photograph shows the Gold Star mother looking out toward the sea, as well as the base of the statue and the benches around it. The base bears the inscription chosen by Cosgrove, while the back of the surrounding granite benches are inscribed with the names of all the New Hampshire sailors lost at sea. (HHS.)

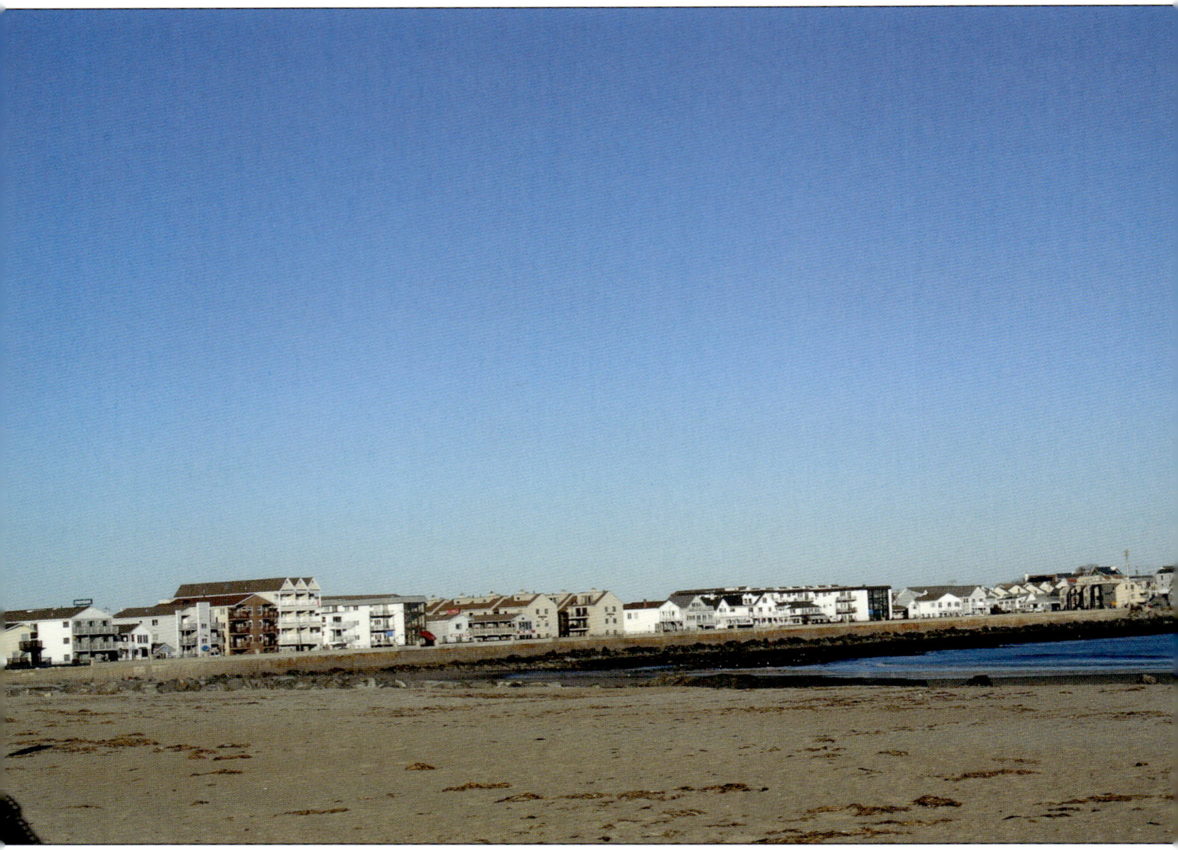

In the 1970s, more visitors wanted to stay longer and spend their whole summers at Hampton Beach. It was not practical to stay in a hotel for such a long time, so businesses began meeting these needs by transforming or even replacing their hotels with condominiums. Most business owners constructed either large buildings with many units or several single units on the same plot of land. This picture, taken in 2015 from the boardwalk, shows Ocean Boulevard lined with all different types of condominium buildings as the road curves toward Great Boar's Head. On the small streets that are set back behind Ocean Boulevard, there are dozens of tiny houses and cottages that make up Hampton Beach's many condominium communities. (Author's collection.)

Three

Annual Festivals, Celebrations, and Parades

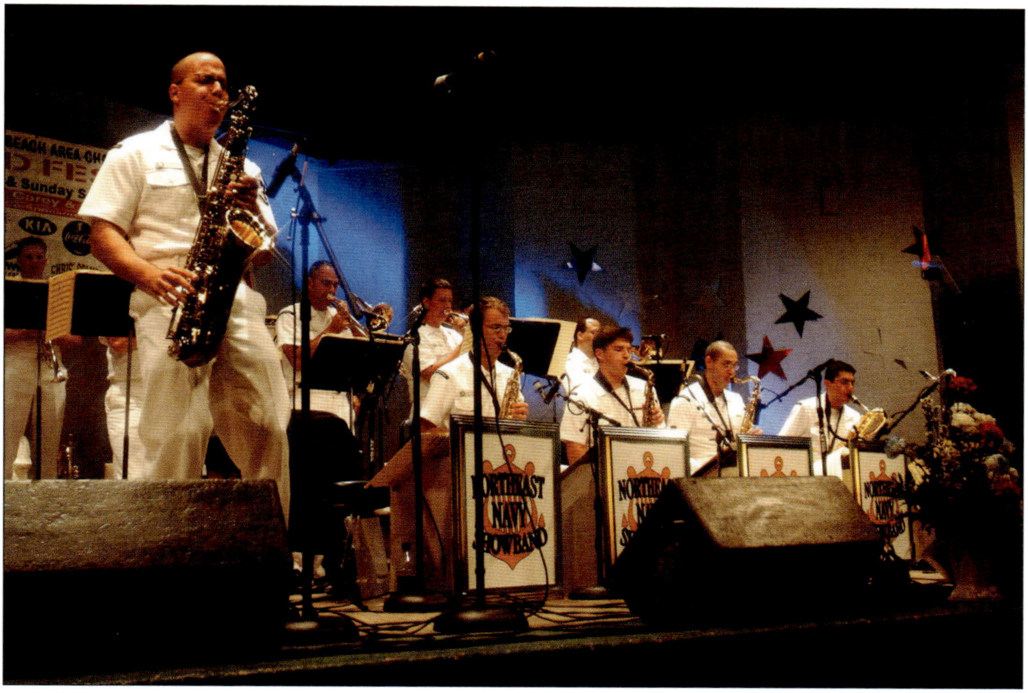

The Northeast Navy Show Band plays on the old Seashell stage during Hampton Beach's annual Seafood Festival. The Navy Band has become such a popular attraction at Hampton Beach that a section of Ocean Boulevard often has to be closed because the audience spills into the street. This is just one of the nightly attractions that is held on the Seashell stage during the Hampton Beach Seafood Festival. Hampton Beach, with its history rooted in leisure and entertainment, puts on almost nightly concerts throughout the summer and into fall for both visitors and locals to enjoy. The Navy Band in particular can be heard for blocks in either direction with its booming, big band sound. (HCC.)

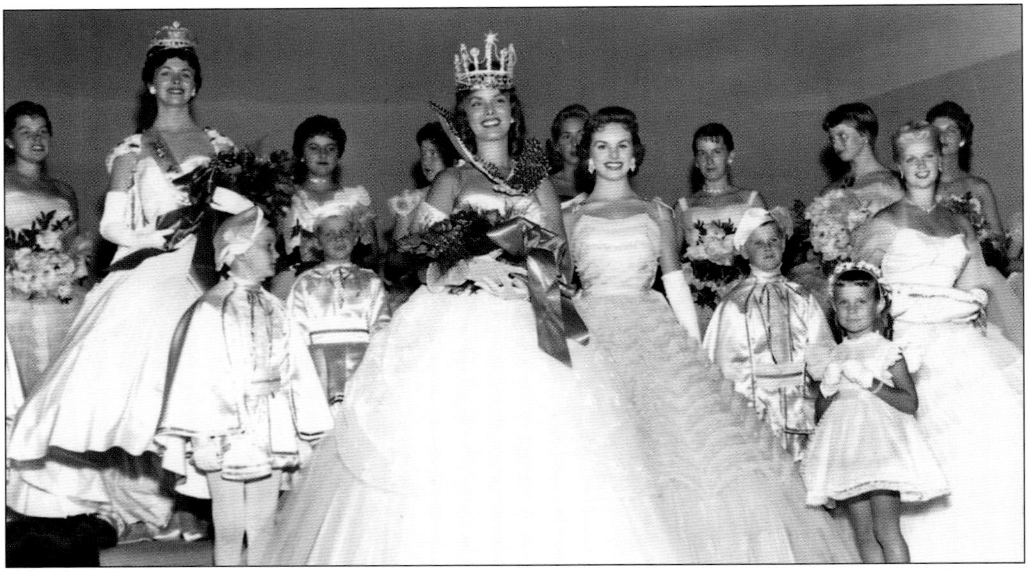

The Miss Hampton Beach beauty pageant has been an annual event at Hampton Beach since 1946, when the pageant was created by the *Beachcomber* newspaper. Pictured here is Carolyn Ann Komant, the winner of the 1958 pageant. According to the 50th-anniversary pageant program, when the event was first created, it contained a tremendous amount of pomp and flash. The winner was crowned at the beginning of Carnival Week, which started off a week of parades and festivals at Hampton Beach. In the same week, a ball was held where Miss Hampton Beach and dozens of other young girls in ball gowns would dance the night away. (HHS.)

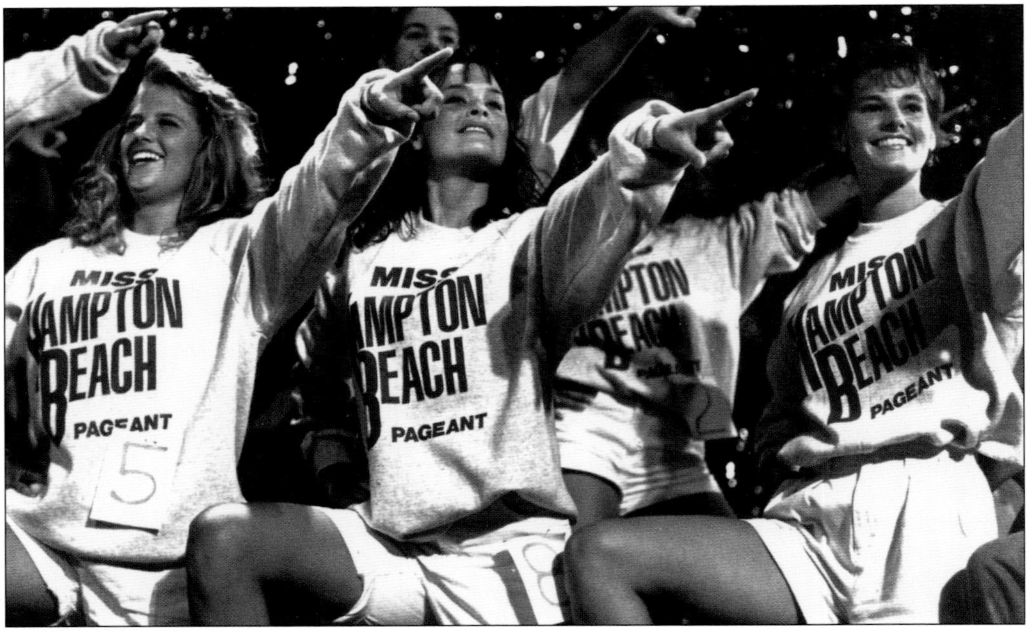

The Miss Hampton Beach competition is still an annual event at Hampton Beach. This picture, taken in the early 1990s, shows contestants dancing in the opening number. According to the 50th-anniversary program, the contestants are judged for their "face, form and personality" by a panel of judges. The pageant also includes a swimsuit competition and an evening gown competition. (HHS.)

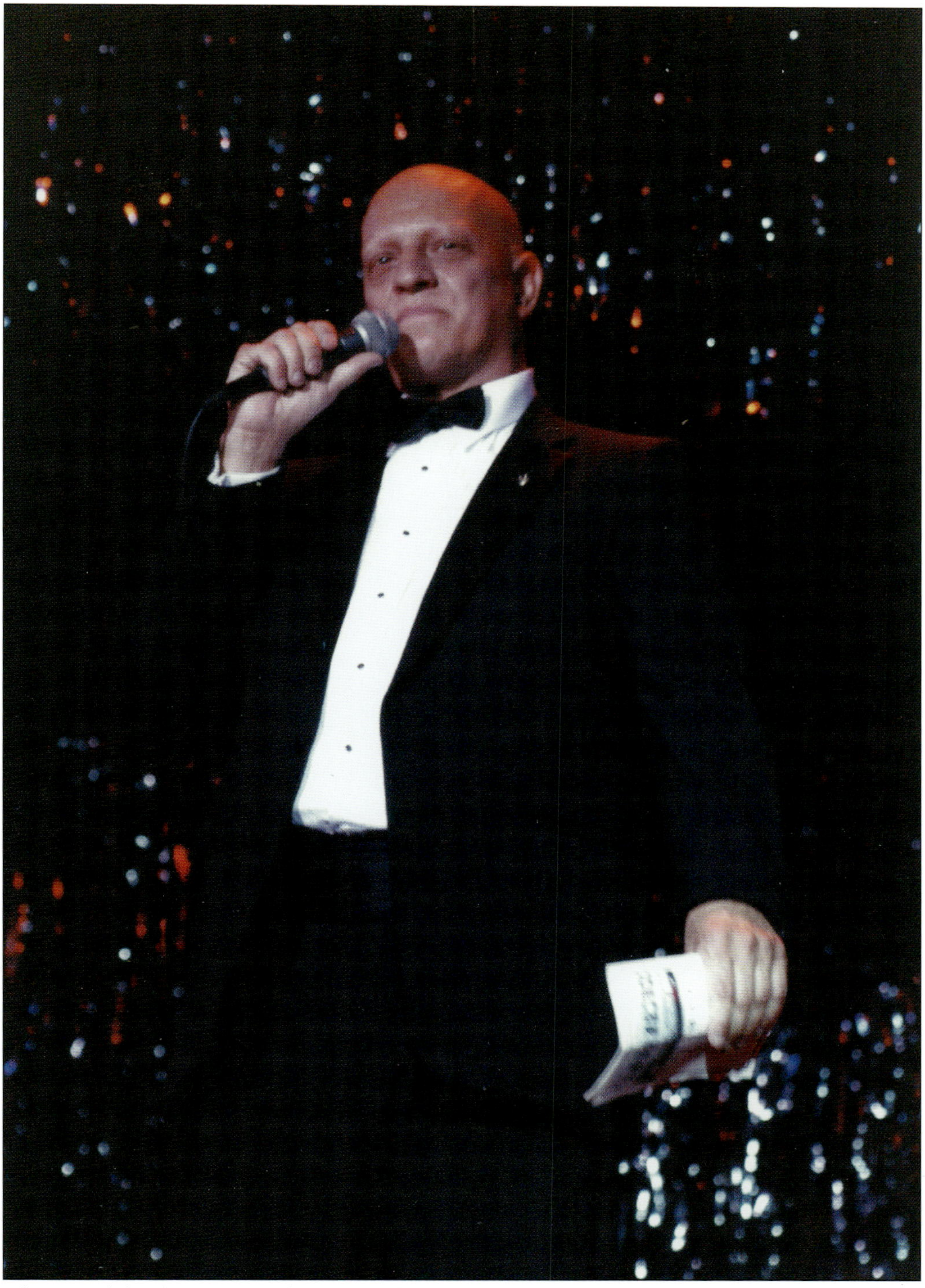

Glen French has been part of planning and directing Hampton Beach entertainment and events for several years. This is a photograph of French speaking at the start of the 1991 Miss Hampton Beach competition as the director of the Hampton Beach Area Chamber of Commerce. (HHS.)

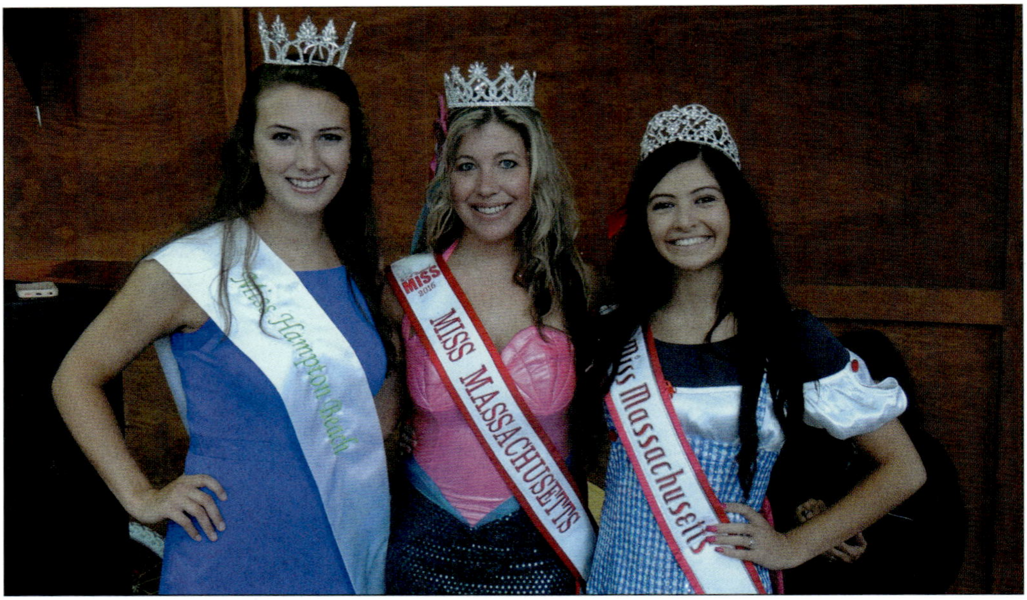

Victoria Soucy, the winner of the 69th annual Miss Hampton Beach Competition in 2015, is seen on the left. At the time she was crowned Miss Hampton Beach, she was 17 years old and lived in Massachusetts. Pageant director Stephanie Lussier says there is no talent competition because all of the focus is on who is the best spokesperson for Hampton Beach, and Soucy stood out. According to a *Seacoast Online* article by Karen Dandurant, Soucy said she believed that Miss Hampton Beach should not only be present at important events, but should also make appearances at the local businesses and social areas, such as arcades and on the beach. (HCC.)

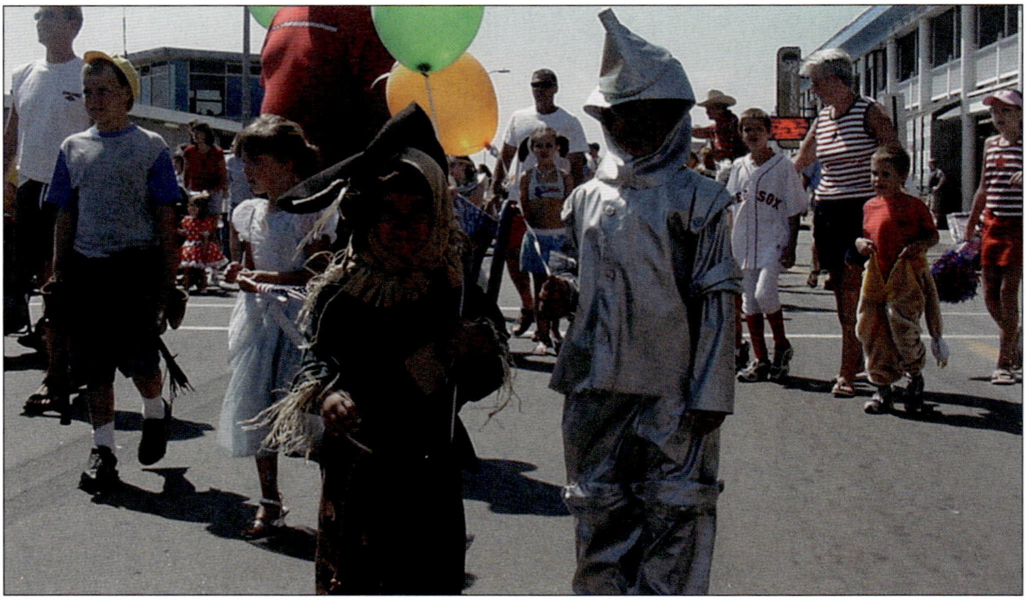

Two young boys enjoy the costume parade during the 2015 Children's Festival. The parade is part of the weeklong festival in which every activity is specifically geared toward kids. These boys are dressed up as characters from *The Wizard of Oz*. They are joined by dozens of other children and their families as they march north along Ocean Boulevard. Here, the parade is just passing the Seashell Complex and the Hampton Beach Casino. (HHS.)

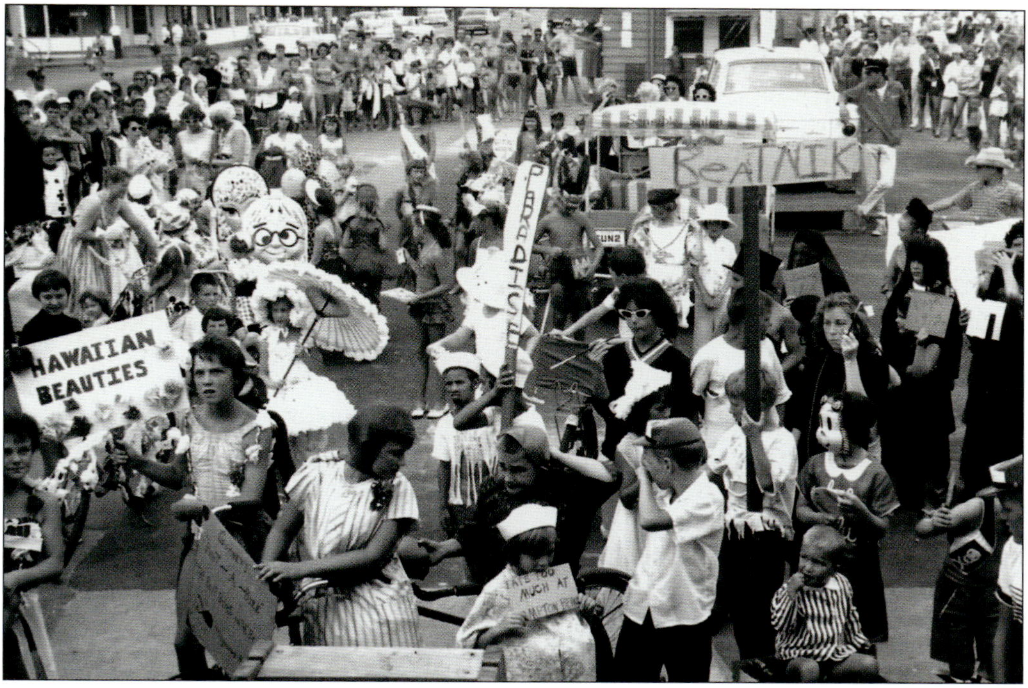

This costume parade took place over 50 years before the parade in the previous image, during the Children's Festival of August 1961. The parade is passing the bandstand on Ocean Boulevard, where the Seashell Complex would be built the next year. Marchers are dressed as a variety of characters and personages. The costume parade has always been one of the main events during the Children's Festivals, giving children the opportunity to win prizes for their costumes. (HHS.)

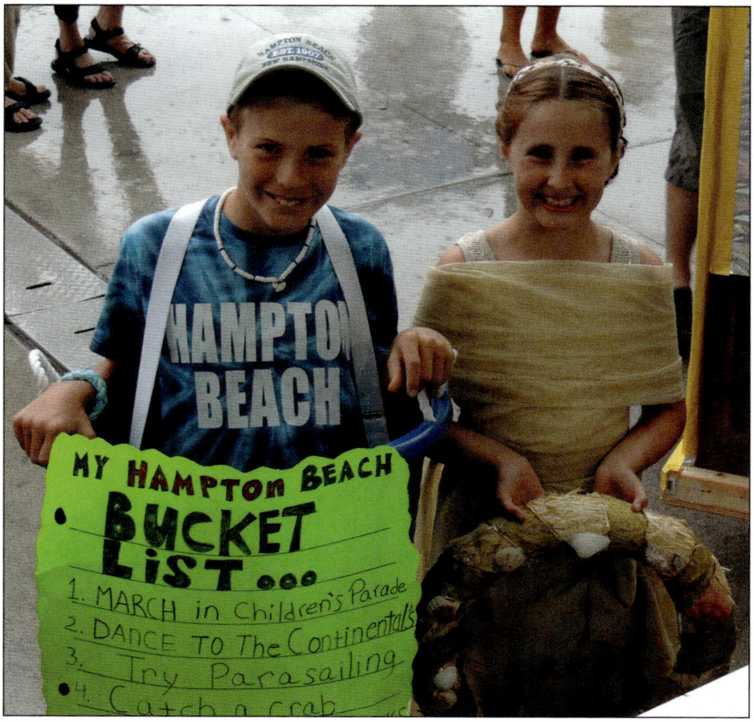

These children are both dressed in costumes that are based on Hampton Beach. While the boy on the left is sporting a list of things that anybody might have the opportunity to do at Hampton Beach, the girl on the right is dressed as the Gold Star mother who stands at the center of the Marine Memorial. (HCC.)

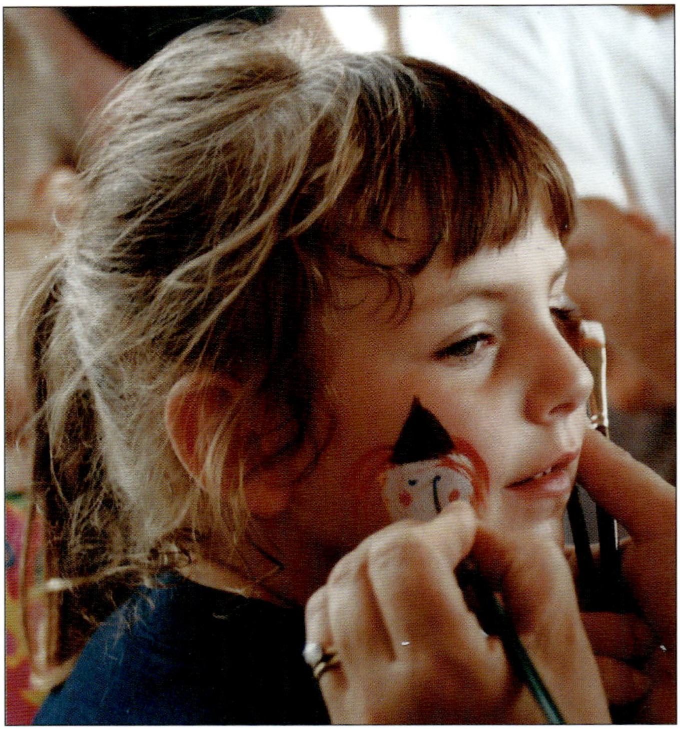

A young girl has her face painted during Hampton Beach's annual Children's Festival in 1998. The festival, one of many throughout the year, has evolved into a weeklong event since its beginning in the early 20th century. The entire week consists of events that aim to celebrate, entertain, and engage families and children from the local area, whether they are visitors or locals. The events include shows, concerts, competitions, parades, and games on and off the sandy beach. (HHS.)

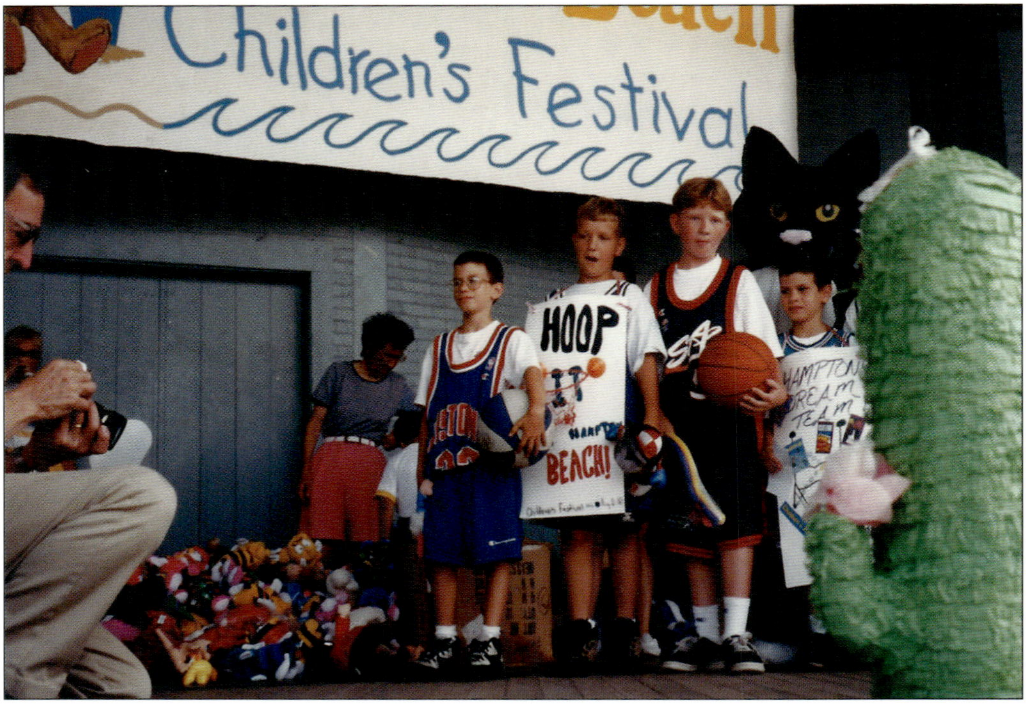

A group of young boys get ready to pose for a picture during the 1998 Children's Festival. The boys are standing on the stage of the original Seashell Complex. Children are encouraged to dress in costume, especially for the costume parade during the week, and these boys have dressed up as basketball players. (HHS.)

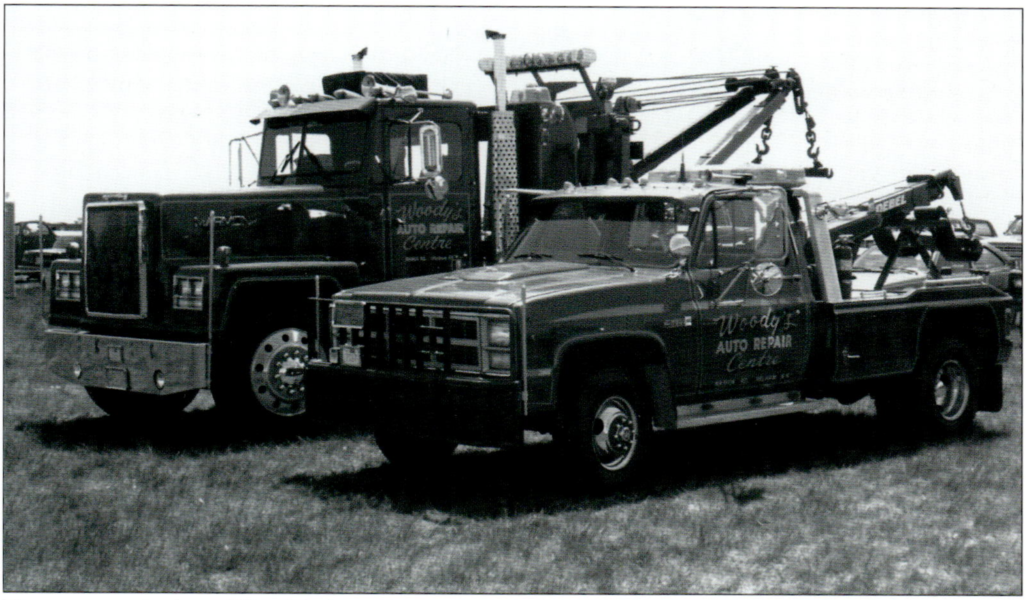

Two tow trucks from Woody's Auto Repair Center from southern New Hampshire line up side by side in preparation for Hampton Beach's annual Tow Truck Rodeo only a few years after it began in 1978. The rodeo includes towing demonstrations, driving contests, and even a truck beauty contest. Each year, the rodeo draws towing companies from all over New England and provides an opportunity for both drivers and businesses to form cooperative relationships. (HHS.)

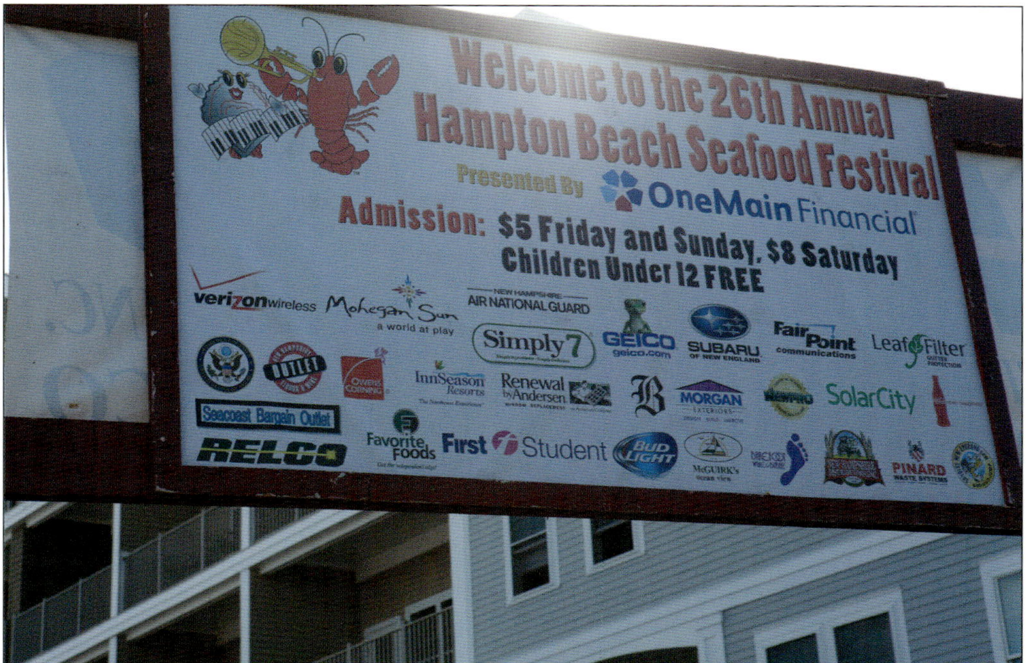

Signs for the Hampton Beach Seafood Festival are put up months in advance and hang over Ocean Boulevard for all to see. The first Seafood Festival was held in 1989 and the event has been steadily growing in size, popularity, and attendance ever since. The festival saw a record amount of people for its 25th anniversary in 2014. (HCC.)

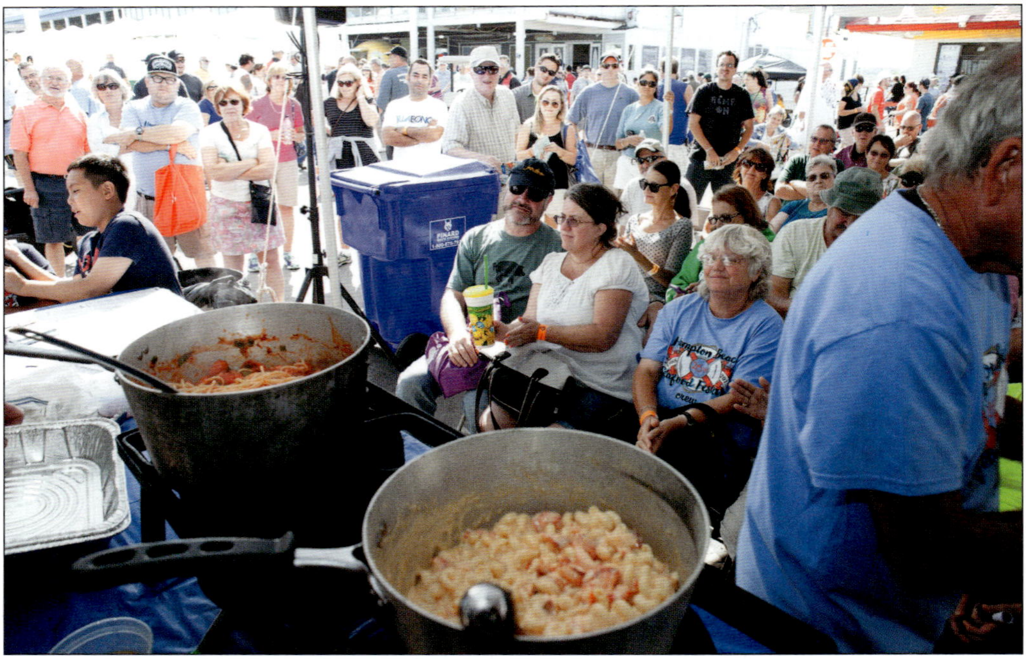

The Seafood Festival started with a few Hampton Beach Area Chamber of Commerce restaurants. These businesses coordinated with each other and set up booths at the southern end of Hampton Beach State Park for a small event in 1988 and offered samples of their seafood specialties to promote business and to showcase New Hampshire's excellent seafood. (HCC.)

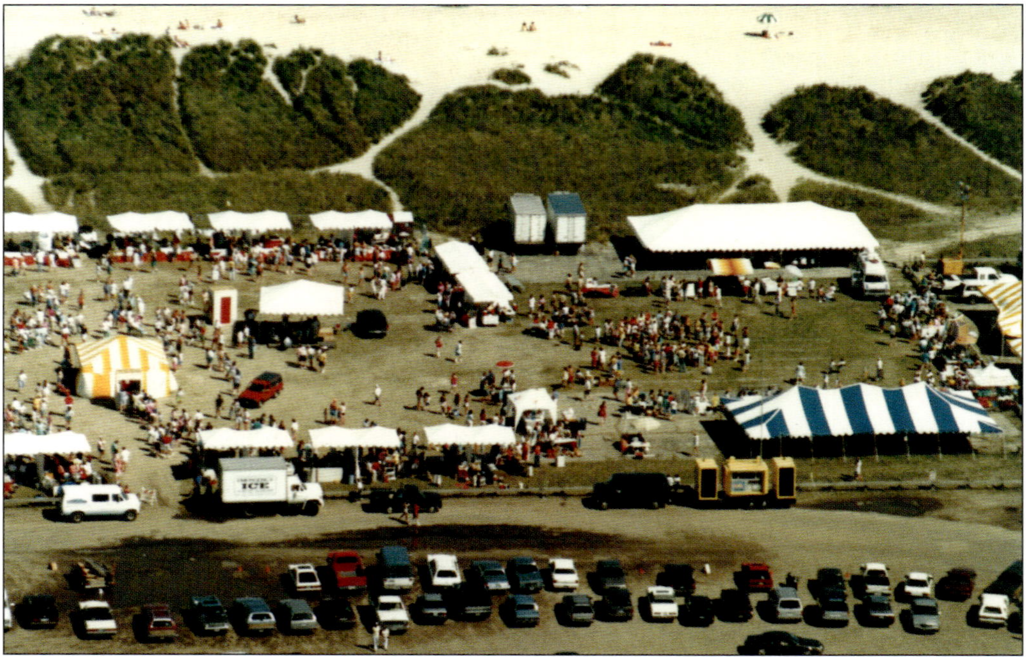

The first few editions of the Seafood Festival were held at the state park at the southern end of the beach. By the time this picture was taken in the late 1990s, the festival was already being held along Ocean Boulevard. However, some of the first festivals would have looked something like this crowd, which is overflowing from the now wildly popular event. (HHS.)

Two young boys are enjoying the Hampton Beach Seafood Festival with their lobster hats. During the festival, the novelty hats are worn by people of all ages. The festival usually occurs later in the season, at the end of August or the beginning of September, and continues for an entire weekend. In recent years, the festival has drawn crowds of over 100,000 from all over the northeast, and in some cases from all over the nation. (HCC.)

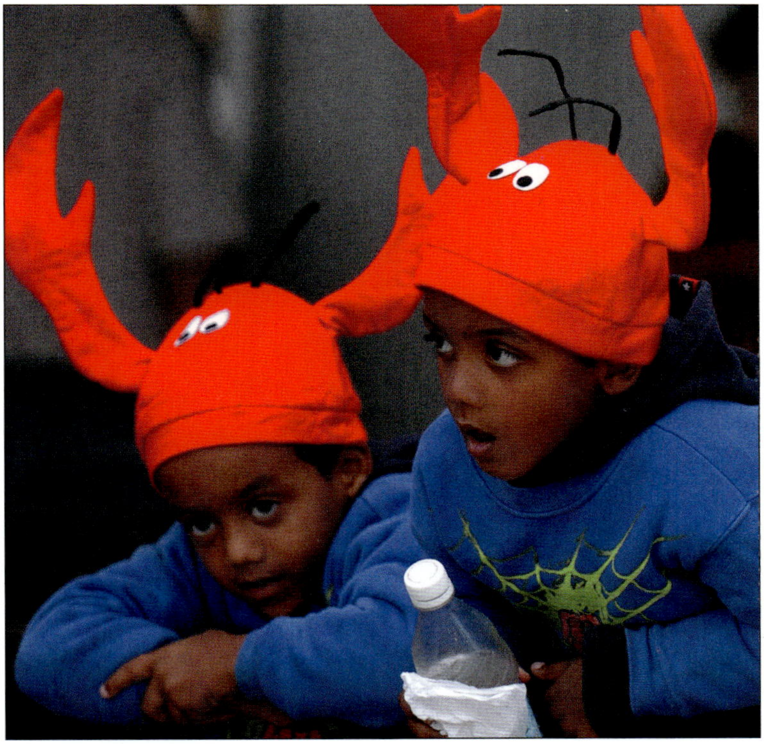

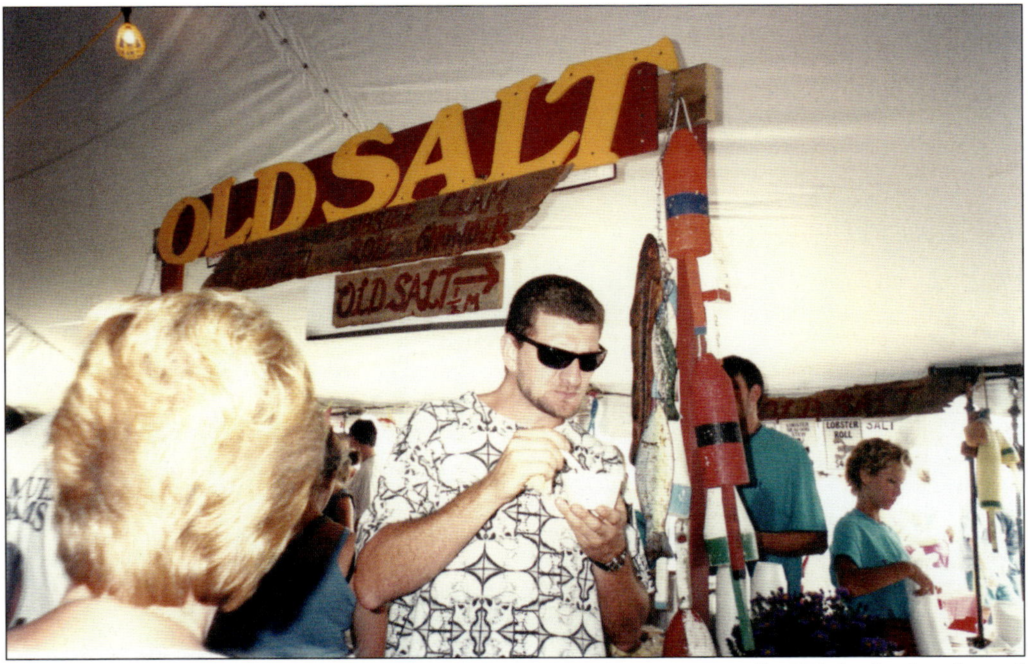

Over the past 25 years or so, the Seafood Festival has grown exponentially. While the first festival involved only a few restaurants, the festival in its present state takes several blocks of Ocean Boulevard and includes dozens of local restaurants and businesses. This picture, taken during the 1997 festival, shows the booth for the Old Salt Eating and Drinking Place, which is now just one of 60 local restaurants showcasing the best of their menus during the festival. (HHS.)

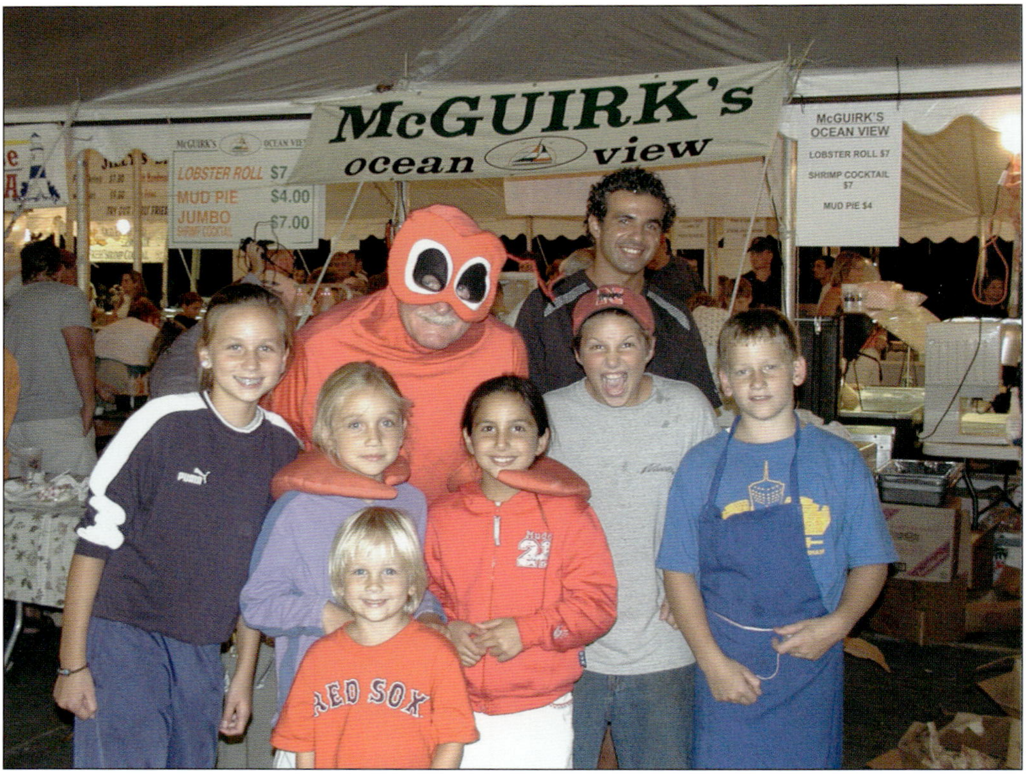

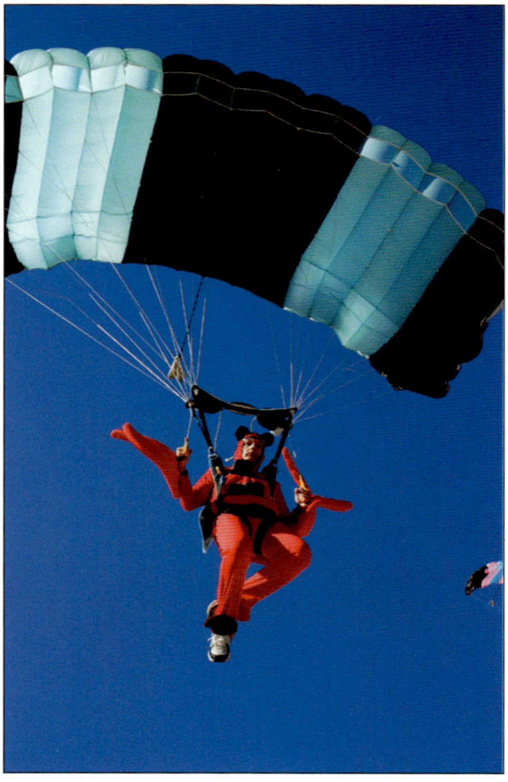

Louie the Lobster and Gladys the Clam are the mascots of the Hampton Beach Seafood Festival. Here, Louie is posing with a group of children in front of McGuirk's Ocean View's booth. Both of the mascots are present throughout the weekend, and even return at different events throughout the year. The Seafood Festival website even reminds potential visitors that "Louie the Lobster and Gladys the Clam will see you there!" (HCC.)

In recent years, the start of the festival has been marked with the exciting entrance of Louie the Lobster and Gladys the Clam. Both of the mascots parachute in to kick off the fun, food, and entertainment. The mascots were originally created by Lorraine Pivirotto, who played a leading role in establishing the Seafood Festival as a recurring event among Hampton Beach's summer activities. (HCC.)

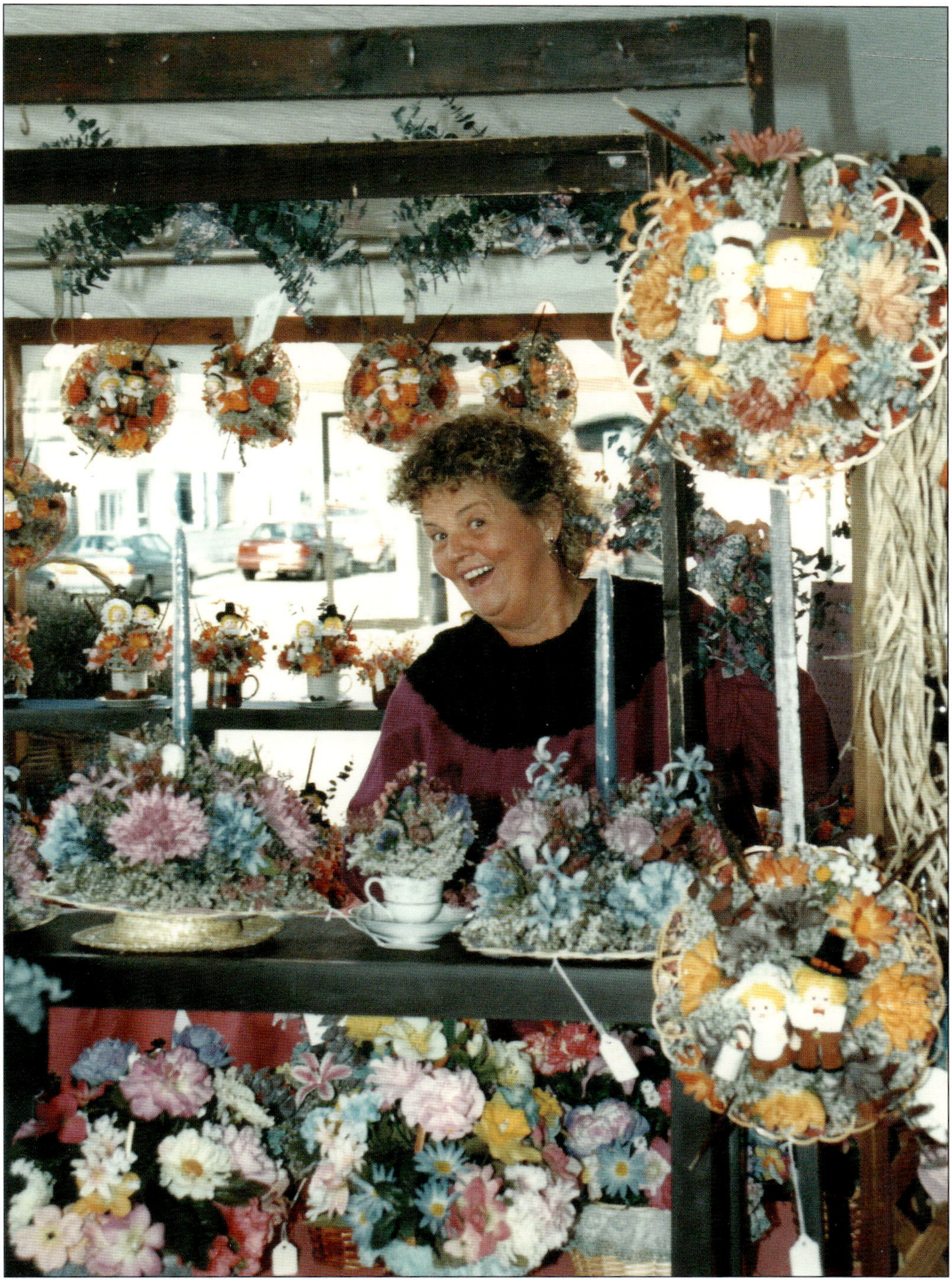

As the Hampton Beach Seafood Festival evolved, it expanded beyond just restaurants and included local businesses from both on and off the beach. Many summer souvenir shops have end-of-season sales and local businesses sell their wares in the open air. This photograph shows just one of the booths selling crafts during the 1998 festival. The festival normally features 60 or more local restaurant booths and 80 or more craft booths where small businesses and individuals can sell their homemade wares. (HHS.)

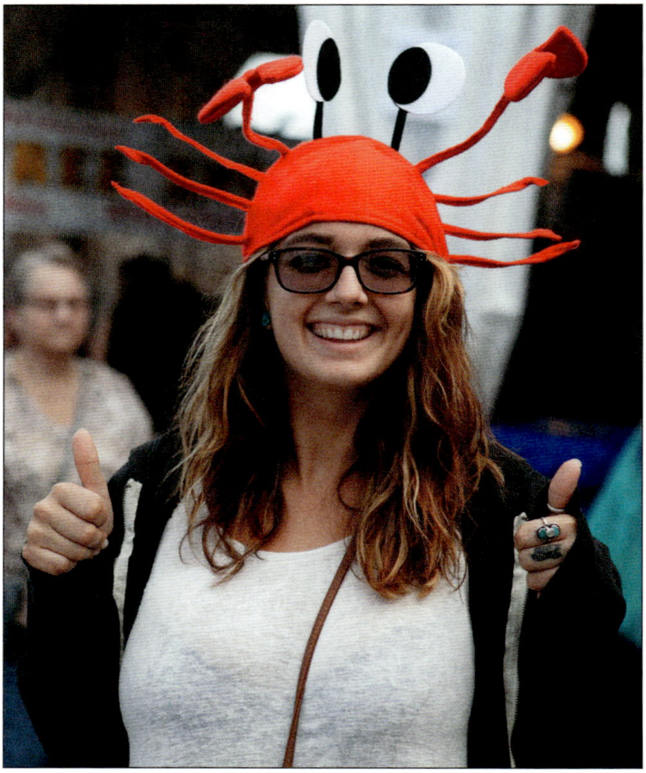

A festivalgoer gives the camera a thumbs-up with her Louie the Lobster hat. Festival attendance has exponentially risen over the years since the event was solidified on Hampton Beach's summer schedule. The 25th anniversary saw a record 150,000 people enjoying the excellent food, fun, and shopping. Some of the special events that are included in the festival are the lobster roll–eating contest, cooking demonstrations by professional chefs, and concerts on the Seashell stage. (HCC.)

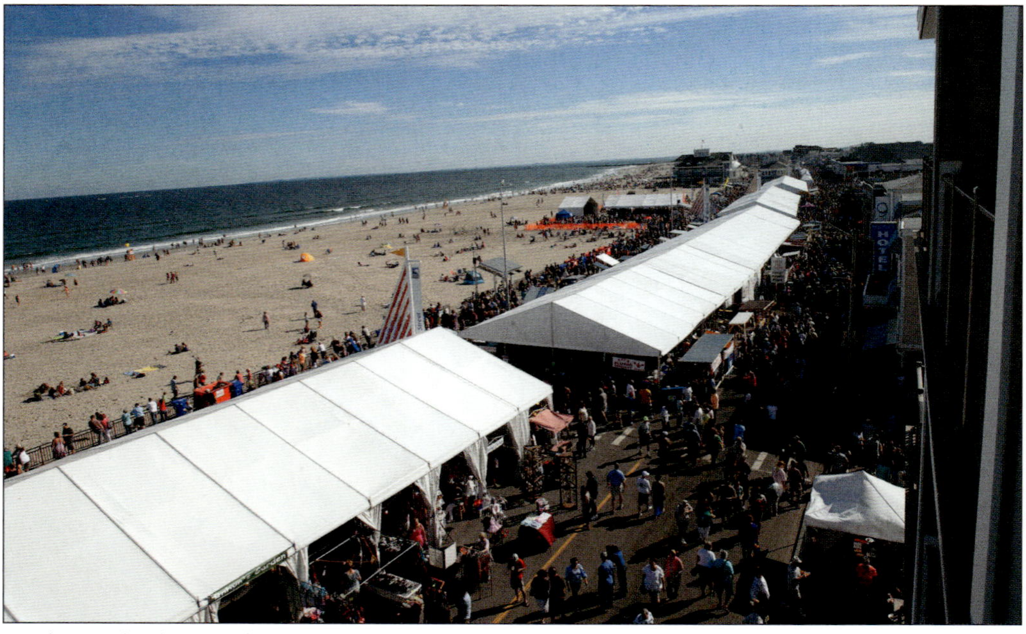

As the Seafood Festival grew in size, it began to take up more and more space. This overhead shot of the 2015 event provides a good perspective on just how popular it really is. Every year, almost the entire length of Ocean Boulevard along the beach is closed down and parts of the beach are even roped off for food and entertainment tents. The main tents extend for four blocks and smaller tents extend the length of the Casino, nearly another two blocks. (HCC.)

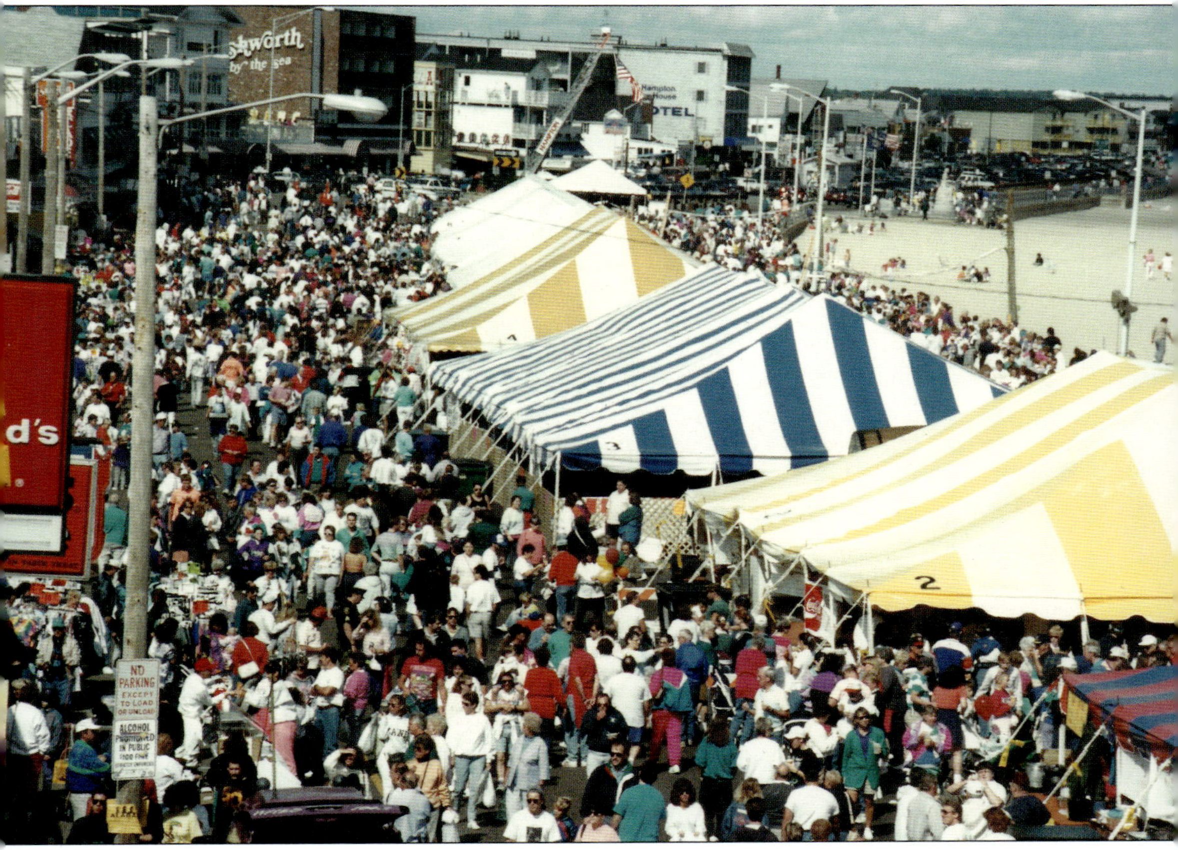

This photograph taken during the 1996 festival shows how far the site extends north. The tents run past A Street and the Surf Hotel and almost reach the Marine Memorial. Even in 1996, when attendance was not nearly as high, the tents extended all the way to the Casino, and the street was packed. Even while the festival goes on, the businesses along Ocean Boulevard continue to run. For example, Blink's Fry Doe, whose sign is hidden behind that of McDonald's, continues to sell fried dough to visitors who are walking outside the tents. (HHS.)

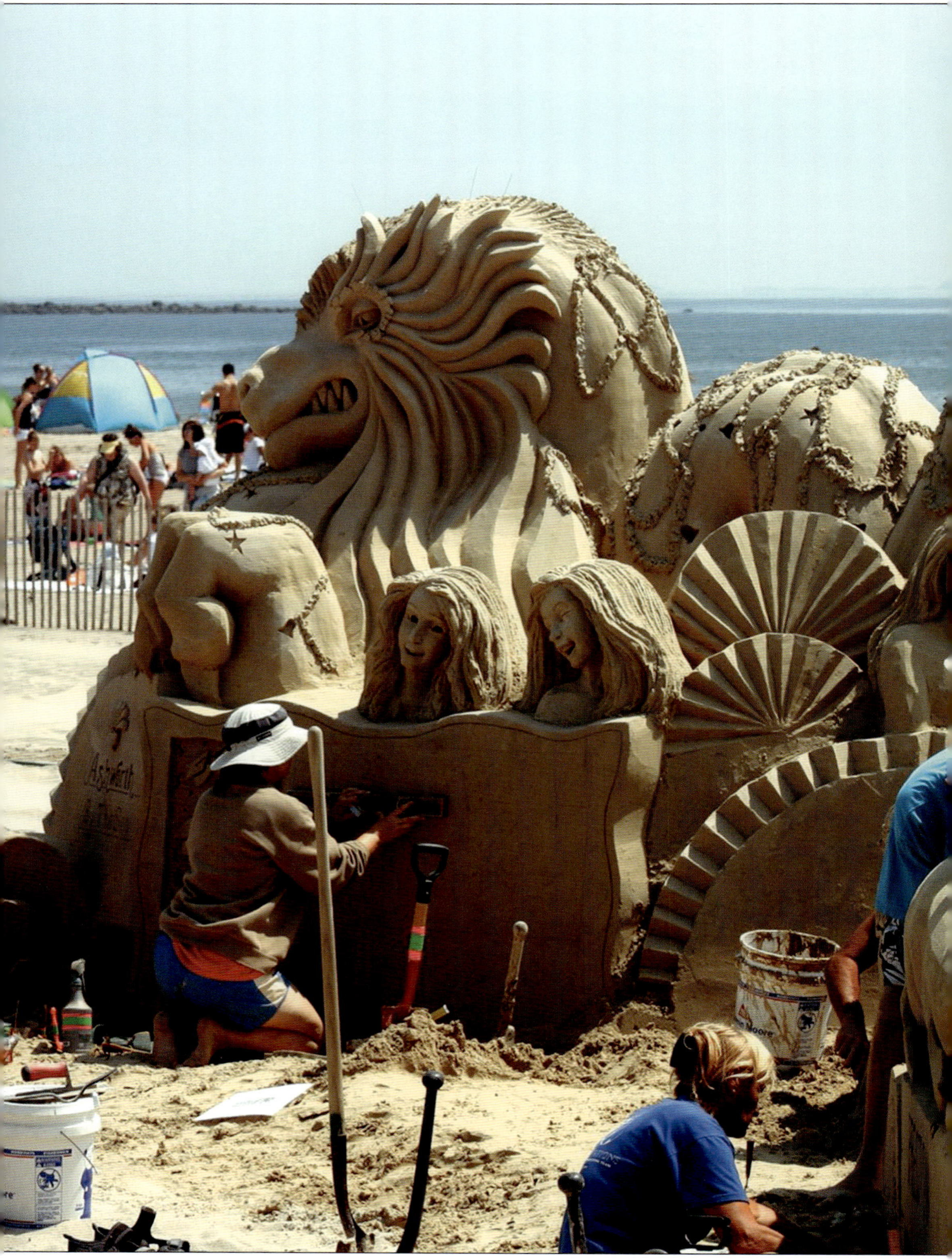

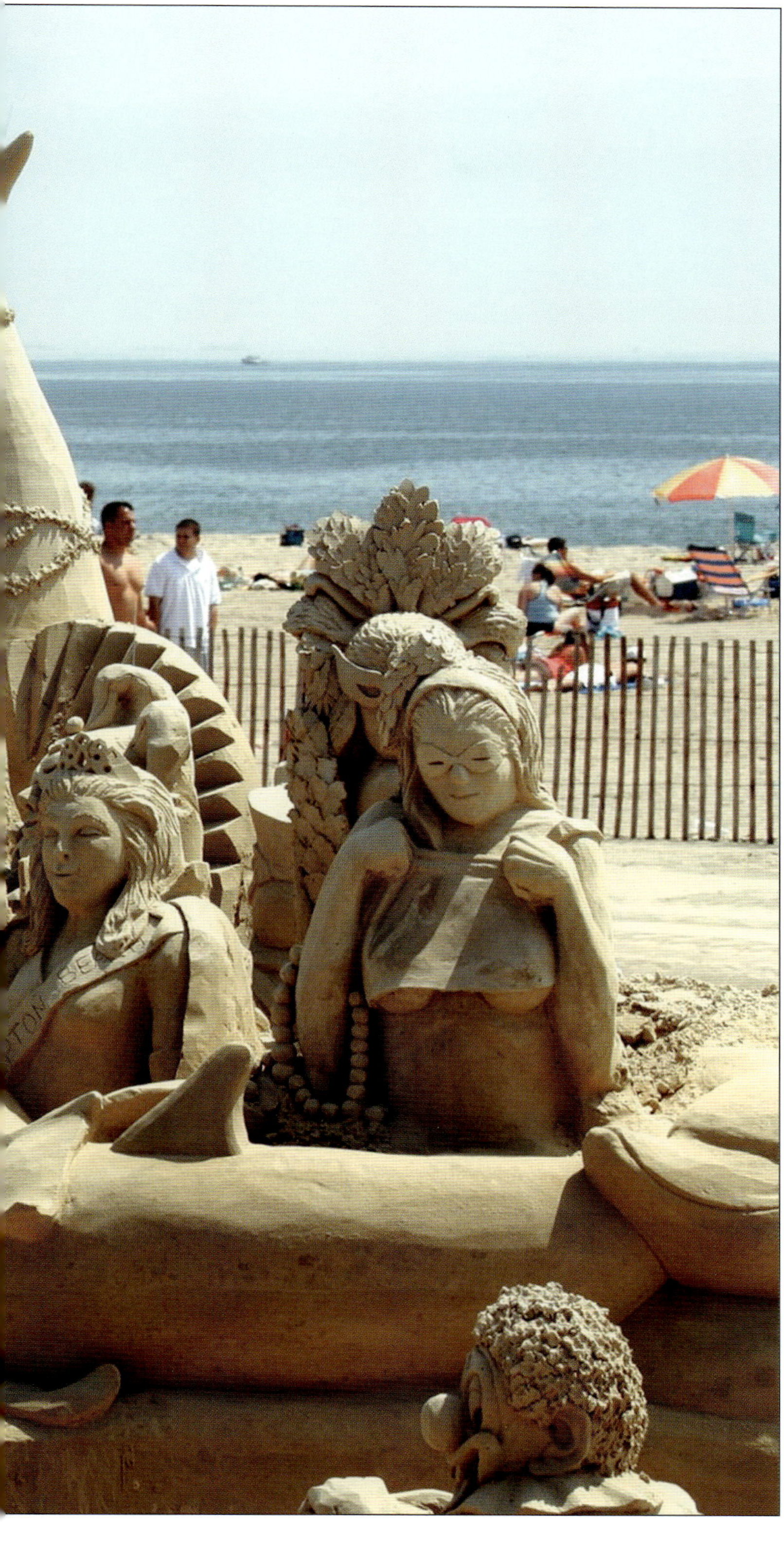

Master sand sculptors work on their projects during the 2015 Hampton Beach Master Sand Sculpting Competition. The competition takes place in a designated part of the beach just north of the Seashell Complex. According to the Hampton Beach Village District, the contest began in 2000 when local master sand sculptor Greg Grady was commissioned by the US Mint to create a massive replica of the New Hampshire Quarter for the start of the Children's Festival. The competition had its first official year in 2001. Every year, 10 entrants spend the first few days creating the sand sculptures that represent the competition sponsors. Only after that is complete does real competition begin. Competitors then have three days to create their masterpieces. (Courtesy of Professional Sculptures By Greg Grady.)

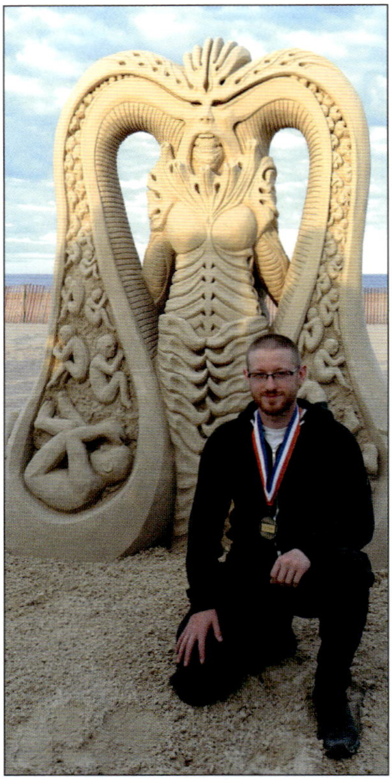

The winner of the 2014 Hampton Beach Master Sand Sculpting Competition was Guy-Olivier Deveau from Québec, Canada. His winning sculpture was *Inseminate*. According to Greg Grady, this was not the first time that Deveau competed in Hampton Beach's master sand sculpting competition, but it was the first time he went home with the top prize. (Courtesy of Professional Sculptures By Greg Grady.)

The Hampton Beach fireworks light up the skies over the old Seashell Complex. The fireworks have been a weekly summer occurrence for nearly a century. According to Peter Randall, author of *Hampton: A Century of Town and Beach*, the idea for a free fireworks show originated with merchants whose businesses were located on the C Street corner. After an event at the Casino, people filed out into the streets and passed by these businesses, having already purchased their late-night refreshments and souvenirs at the Casino complex. In order to lure people's attention away from the Casino shops, the merchants, namely John White and Joseph Dudley, put on a free fireworks display. After having huge success in increasing revenue with the fireworks, White and Dudley continued the show a few nights a week and eventually chose Wednesday nights for the summer tradition. (HBCC)

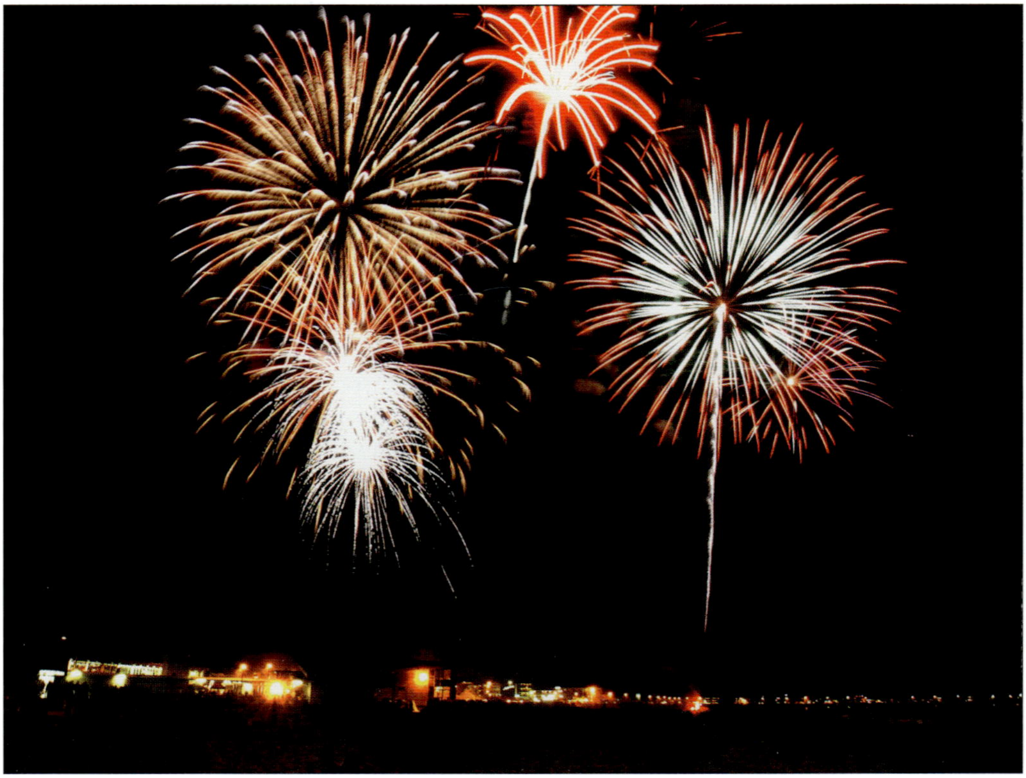

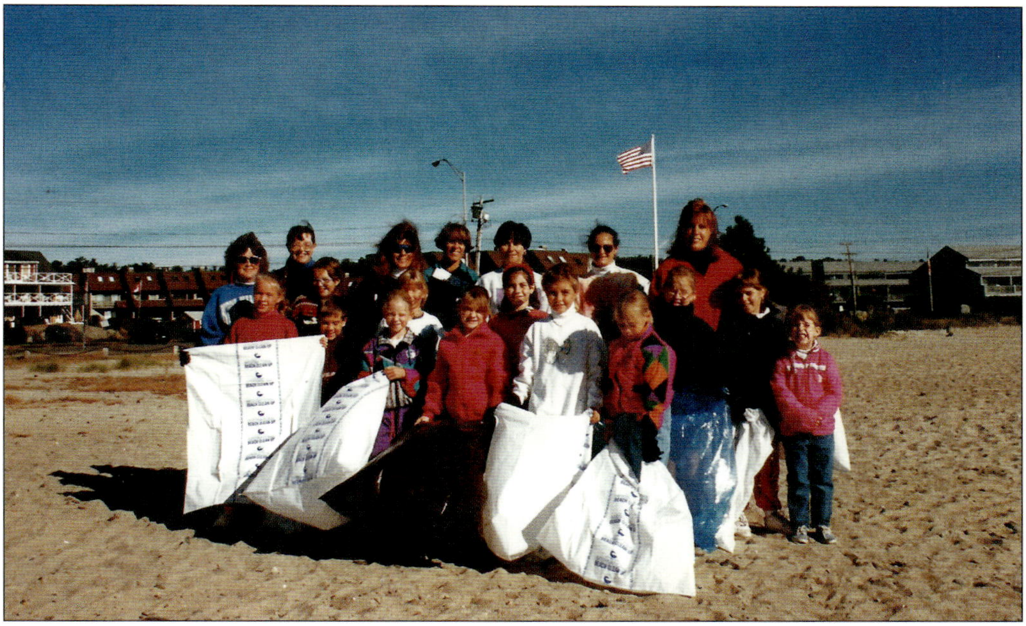

Girl Scout Troops 292, 738, and 654 pose for a picture before participating in the annual Coastal Cleanup event, put on by the Blue Ocean Society every fall. Volunteers from all over the state spend the day cleaning up one of New Hampshire's beaches. These Girl Scouts are at Bicentennial Park, one of the northernmost points of Hampton Beach. (HHS.)

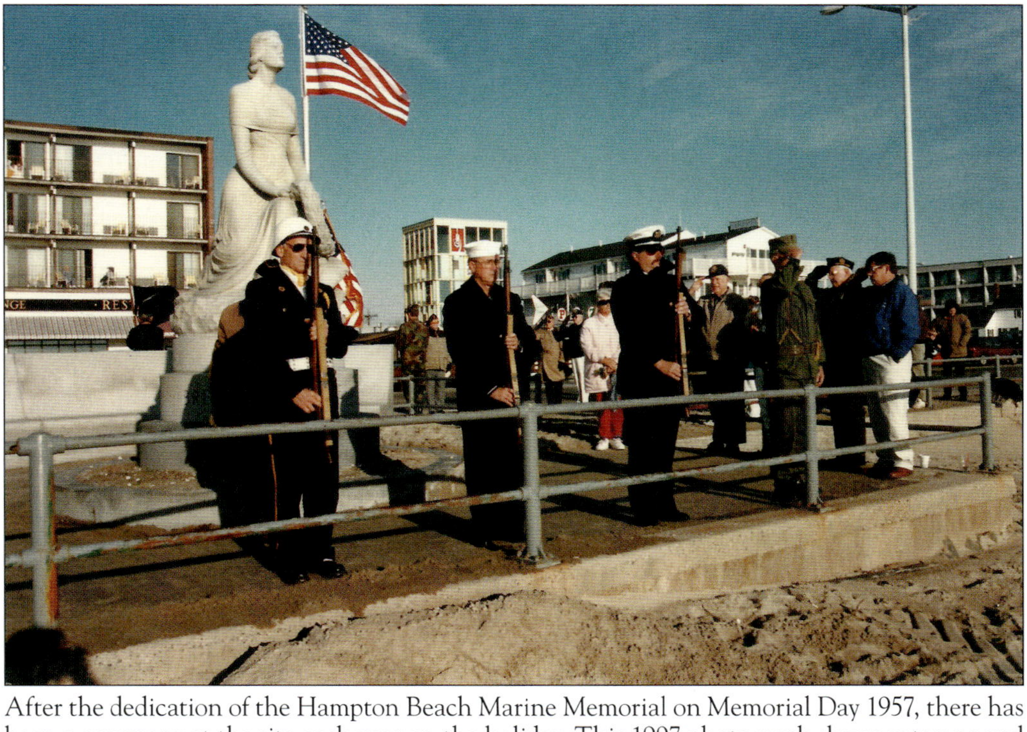

After the dedication of the Hampton Beach Marine Memorial on Memorial Day 1957, there has been a ceremony at the site each year on the holiday. This 1997 photograph shows veterans and servicemen facing the ocean, saluting those New Hampshire men and women lost at sea during every US war. (HHS.)

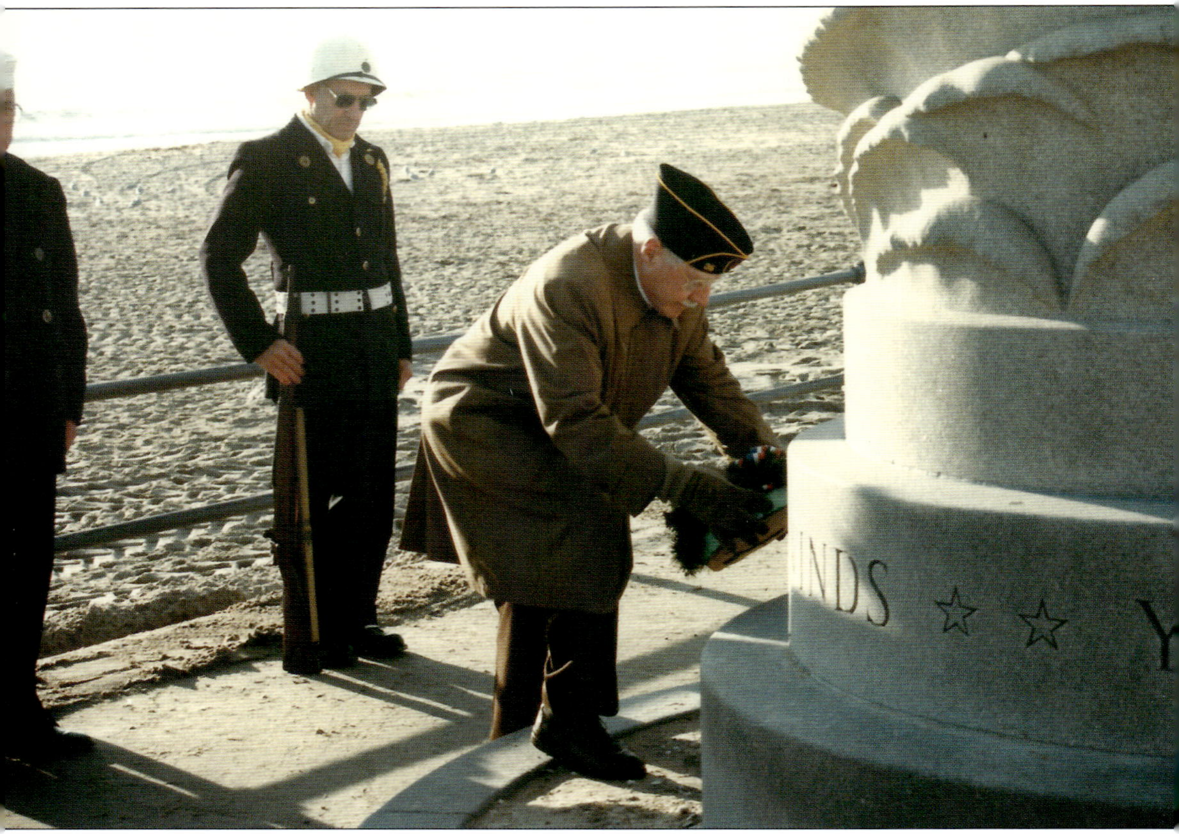

Tom Gillick, a World War II veteran and longtime beach visitor, lays a wreath on the New Hampshire Marine Memorial on Memorial Day 1997. The annual Memorial Day parade leaves from the town offices and travels down Winnacunnet Road from the town center toward the beach. The parade ends at the Marine Memorial, with local and special guest speakers, a gun salute, and the laying of the wreath. (HHS.)

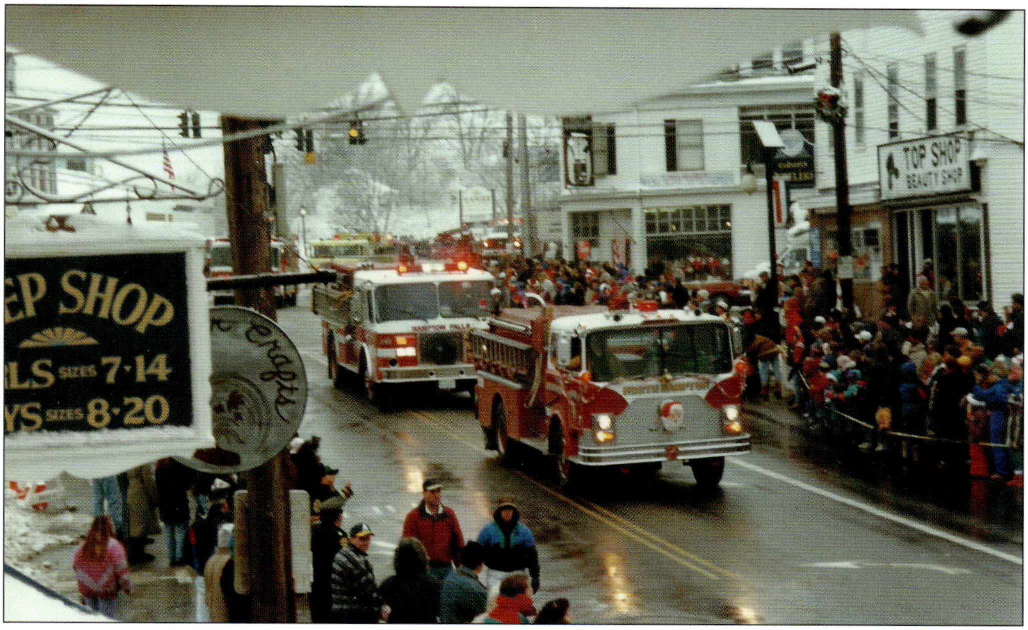

The annual Christmas parade heads south on Lafayette Road. In true Hampton fashion, the Christmas parade is as extravagant as Hampton Beach's summer festivals and parades. This 1996 parade included the Winnacunnet Warrior Band, several floats, the mounted police, and emergency vehicles from many of the surrounding towns. The parade is seen here passing through Marelli Square. (HHS.)

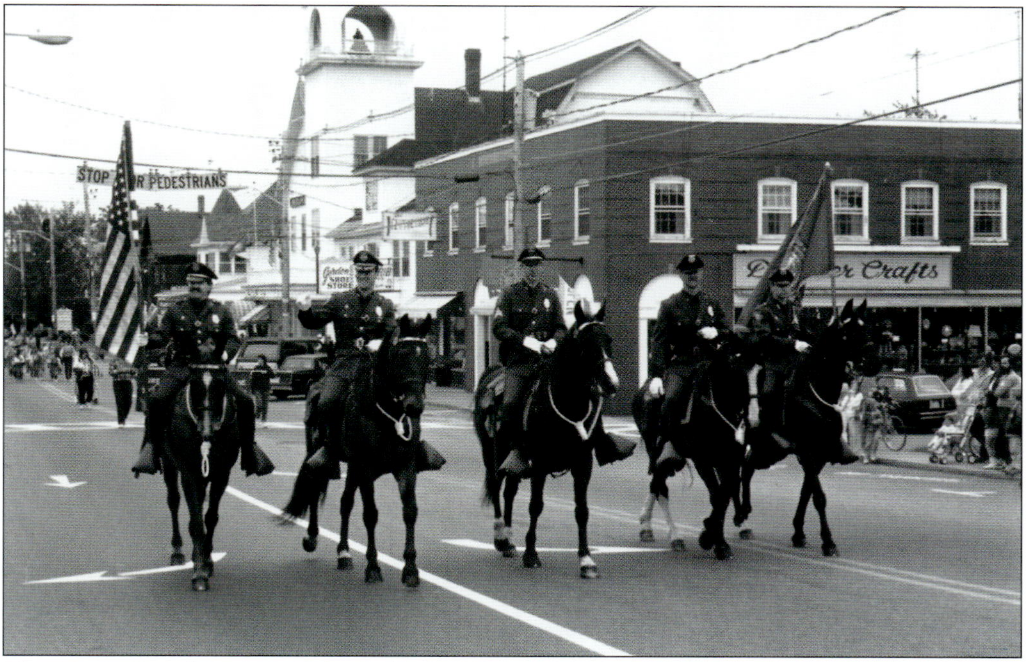

The Hampton Police Mounted Patrol Unit marches north on Lafayette Road during what is most likely a summer parade in 1987. The mounted police have also walked in the annual Christmas parade for many years. During the Christmas parade, the unit's horses are extravagantly dressed in holiday decorations and are a staple of the parade procession. (HHS.)

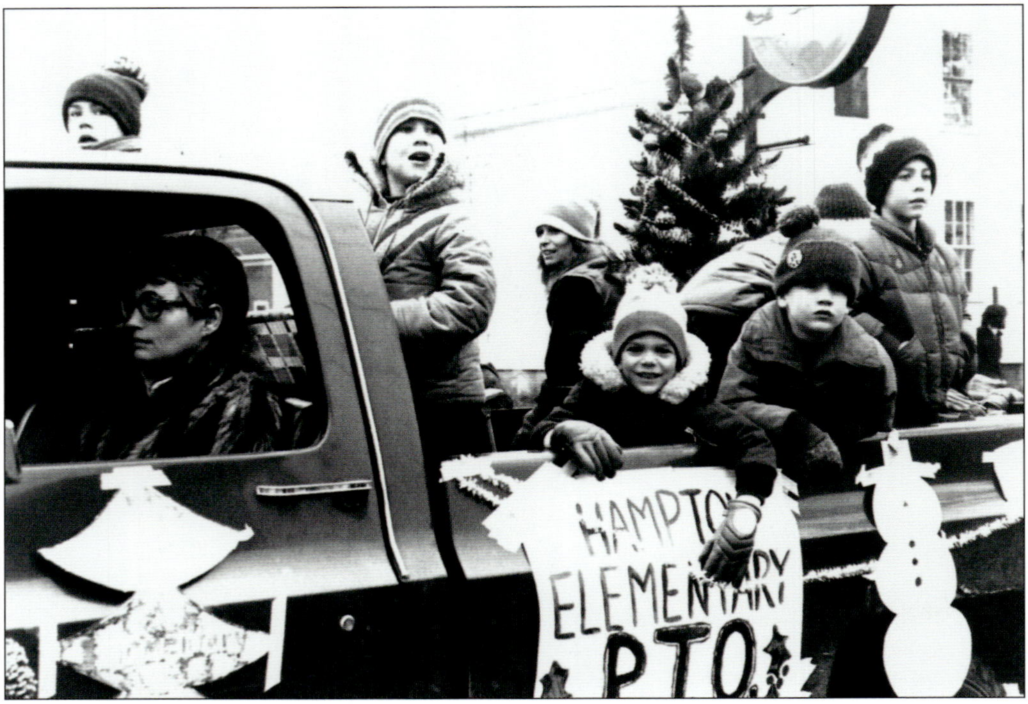

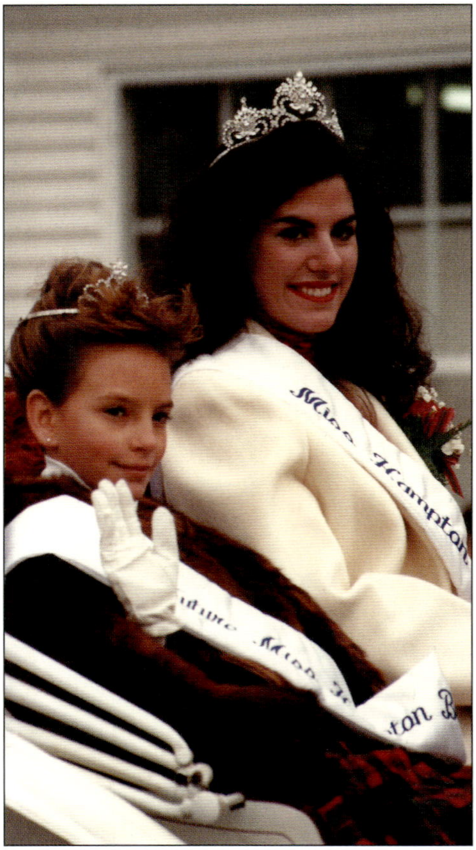

One of the floats in the 1981 Christmas parade was the truck float for the Hampton Elementary PTO. Hampton schools have always been involved in the parade though floats and the yearly appearance of the Winnacunnet Warrior Marching Band. According to a *Hampton Union* article by Jason Schreiber, the parade was cancelled in 2007 because a young boy in the nearby town of Greenland, New Hampshire, was killed because of unsafe float conditions during a parade earlier that year. The Hampton parade was not held again until 2010, when, to the great delight of Hampton residents, it was brought back in full force. The town also intentionally made sure the parade maintained all the splendor and spirit it had in previous years to help recover from the three-year gap. (HHS.)

Another important entry in the Hampton Christmas parade is the Miss Hampton Beach float. The float carries the winner of the Miss Hampton Beach pageant as well her younger counterpart, the winner of the Future Miss Hampton Beach pageant. This float in the 1997 parade carries Miss Hampton Beach, Julie Russell from Woburn, Massachusetts, and an unidentified Future Miss Hampton Beach. (HHS.)

Four

AROUND TOWN

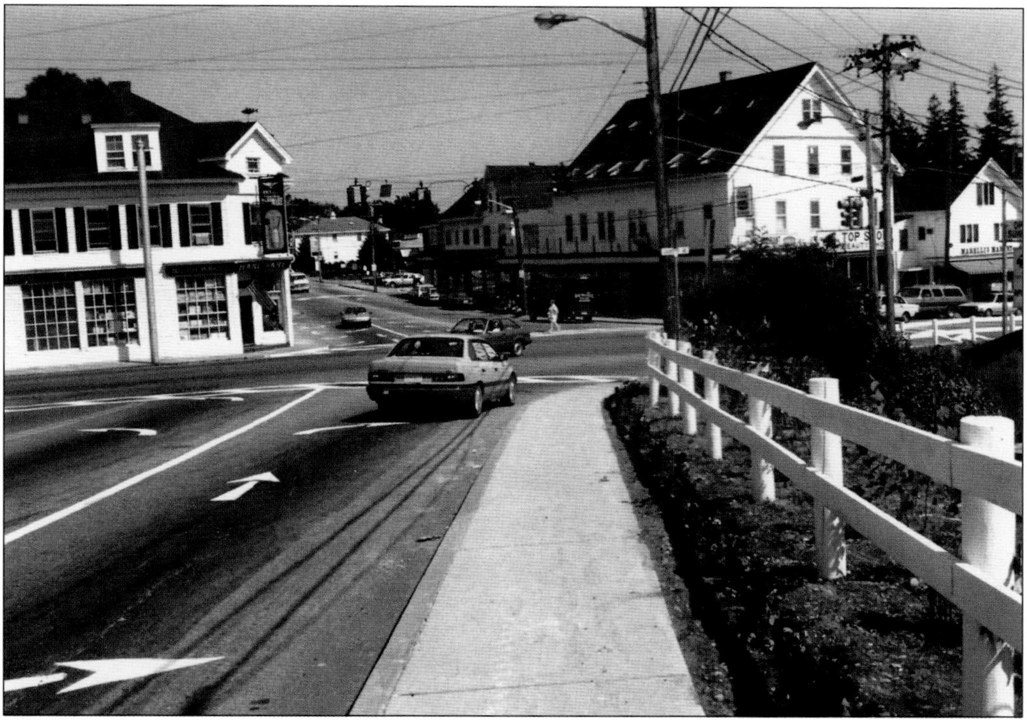

The intersection of Lafayette Road, also known as New Hampshire Route 1, and High Street, is near the center of Hampton and is a hub for local businesses. The square is called Luigi Marelli Square, known as Marelli Square, and was named for the man who owned the market in the small building at far right. The square was given its name on March 9, 1960, to memorialize Marelli for being an outstanding citizen. This view is looking east on High Street, which leads to the beach. Just outside of the view, at the back left corner of the intersection, is Lamie's Tavern, which will later become the Old Salt at Lamie's Inn. Hampton Village Hardware is on the corner at far left. (HHS.)

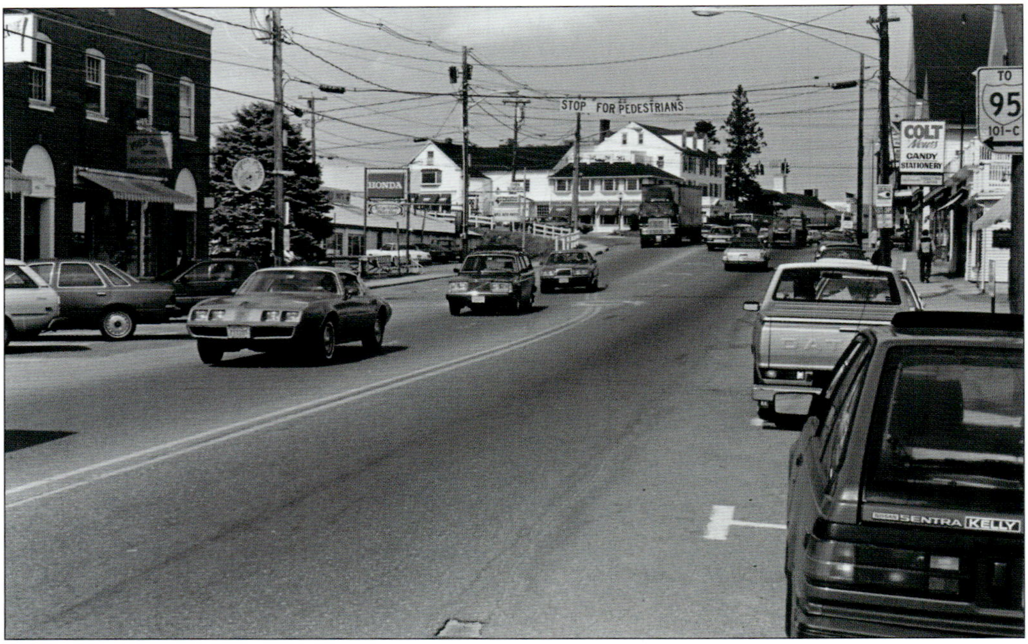

New Hampshire Route 1 goes right through the center of Hampton and is one of the roads that forms Marelli Square. Many of Hampton's well-known, family-owned businesses line this street, including Colt News, Marelli's Market, and Lamie's Inn. By the time this picture was taken in the early 1990s, many of these businesses had already been open for decades. (HHS.)

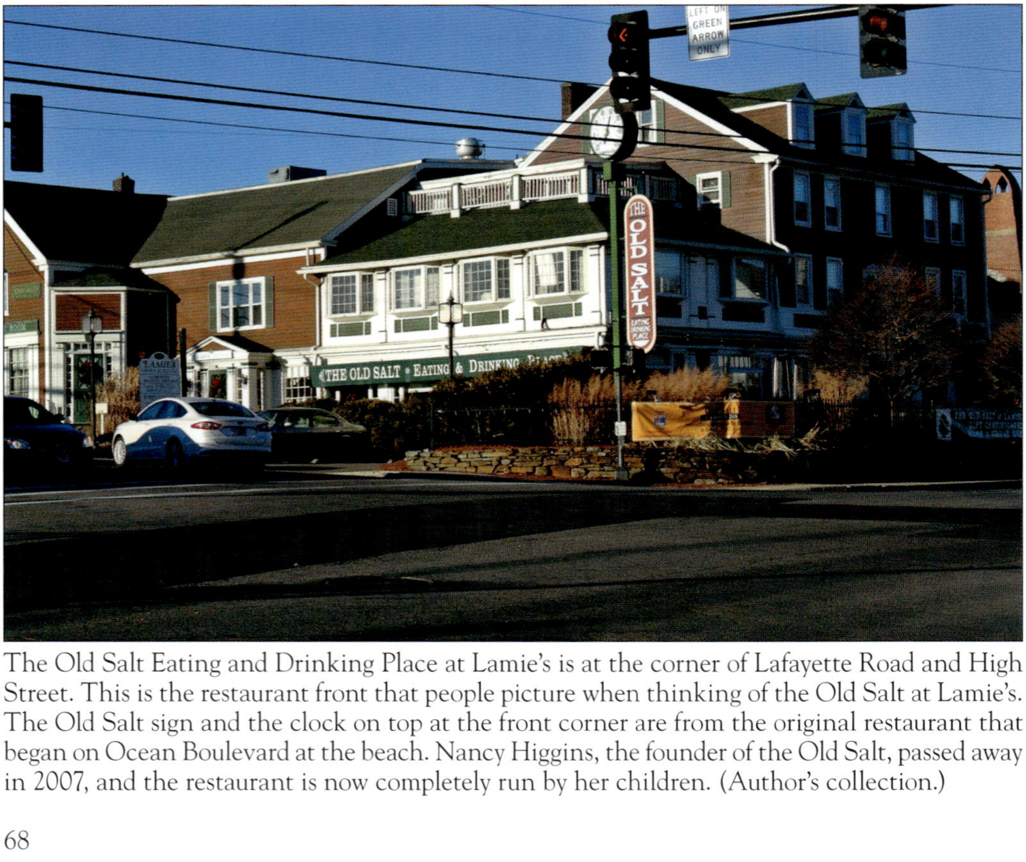

The Old Salt Eating and Drinking Place at Lamie's is at the corner of Lafayette Road and High Street. This is the restaurant front that people picture when thinking of the Old Salt at Lamie's. The Old Salt sign and the clock on top at the front corner are from the original restaurant that began on Ocean Boulevard at the beach. Nancy Higgins, the founder of the Old Salt, passed away in 2007, and the restaurant is now completely run by her children. (Author's collection.)

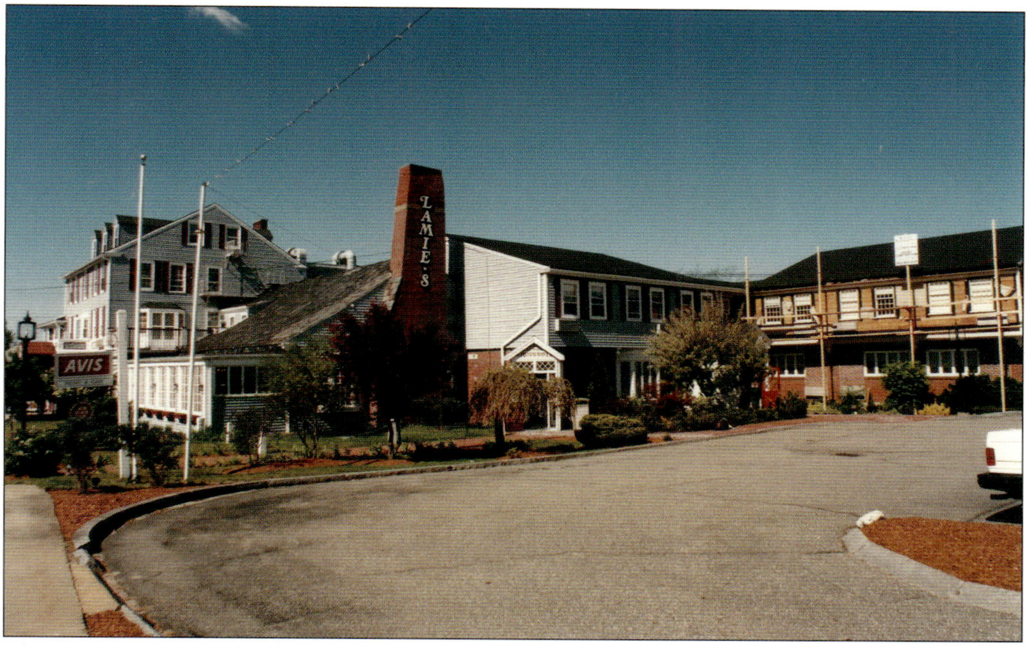

This 1997 picture shows one of the entrances to Lamie's Tavern. In just four years, the establishment would be sold to the Higgins family and become the Old Salt at Lamie's Inn. When the Old Salt Eating and Drinking Place on Ocean Boulevard burned down and the Higgins family finally purchased Lamie's, the original sign and clock were both moved to the new location. (HHS.)

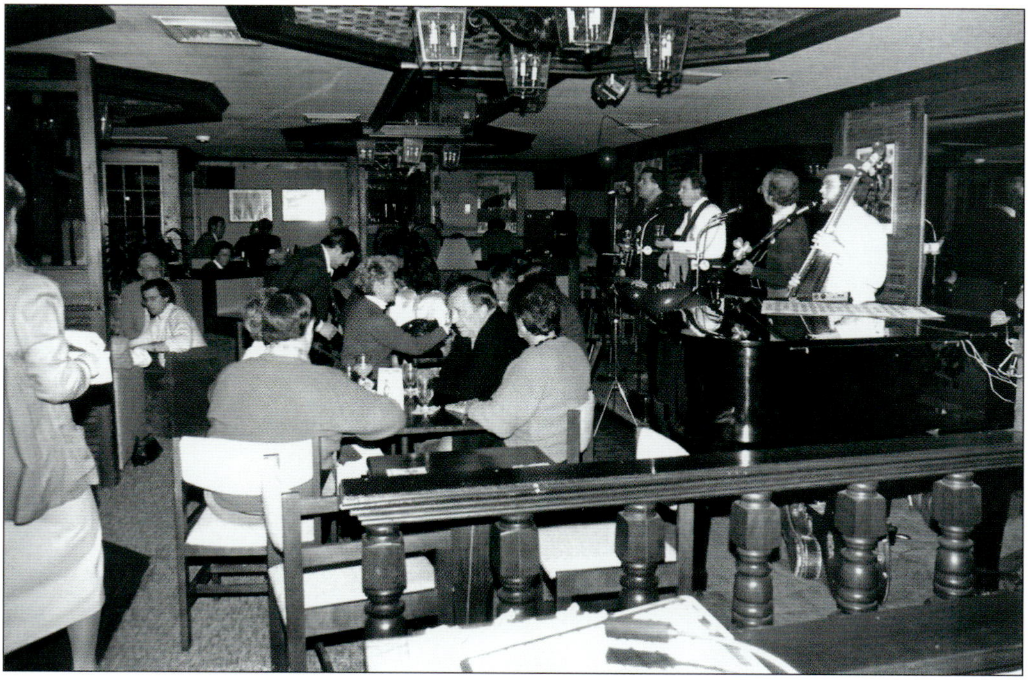

This photograph, captured in 1987, shows a busy night in Lamie's Tavern Tap Room. It is one of many specific rooms in the tavern. Some of the other rooms are the Goody Cole Room, named after Hampton's 17th-century witch, and the Eisenhower Room, which once hosted President Eisenhower and his family for a meal. (HHS.)

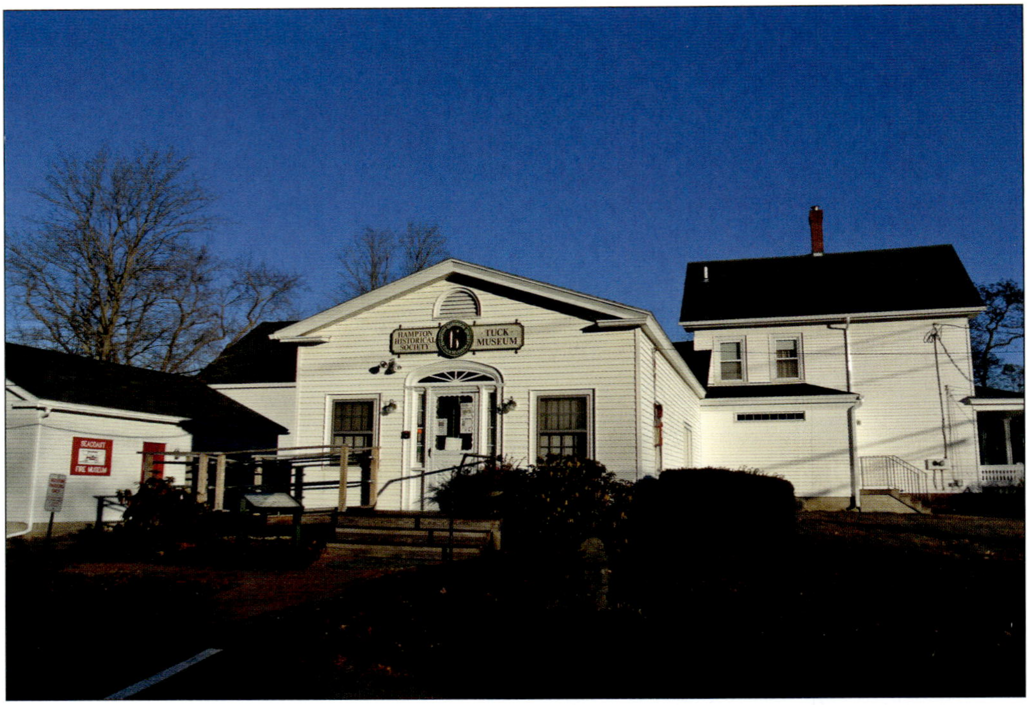

The Hampton Historical Society, Tuck Museum, and Tuck Field are located on Park Street just off Route 1 near Hampton's town center. The historical society was originally incorporated in 1925 as the Meeting House Green Memorial Association to honor Hampton's settlers. Edward Tuck generously donated funds for a house to be built on the original meeting house green. The house is now the Tuck Museum and is surrounded by several other buildings, including a schoolhouse and a firefighting museum. The society contains records and artifacts from Hampton's settlement to the present. (Author's collection.)

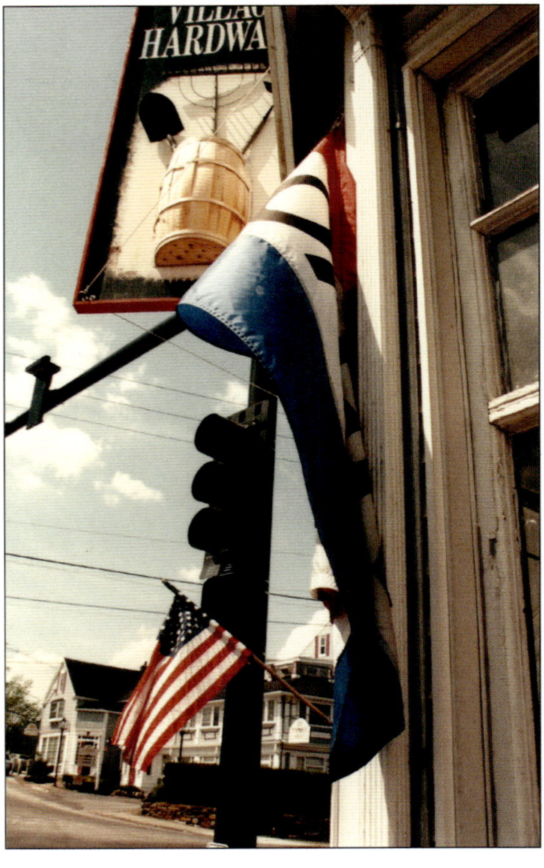

Hampton Village Hardware was located at 2 High Street, directly across from the Old Salt at Lamie's Inn. The hardware store was established in 1973 by owner Bob Wallace, and though the owners and name have changed, it continues as a hardware store. The sign in this photograph was not original to the business but was added much later, in the 1990s. (HHS.)

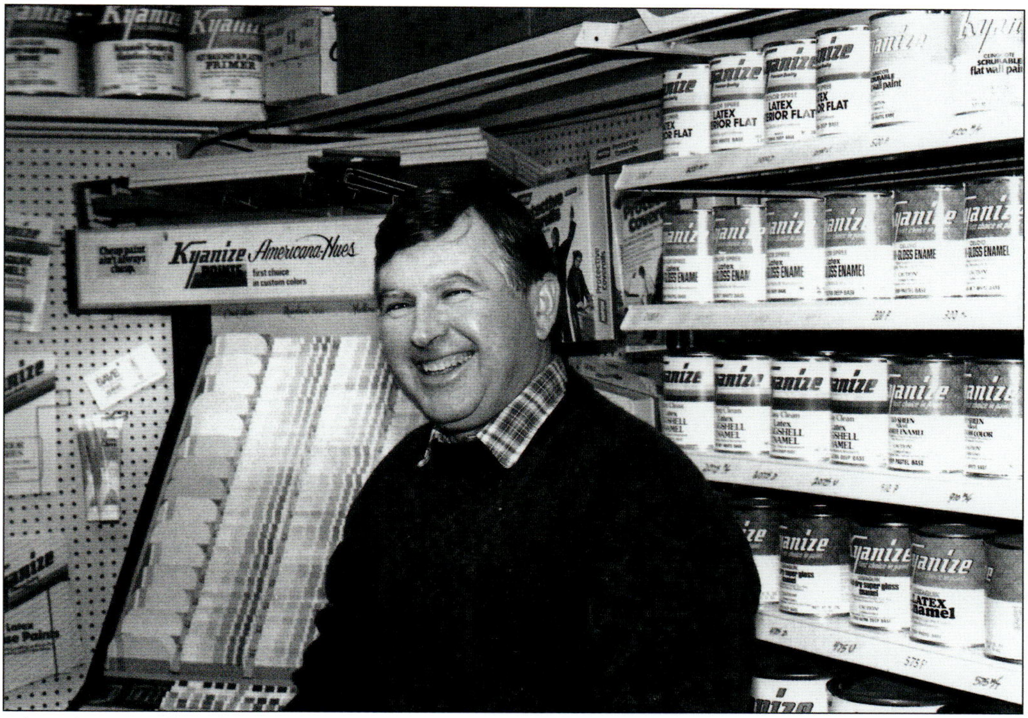

This photograph, taken in 1984, shows Hampton Village Hardware owner and manager Bob Wallace, a longtime Hampton resident. As reported in the *Atlantic News* by Steven Tobias, Wallace finally sold his store after 23 years of management to another longtime Hampton resident, Alexander J. Stephens, in 1996. Stephens intended to keep the hardware store as it was and honor the history of the building and the successful business itself. (HHS.)

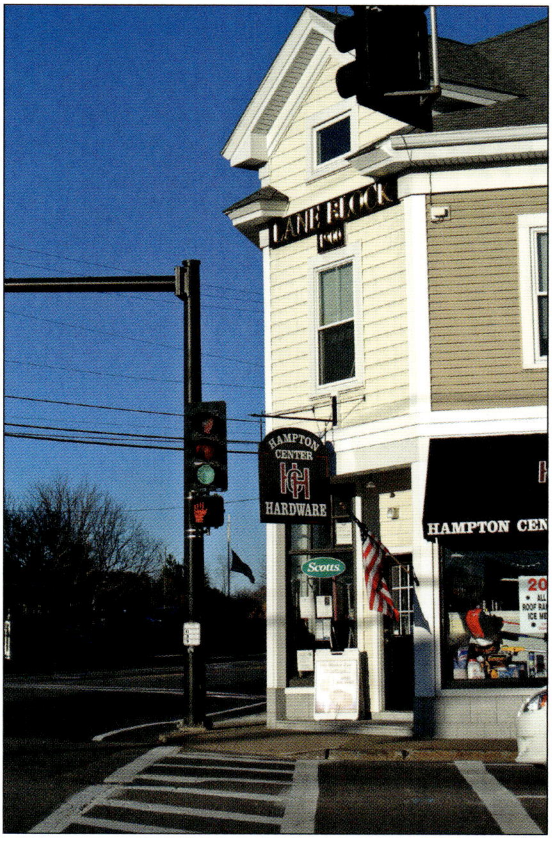

The corner shop across the street from Lamie's Tavern, Hampton Village Hardware, went out of business in 1997. By 1998, the new Hampton Center Hardware had already opened in the same storefront. Although it was sad to see a local business that had been a part of the community for over 20 years go out of business, the fact that the new hardware store was also a small business made the transition easier. (Author's collection.)

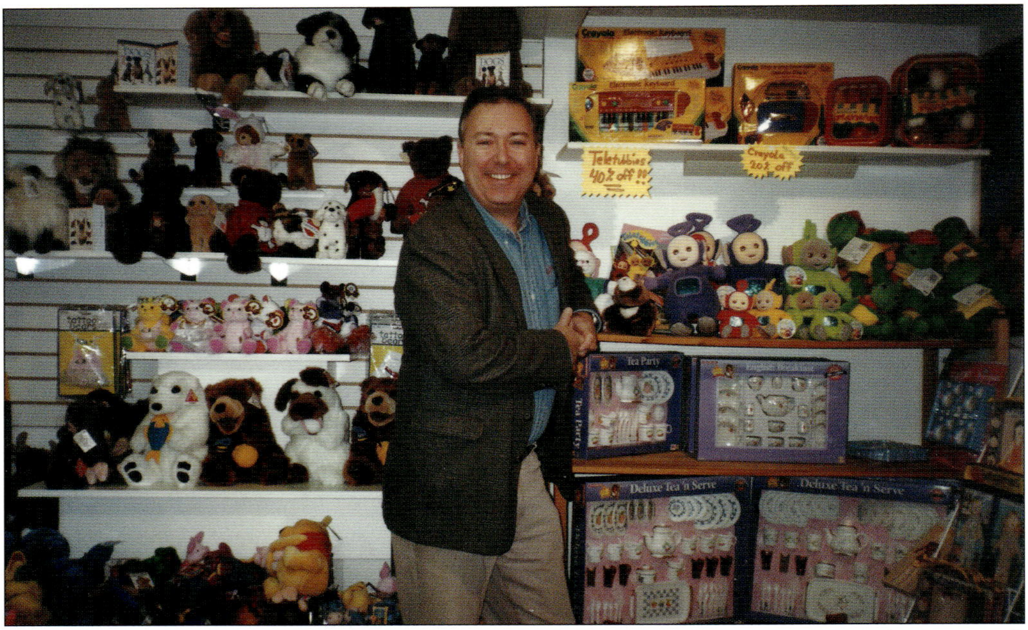

Funny Bones Toys first opened its doors at the end of September 1998 at 441 Lafayette Road. David Schwab and his wife, Rose, run the store, in which every toy is intended not only to be fun but also educational. *Atlantic News* reporter Kathie Bowen wrote that the unofficial philosophy of Funny Bones Toys, according to Schwab, is to only provide toys that are both enjoyable and encourage the exploration of "science in particular, and of learning in general." (HHS.)

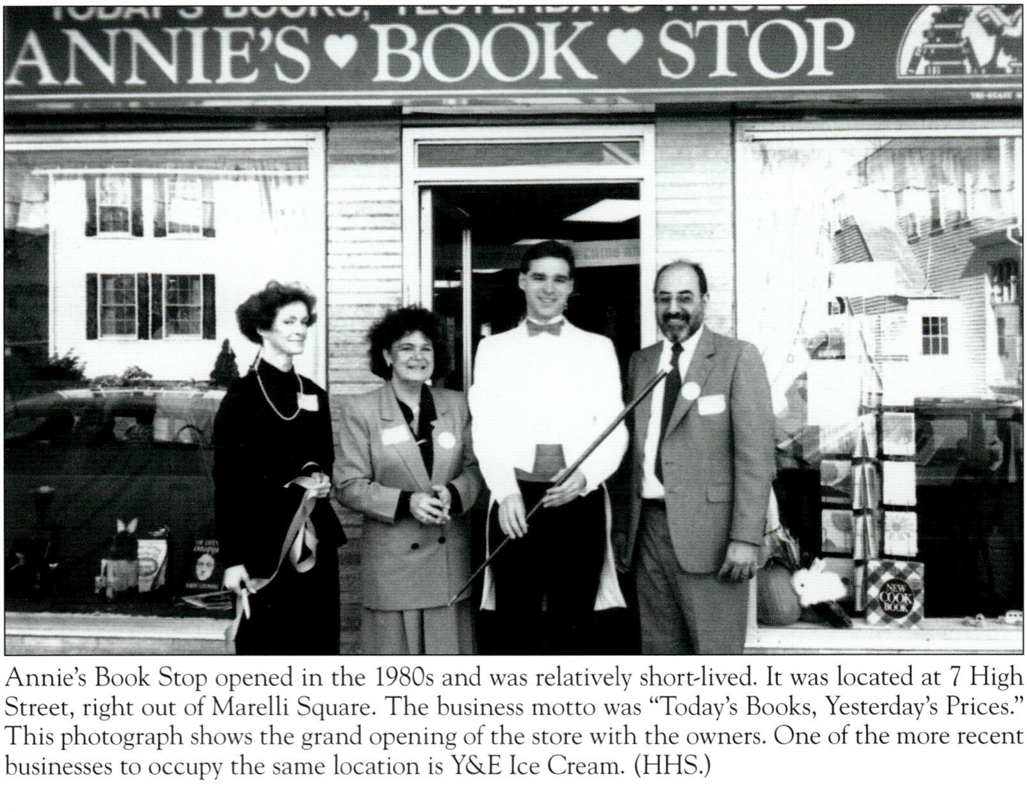

Annie's Book Stop opened in the 1980s and was relatively short-lived. It was located at 7 High Street, right out of Marelli Square. The business motto was "Today's Books, Yesterday's Prices." This photograph shows the grand opening of the store with the owners. One of the more recent businesses to occupy the same location is Y&E Ice Cream. (HHS.)

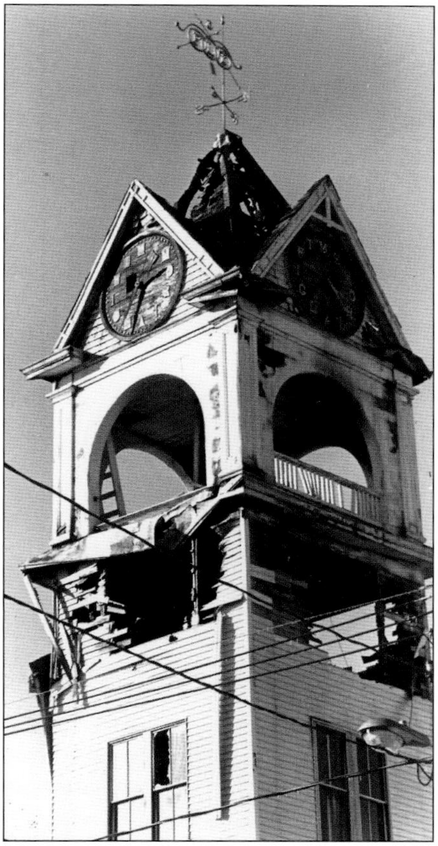

The Odd Fellows Building was erected on Lafayette Road near Hampton's town center. The clock tower stood above the surrounding buildings and contained a century-old bell. One night in January 1990, the Odd Fellows Building caught fire and was mostly destroyed before it was extinguished. This photograph was taken not long after the fire. According to articles in the *Hampton Union*, firefighters and onlookers heard the bell toll for the last time at 3:00 a.m. while the structure was engulfed in flames. The town is currently fundraising to build a courtyard and small tower to house the bell on the grounds of Hampton's Centre School. (HHS.)

Parker Ryan opened Widow Fletcher's Tavern in 1983. According to an article by Shir Haberman in the *Hampton Union*, Ryan chose the name because it was unique among British pubs, many of which are named after generals and popular drinks. He had read about a woman opening a tavern in her home in 18th-century England after she was widowed and liked the idea of naming it after a unique and independent woman. In 2009, after over 25 years of success, Ryan sold Widow Fletcher's Tavern to Daniel "Desi" Lanio, who owns many other businesses on Hampton Beach. The restaurant, which retained its location and atmosphere, is now the 401 Tavern, named after its address on Lafayette Road. (HHS.)

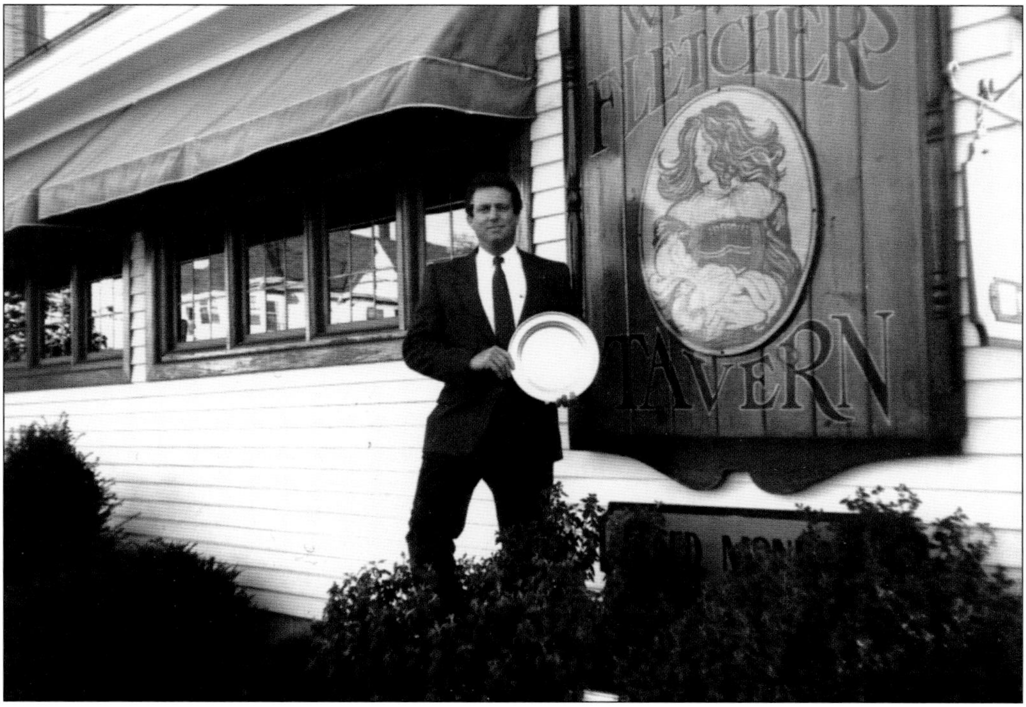

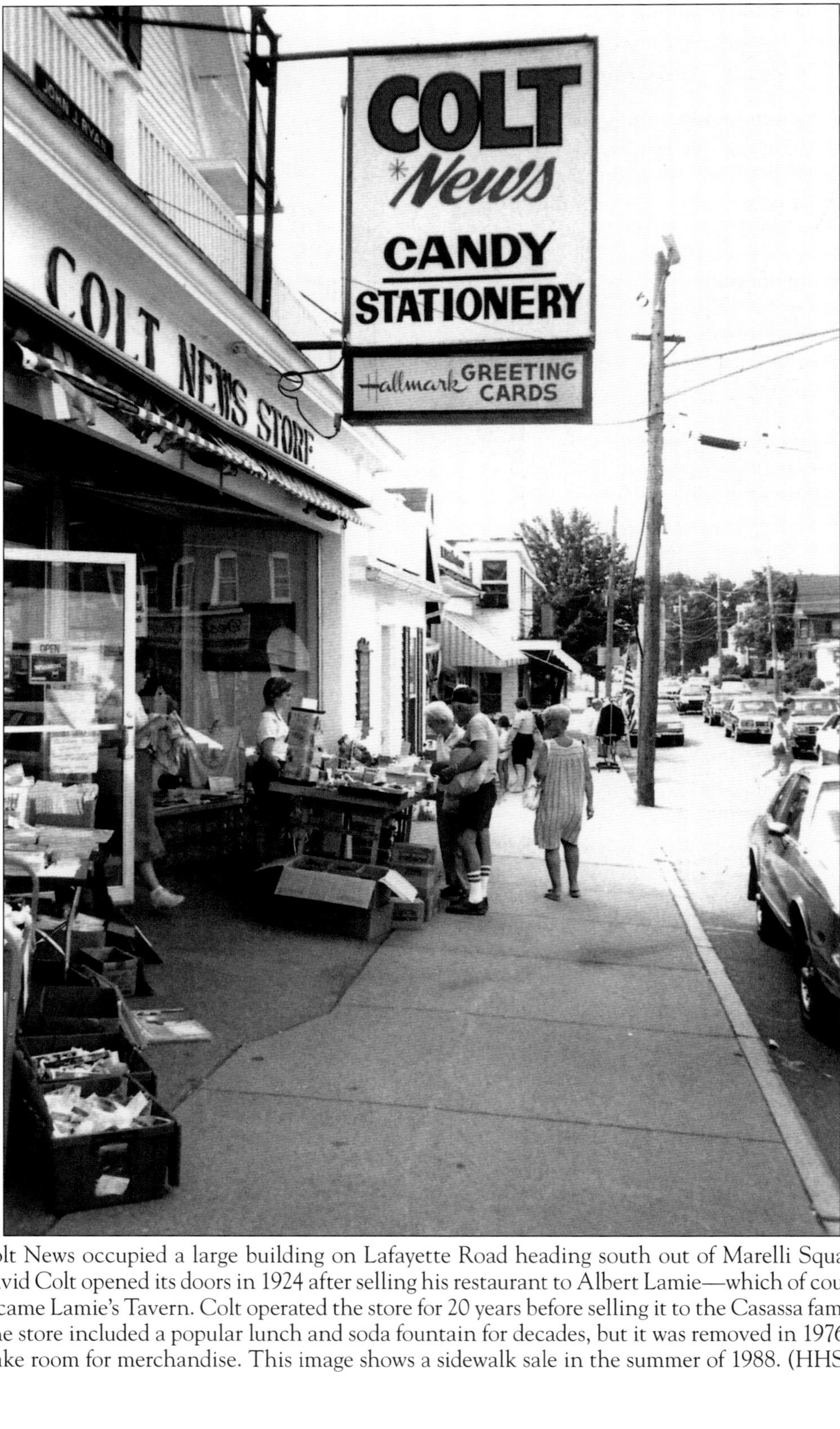

Colt News occupied a large building on Lafayette Road heading south out of Marelli Square. David Colt opened its doors in 1924 after selling his restaurant to Albert Lamie—which of course became Lamie's Tavern. Colt operated the store for 20 years before selling it to the Casassa family. The store included a popular lunch and soda fountain for decades, but it was removed in 1976 to make room for merchandise. This image shows a sidewalk sale in the summer of 1988. (HHS.)

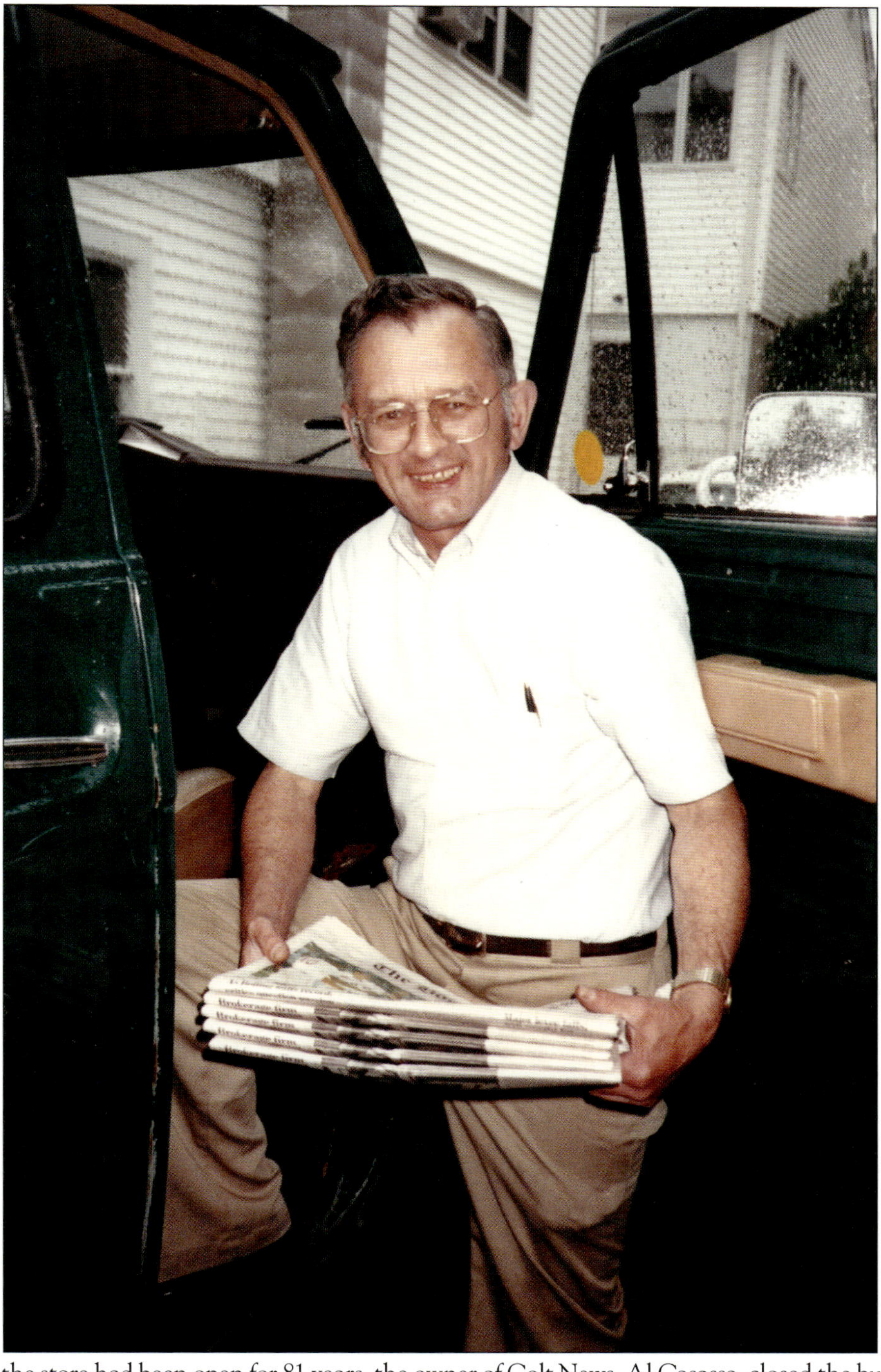

After the store had been open for 81 years, the owner of Colt News, Al Casassa, closed the business at the end of 2005. He said it was a tough decision, but with new technologies and new traffic patterns in Hampton, people's shopping habits had changed. Casassa gave a special thanks to a few people, one of whom was Glyn Eastman. According to a *Hampton Union* article by Patrick Cronin, Eastman had been with the company for over 50 years and was instrumental in the store's operation, especially in managing paper distribution. (HHS.)

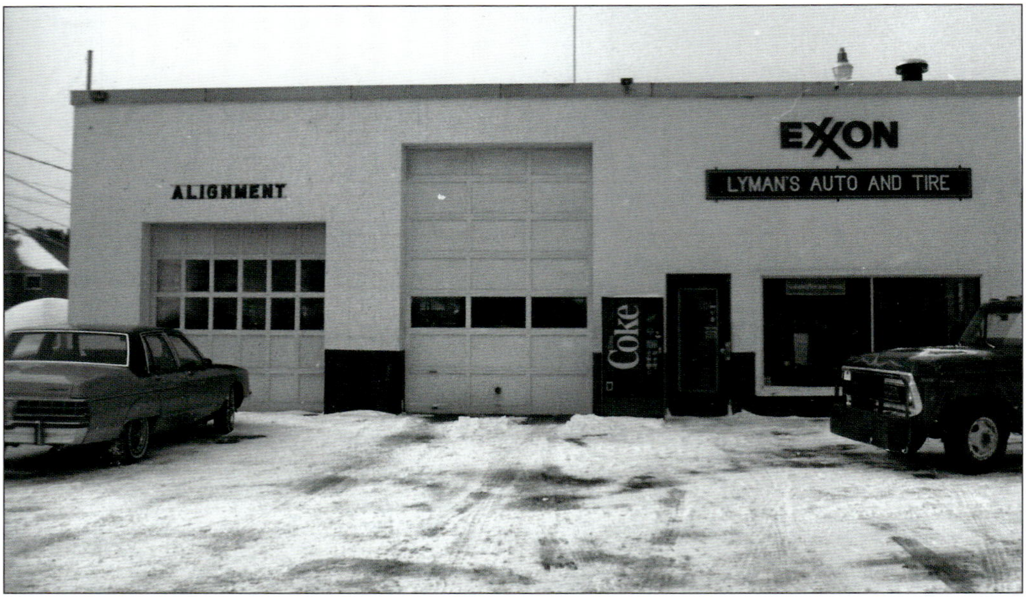

Lyman's Auto and Tire is located at 775 Lafayette Road, which is about a half mile north of Marelli Square. The garage was founded in 1975, and this photograph was taken in 1984. The building may have changed in its 40 years of business, but Lyman's is still in the same place and is highly recommended by locals and visitors for its personalized service. (HHS.)

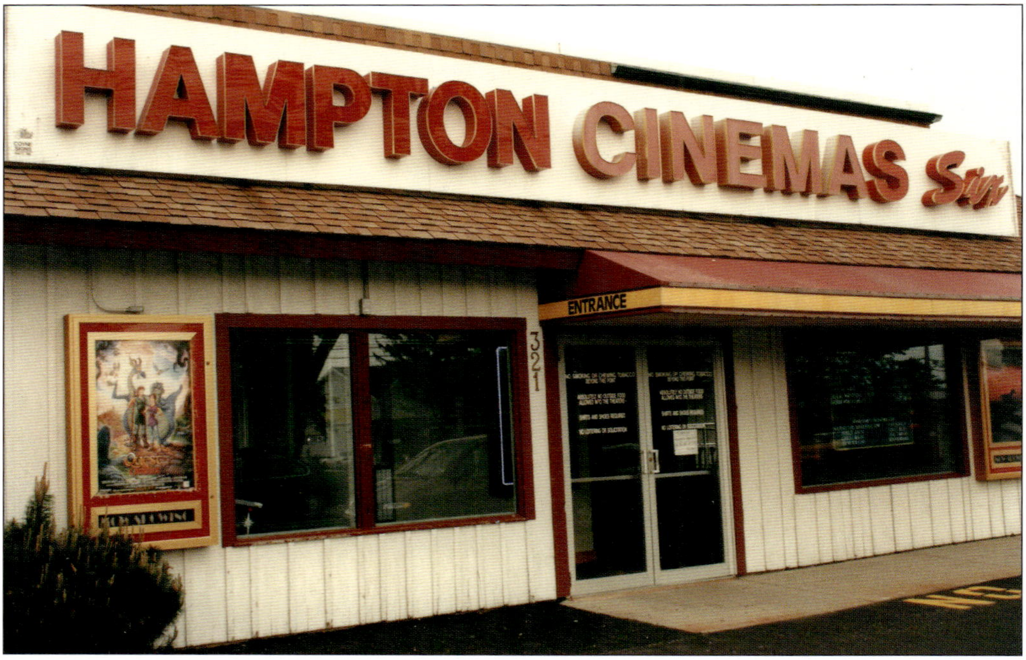

Hampton Cinemas, shown here in 1998, was in business for 29 years. It opened in 1980 and stood at 321 Lafayette Road across the street from Fast Eddie's Diner. According to an article written by Gina Carbone in the *Herald Sunday*, much of the staff and long-term patrons were "heartbroken" when the cinema closed. The front windows reveal that at the time, *Deep Impact*, *Godzilla*, *City of Angels*, *The Horse Whisperer*, and *Quest for Camelot* were showing. A CVS now stands at this location. (HHS.)

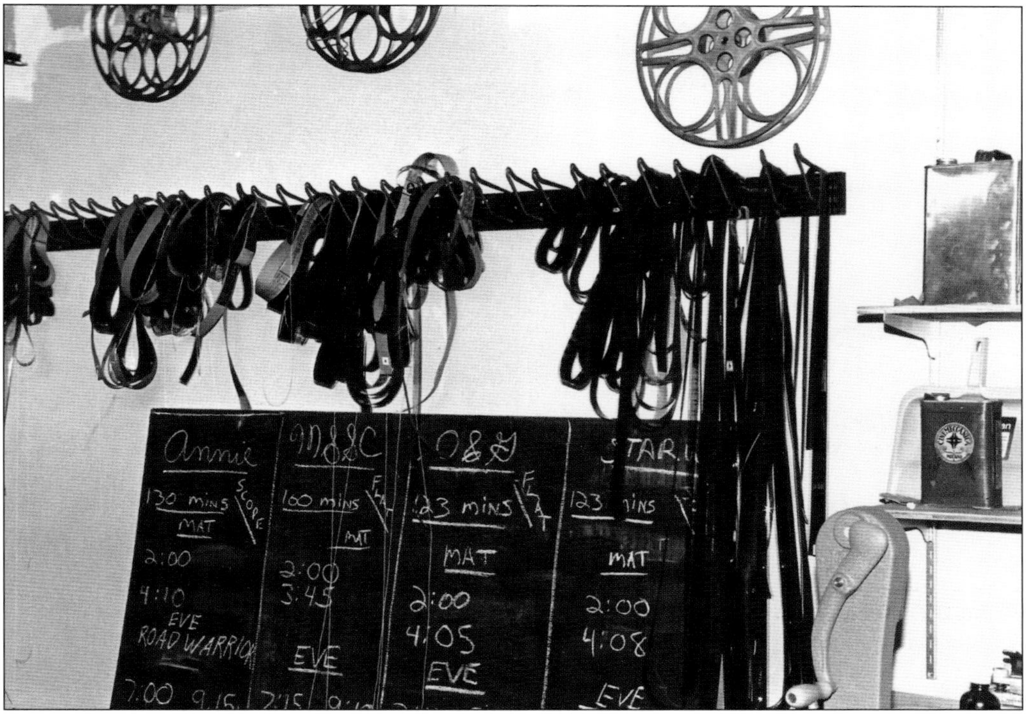

This photograph, taken in September 1982, shows the movies that Hampton Cinemas was playing that night, including *Annie*, *A Midsummer Night's Sex Comedy*, *An Officer and a Gentleman*, and *Star Trek: The Wrath of Khan*. As Gina Carbone wrote, during the last few days in 1999, the theater celebrated its time in business by offering tickets at 1980 prices. (HHS.)

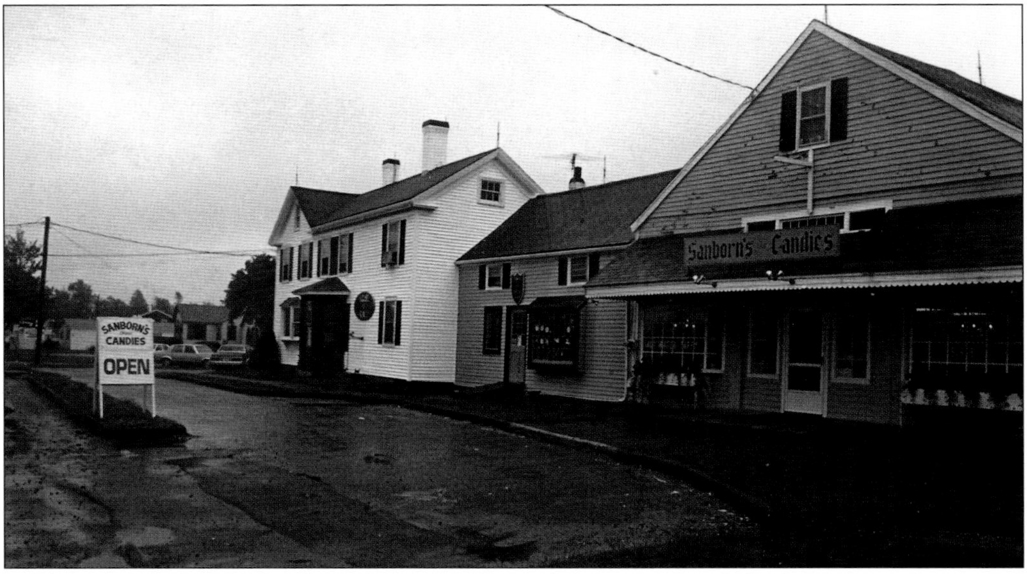

Sanborn's Fine Candies has been on Lafayette Road since 1984, and the family-owned company also has a store in the Hampton Beach Casino complex. This 1984 photograph shows where the Sanborn Candies shop was originally located on Lafayette Road, over a half mile north of Marelli Square. The new and current location is just south of the town center, close to where the Hampton Cinemas once stood. (HHS.)

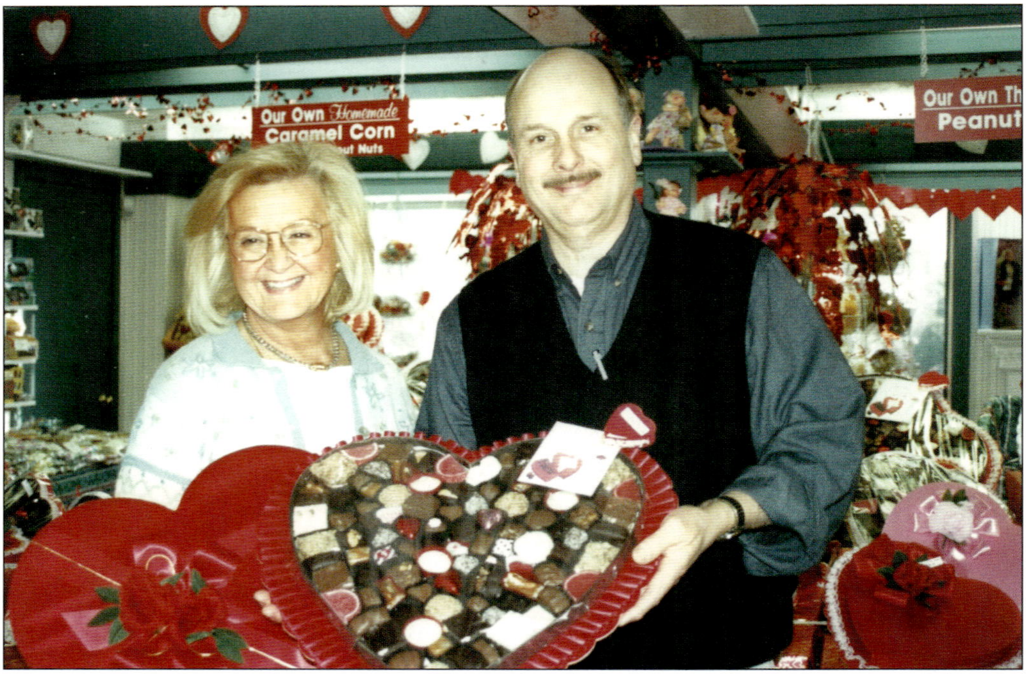

This picture, taken around Valentine's Day 1999, shows Billie and Bob Cooper holding up one of their large heart-shaped boxes filled with homemade chocolate. Sanborn's is unique because all of its candy is homemade and the company has been kept within the family since its establishment in the 1950s. Since this particular store was established, Billie Sanborn-Cooper and Robert C. Cooper have been the owners. (HHS.)

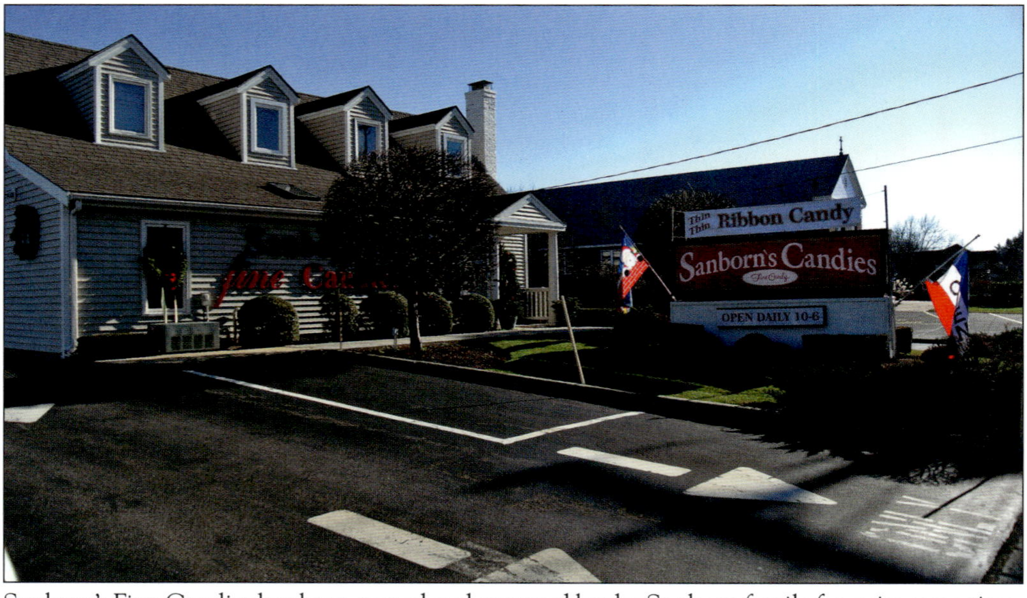

Sanborn's Fine Candies has been owned and operated by the Sanborn family for quite some time. This picture, taken in 2015, shows its current location on Lafayette Road between Our Lady of the Miraculous Medal Church and CVS. The family-owned confectionary business has always fit in well with Hampton's culture of fun and celebration, and has become even more popular since moving to this central location. (Author's collection.)

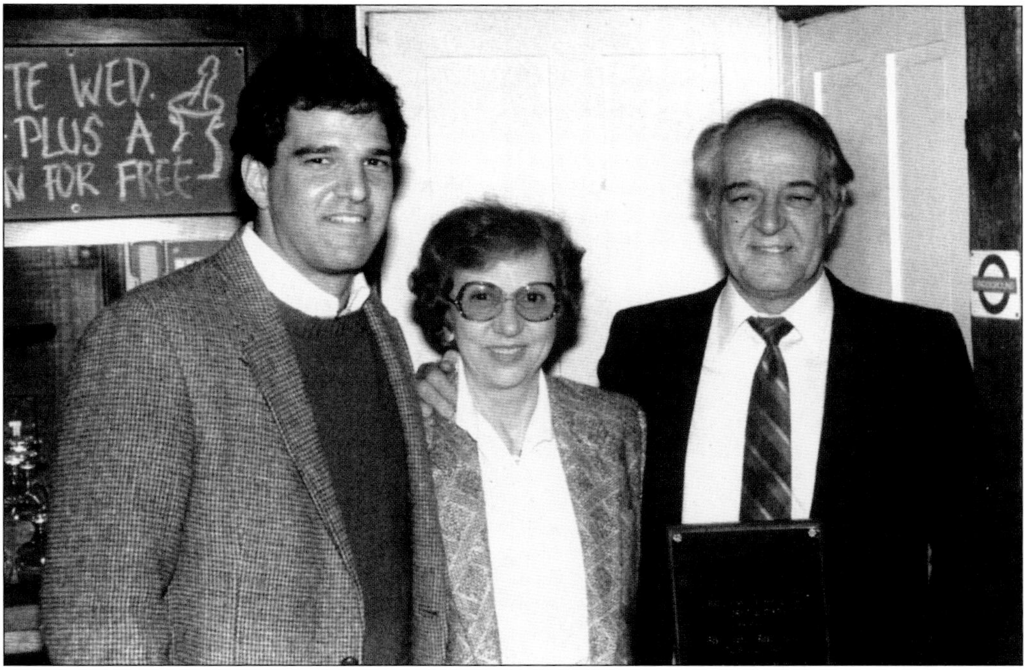

The Galley Hatch is a well-known restaurant on the corner of Lafayette and Winnacunnet Roads. In 1987, the restaurant's owners, John and Kay Tinios, received the Best Overall Restaurant Award from *Seacoast Life*. The Galley Hatch is said to serve some of the area's best seafood and always has extravagant desserts to offer its patrons. (HHS.)

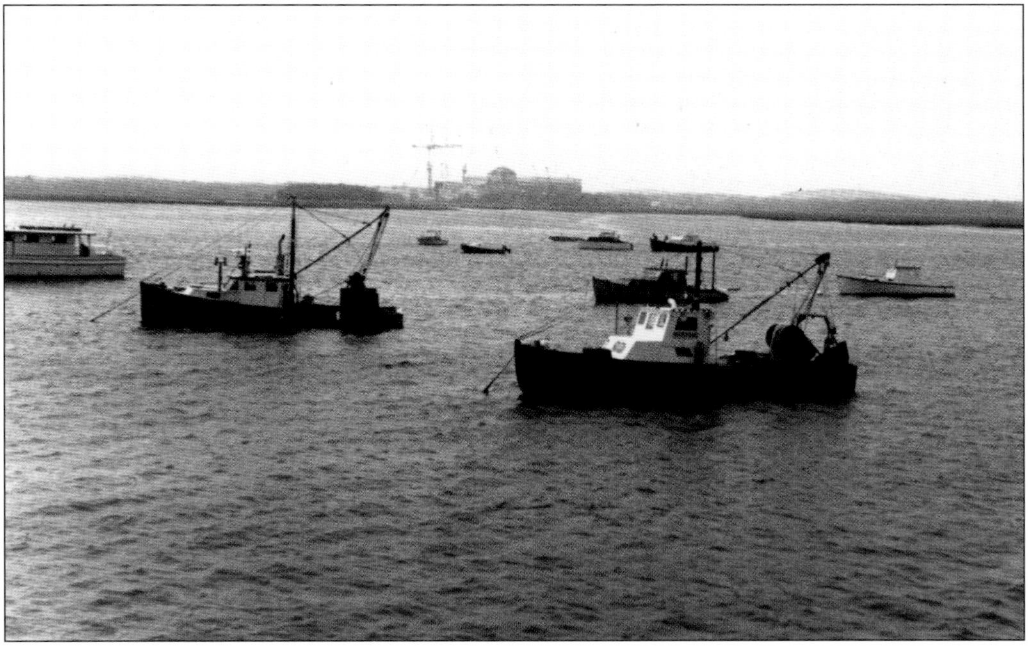

The Seabrook Station Nuclear Power Plant is located in Seabrook, just south of Hampton. The power plant can be seen here across the Hampton River and the Hampton-Seabrook Marsh. While the power plant is not actually in Hampton, it was thought it would have major implications for Hampton Beach and town residents when permission was granted to build it. (HHS.)

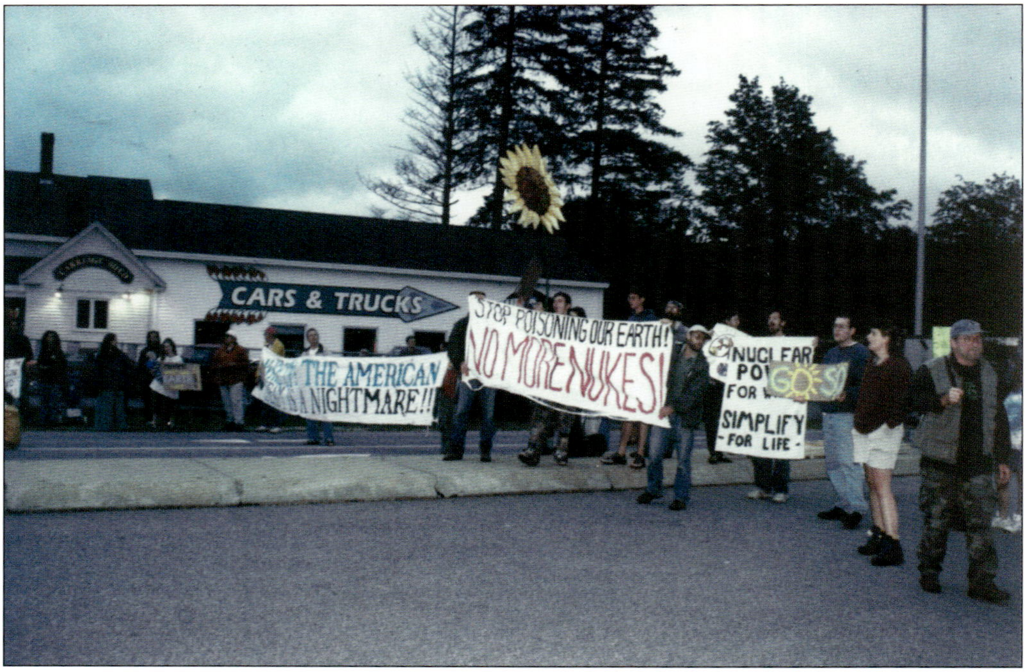

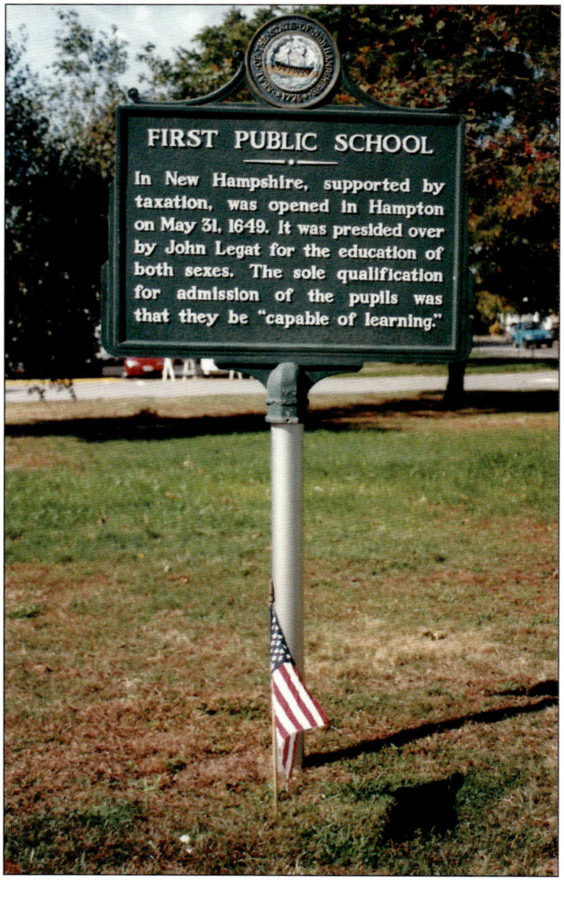

While permission was being sought to build the nuclear power plant, there was a large amount of protesting from several environmental groups as well as groups who were concerned for their safety. One of the major issues that residents were grappling with was whether or not town evacuation was feasible if something were to go wrong. One of the most controversial photographs ever taken of Hampton Beach was a product of this debate. Using a special lens, a *National Geographic* photographer made it look like the two miles between the nuclear power plant and Hampton Beach was only a few yards, perfectly capturing how many people felt about the plant. (HHS.)

This historic site sign stands on the front lawn of Hampton Centre School, a public school on Winnacunnet Road. The school is part of Hampton School District, which includes at least one other historic school. Hampton was originally settled in 1638, so it was a full 13 years before a proper school was established. The school currently offers preschool through second grade. (HHS.)

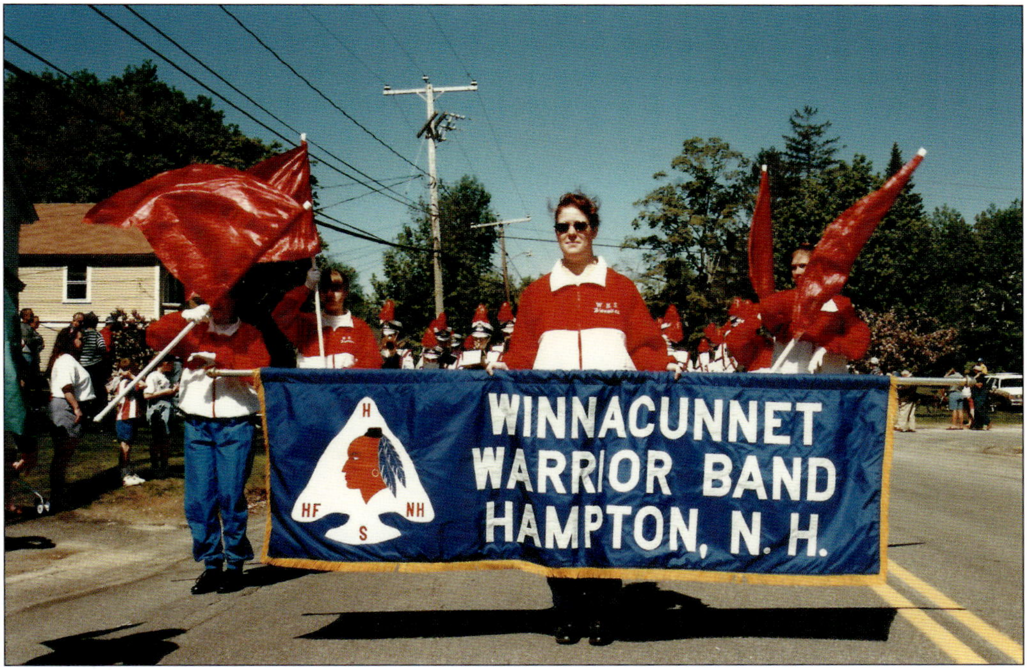

This photograph shows the Winnacunnet High School Warrior Band marching in the Memorial Day parade of 1997. The band marches in nearly every parade held in the town, and quite a few occur throughout the year. Winnacunnet is what the Native Americans had named the area later known as Hampton when the European settlers arrived in 1638. The name is said to mean "Beautiful Place of Pines." (HHS.)

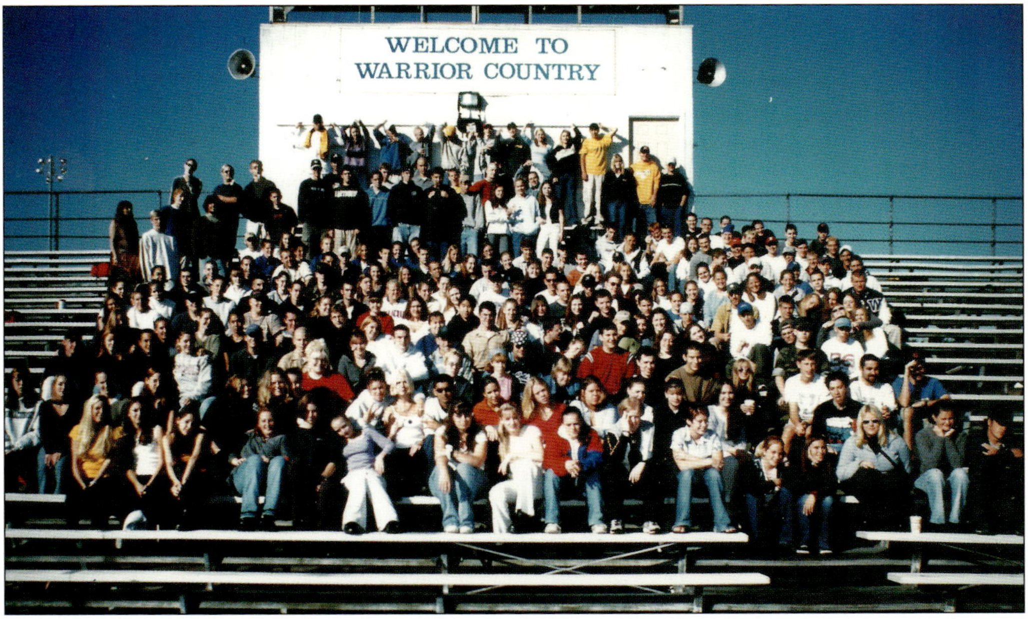

A large group of Winnacunnet High School students pose on the bleachers in front of a banner that reads, "Welcome to Warrior Country." Winnacunnet High School has a comparatively large athletic program compared to other schools in the area. It offers football, lacrosse, hockey, swimming, and many more traditional and nontraditional sports. (HHS.)

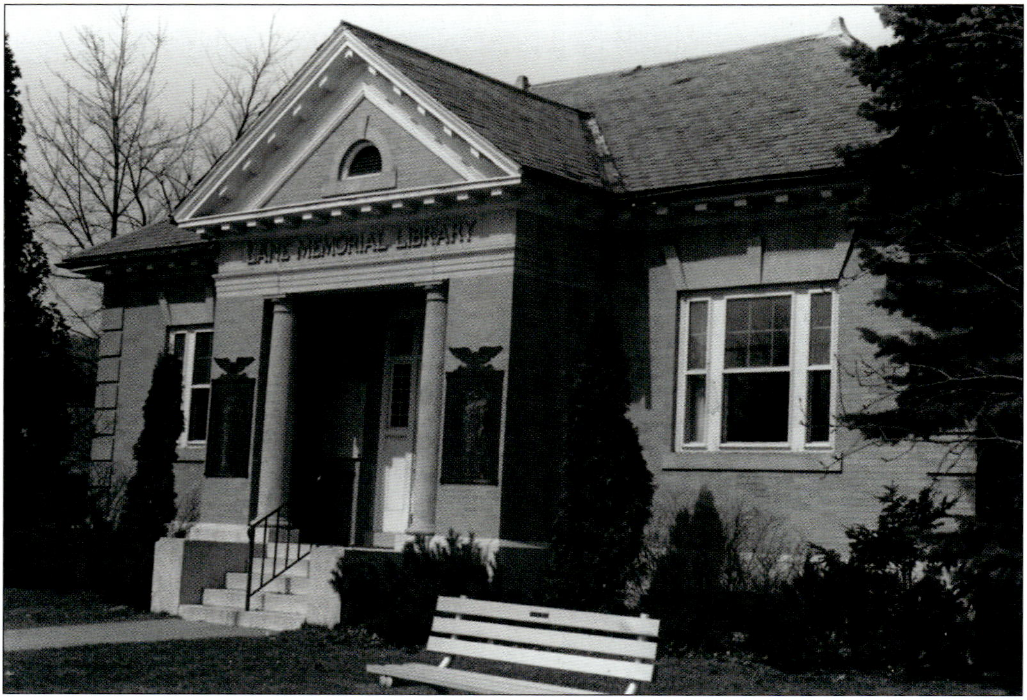

The Lane Memorial Library became a public library exactly 100 years before this picture was taken in 1981. The library received its current name in 1958 after additions and renovations were completed with funds generously donated by Howard G. Lane and his son Wheaton J. Lane. According to William Teschek, the library only endured three librarian changes in 100 years. There seemed to be the same amount of cataloguing system changes in a shorter period of time. The Lane Memorial Library is located at 2 Academy Avenue in Hampton, and the current head librarian in 2016 is Amanda L. Reynolds Cooper. (HHS.)

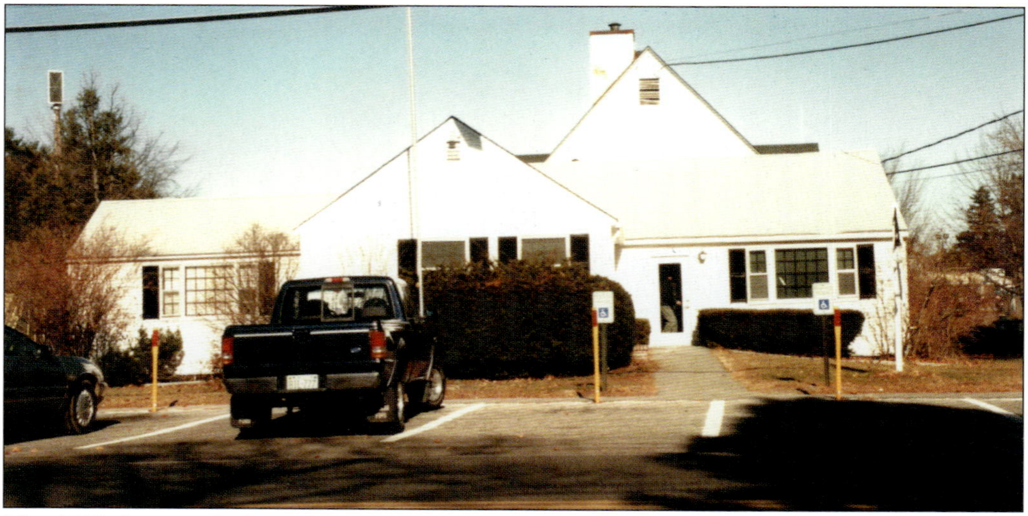

This 1997 photograph shows the Hampton Town Offices at their previous location on Winnacunnet Road. According to the Lane Memorial Library, the offices were moved in 1999 to the old Citizens Bank building next to the library. The old town office building remained vacant for several years and was demolished in 2011. (HHS.)

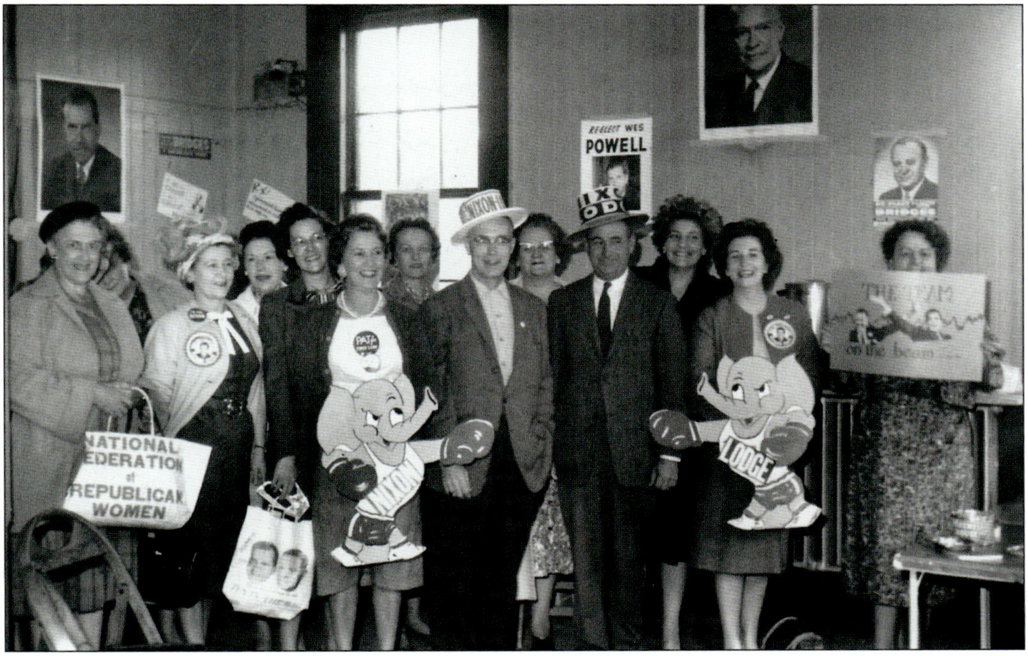

This Republican Party meeting took place in October 1960 as New Hampshire was getting ready to vote. President Eisenhower was particularly loved by some Hampton residents because he and his family had come especially to Lamie's Tavern for a meal. The identified people in this picture are Minnie Philbrook at far left, Hazel Coffin at far right, Malcolm Hamilton front and center with the white hat, Donald Ring to his left, and Edna Pearl Parr to his left. (HHS.)

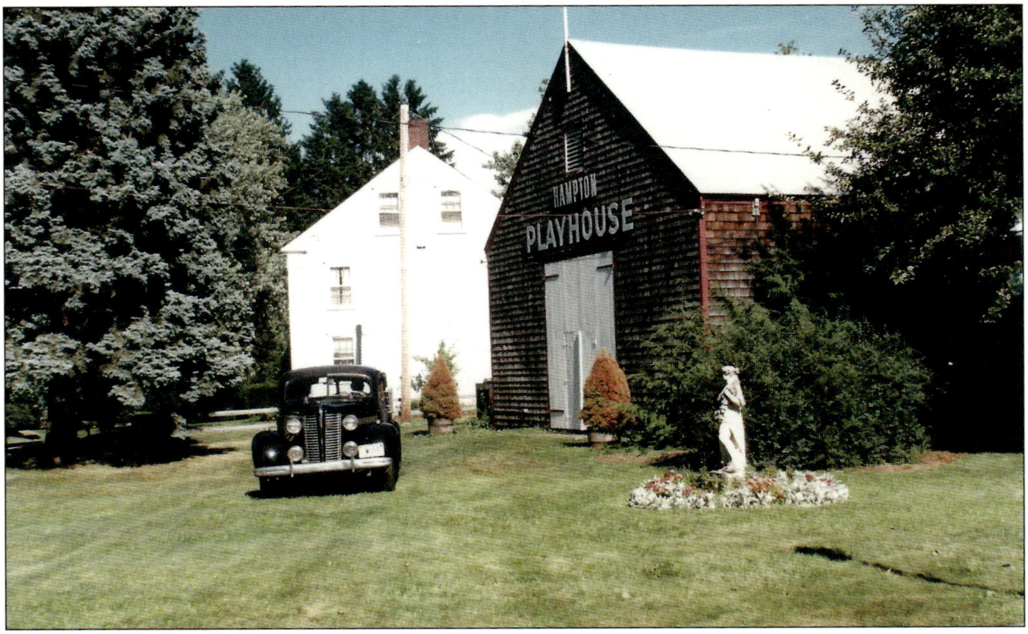

The Hampton Playhouse was a widely renowned theater in a 200-year-old remodeled barn on Winnacunnet Road. The theater was established in 1948 and put on several shows every summer for over 50 years. The barn was regarded as a cultural institution but unfortunately was demolished in 2001, even after many Hampton residents fought strongly for it to be saved. (HHS.)

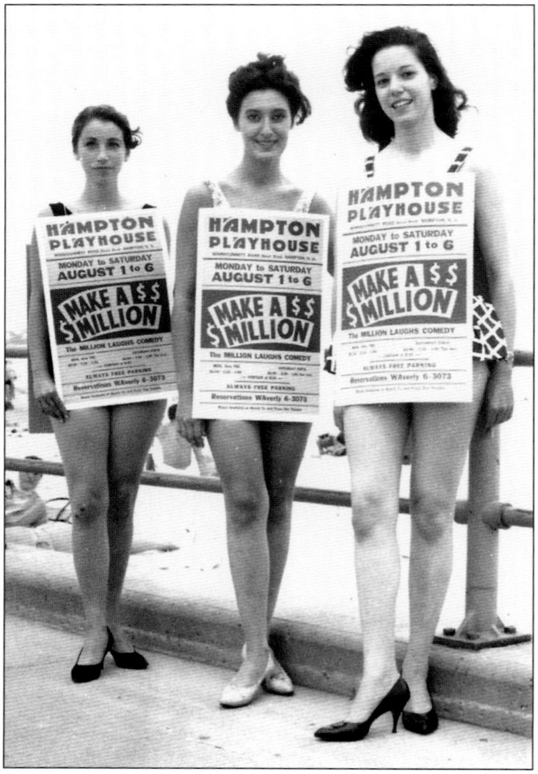

Three young women wear advertisements for an upcoming play at the Hampton Playhouse as they enjoy the sun on the seawall. When this photograph was taken in August 1960, the Hampton Playhouse, located farther inland, was already in the middle of its 12th season. What better way to end a day of relaxation and recreation than to go see the show that promises a million laughs? (HHS.)

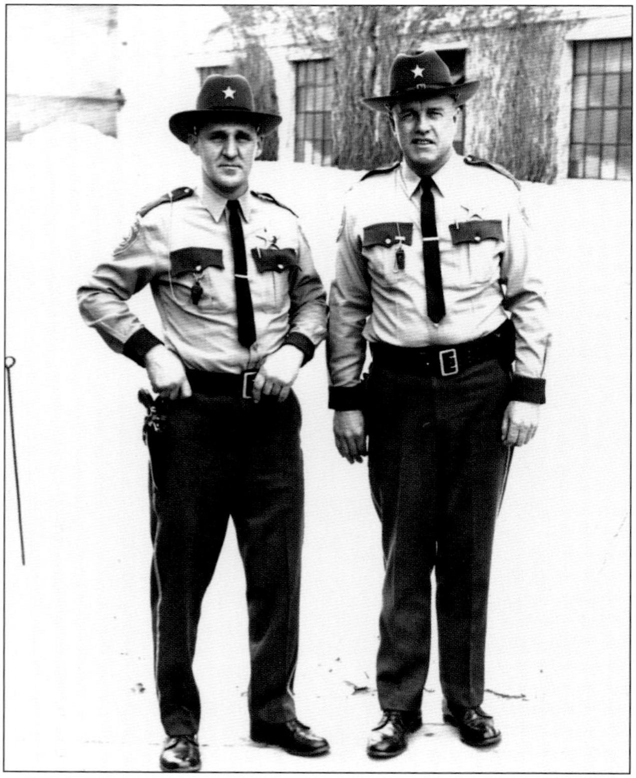

Officers George Hardheart (left) of Hampton and Mike Kirkstead of North Hampton pose for a photograph in 1960. Just four years later, Hampton police officers would face one of their toughest internal challenges. According to Randall, the 1964 Hampton Beach Riots were brought on by rebelling local youths, years of pent-up anger, and young people's dissatisfaction. By the end of it, both rioters and police officers had received numerous injuries, but somehow no one was killed. (HHS.)

This December 1997 photograph shows William "Skip" Sullivan speaking to some of his fellow firefighters. Sullivan was the Hampton fire chief from 1987 to 1999 and led the fire department in one of its greatest eras. Reporter Steve Haberman writes in an article in a 1999 *Herald Sunday*: "In some dictionary somewhere, next to the definition of a public servant, there must be a small, but detailed photograph of Hampton Fire Chief William 'Skip' Sullivan. And if there isn't, there certainly should be." (HHS.)

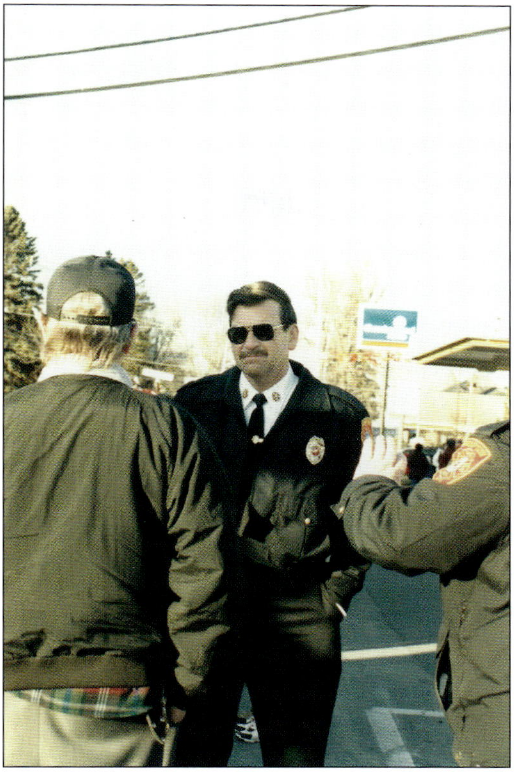

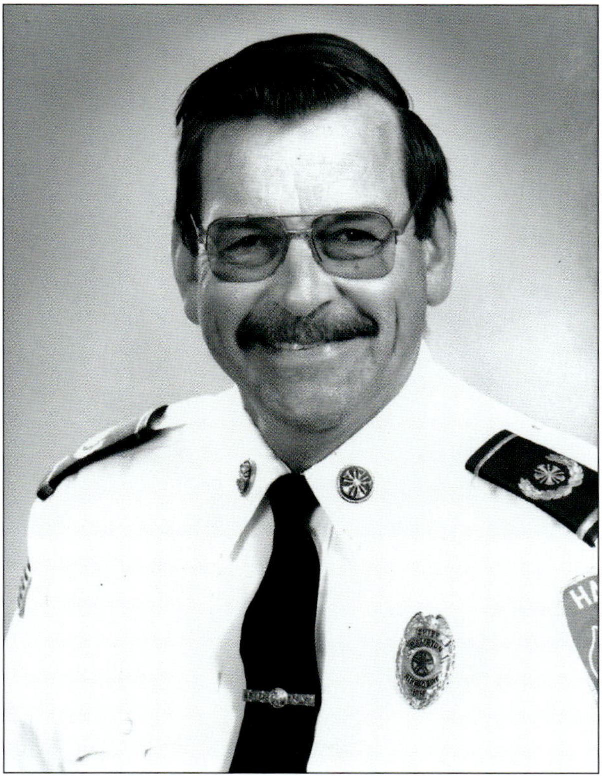

Sullivan had previously been a Hampton firefighter from the 1950s to 1977, when he resigned. He was later hired as fire chief and retired for good in 1999. The public opinion was that his retirement would be the end of an era. According to the Steve Haberman article, not only was Sullivan one of the best leaders the fire department ever had, he was also a community leader who always aimed to solve a problem, not to assign blame. (HHS.)

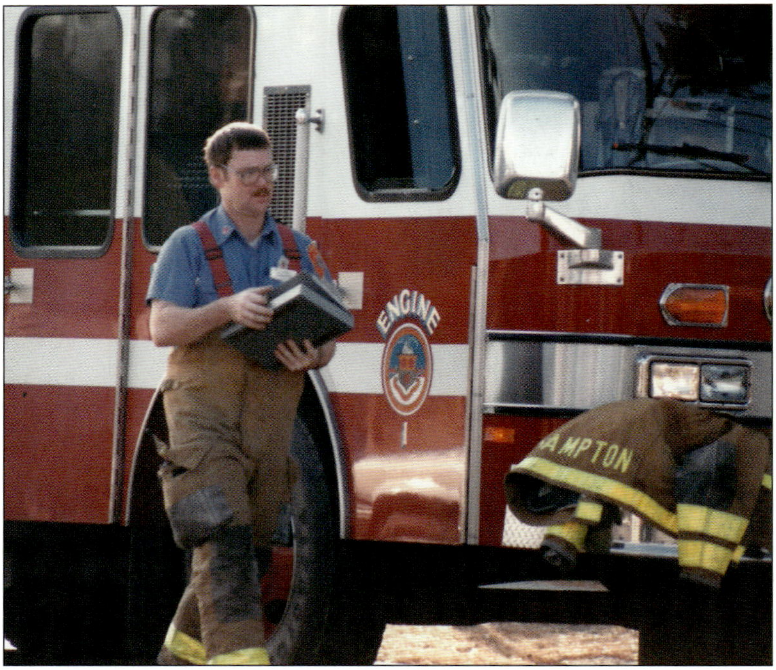

A Hampton firefighter walks next to Hampton's Engine 1 fire truck. The vast majority of businesses and buildings on Ocean Boulevard were constructed of wood and were always bustling with activity. According to the *Herald Sunday*, "the nature of the summer tourist season makes each fire, however small, a potential disaster." (HHS.)

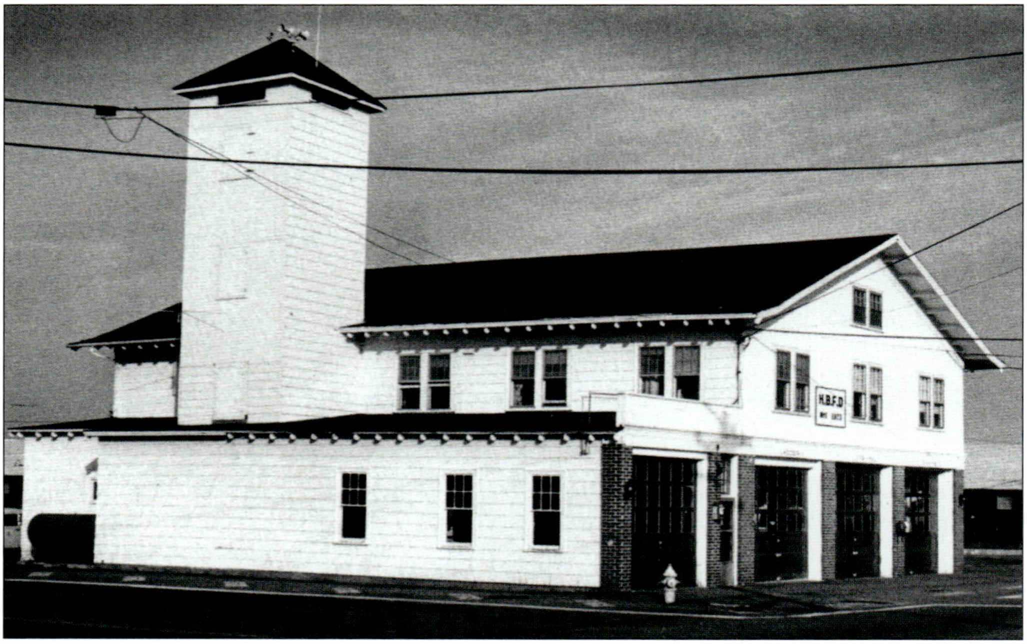

The Hampton Beach Fire Department was originally built in 1923 on the corner of Brown and Ashworth Avenues, directly across from the rear entrance of the Casino Ballroom. This photograph was taken in 1960 when the building and tower were already beginning to look worn. The fire station was finally torn down over 50 years later, in 2013, after a new station was completed just behind it on Brown Avenue. According to an article by Nick B. Reid in the *Hampton Union*, the retired firefighters had mixed emotions about the old station's demolition, with many feeling like it was long overdue. Hampton Fire Department operates out of two buildings, one on Brown Avenue and the other in town on Winnacunnet Road. (HHS.)

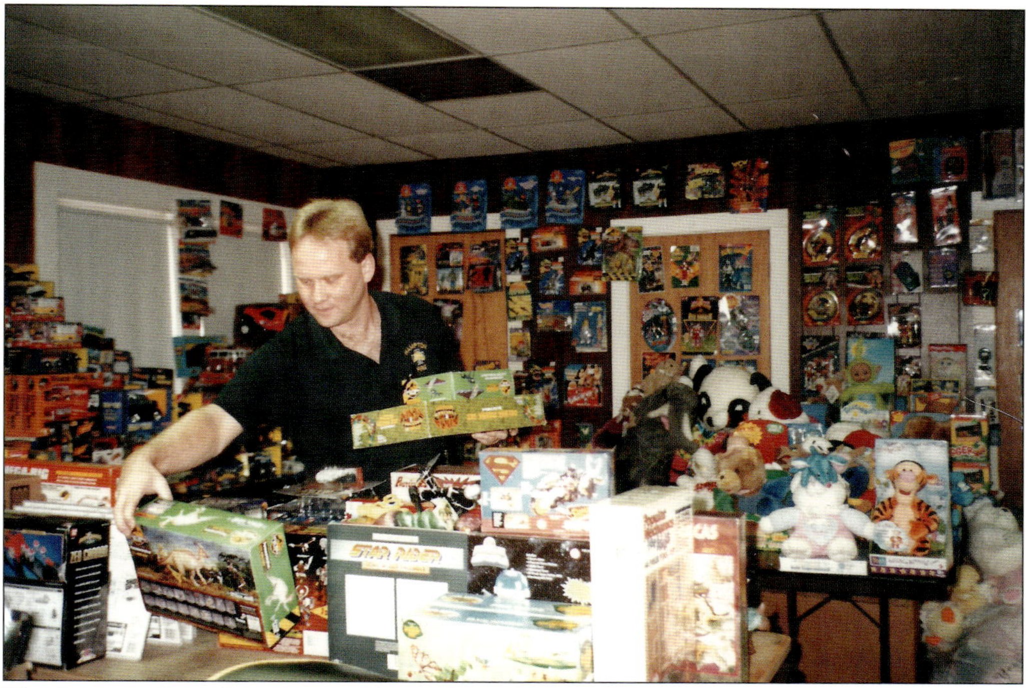

The Seacoast Firefighters Toy Bank is run by firefighters from several seacoast stations, including the Hampton and Seabrook Fire Departments. This photograph was taken at the old fire department on the beach. According to a 2002 article in the *Hampton Union*, the organization aims to provide gifts for children who would not be spending Christmas at home, whether it was because they were in a hospital or had lost a home due to fire or other reasons. (HHS.)

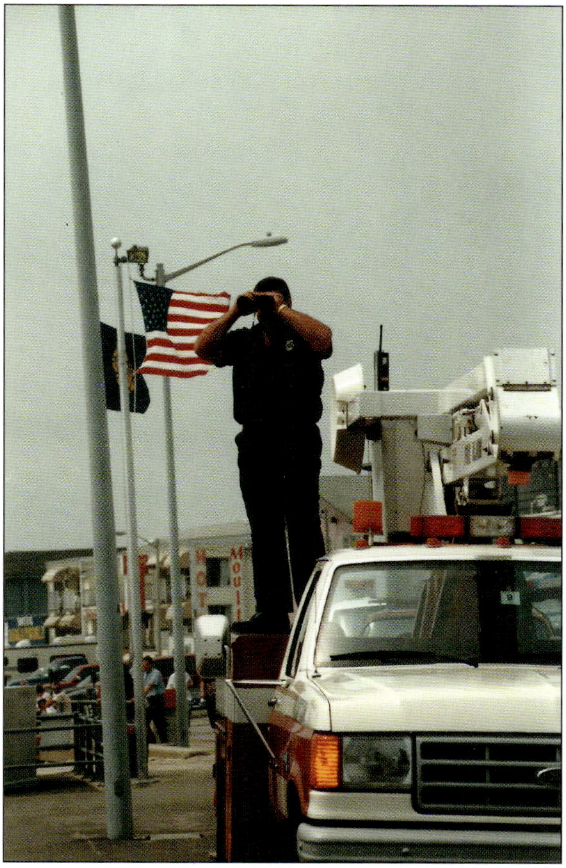

A firefighter stands on a Hampton emergency vehicle during a search-and-rescue mission in 1999. During missions like this, the Hampton Fire Department, Hampton Beach State Park staff and lifeguards, and sometimes even other state employees work together to achieve a successful rescue or to complete a recovery. (HHS.)

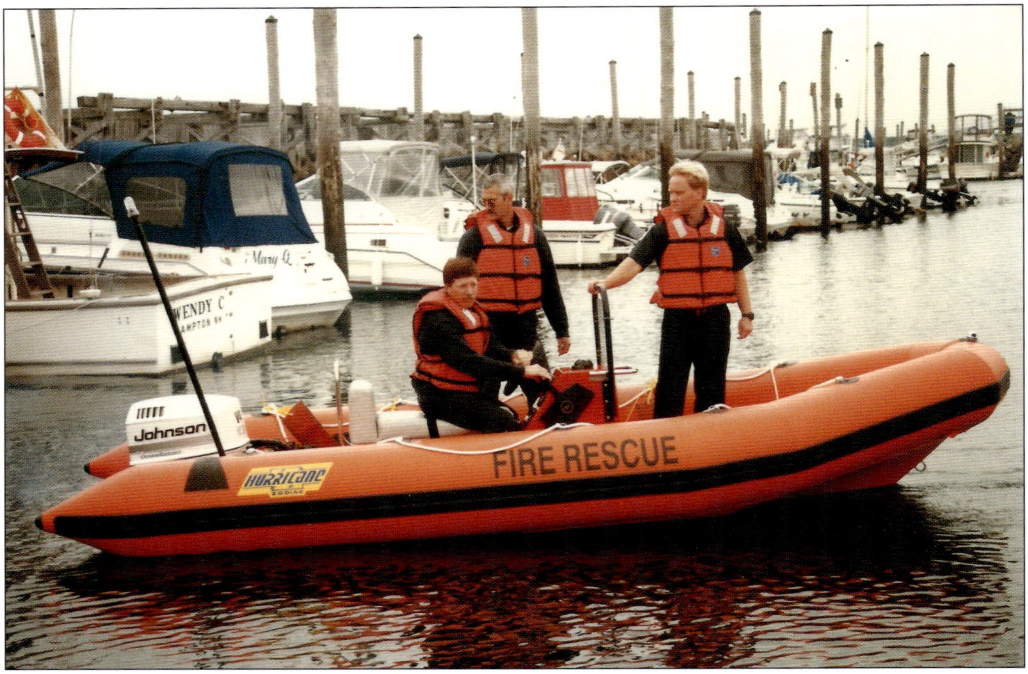

Three Hampton firefighters use the town's search and rescue raft in Hampton Harbor. The harbor connects to the Hampton River and sits just behind the beach community near the Hampton-Seabrook Marsh. Hampton firefighters are highly trained in water rescue and often work with Hampton Beach State Park lifeguards. (HHS.)

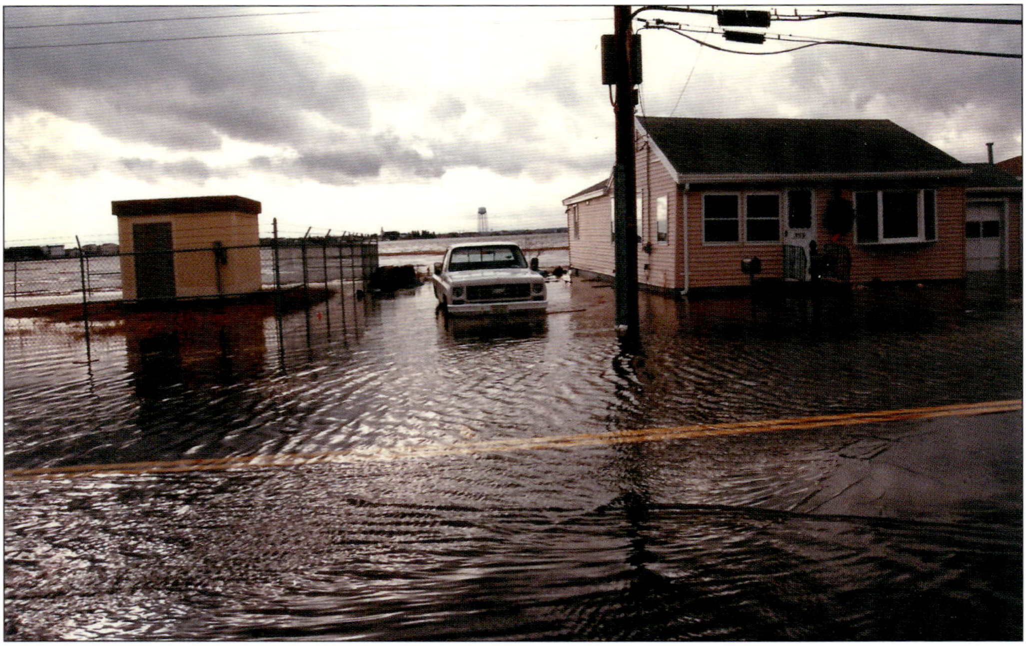

This picture shows a home and the surrounding lot being flooded by the Hampton River and the Hampton-Seabrook Marsh. Flooding happens throughout the year, with the worst floods occurring in the winter and the spring. The Hampton Beach Water Tower, an iconic structure, can be seen across the water in the background. (HHS.)

Five

The Master Plan and the New Seashell Complex

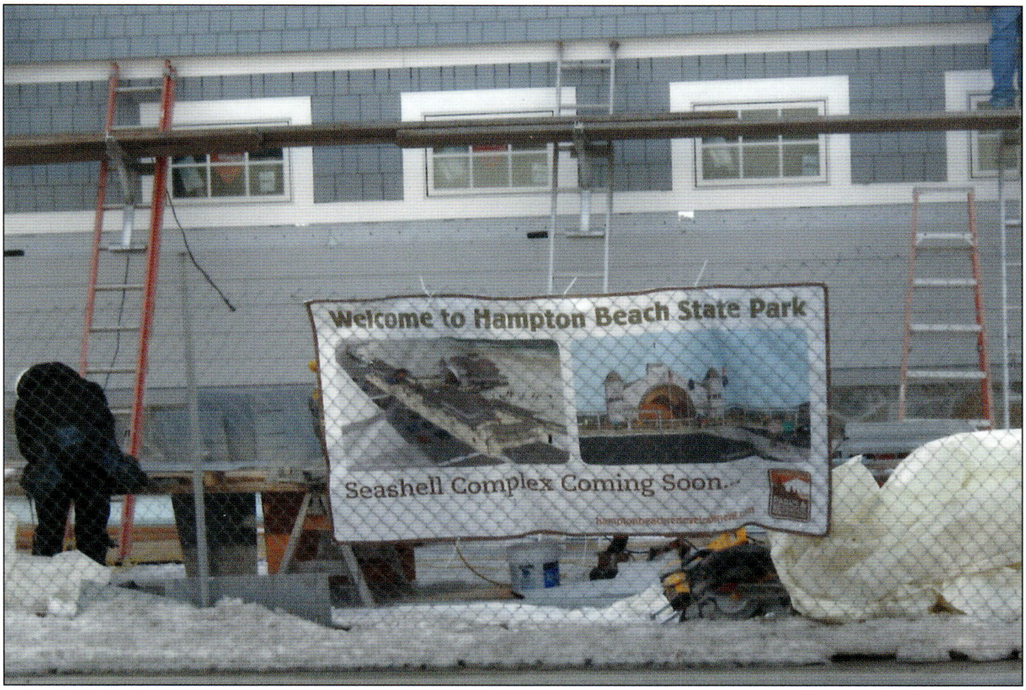

In 2010, plans for a new Seashell Complex and Hampton Beach center were put into action. This rough sign of what was to come reads, "Welcome to Hampton Beach State Park, Seashell Complex Coming Soon . . ." After the 99-year lease to the Hampton Beach Improvement Company expired in 1997, development rights for the beach reverted back to the town. In response to this, the Hampton Beach Area Master Plan was drafted in 2001 to continue the development of the beach. Through a partnership between the New Hampshire Department of Resources and Economic Development, the Town of Hampton, and the New Hampshire Office of Energy and Planning, the master plan was drafted to lay out the next 50 years of beach development and improvement. (DRED.)

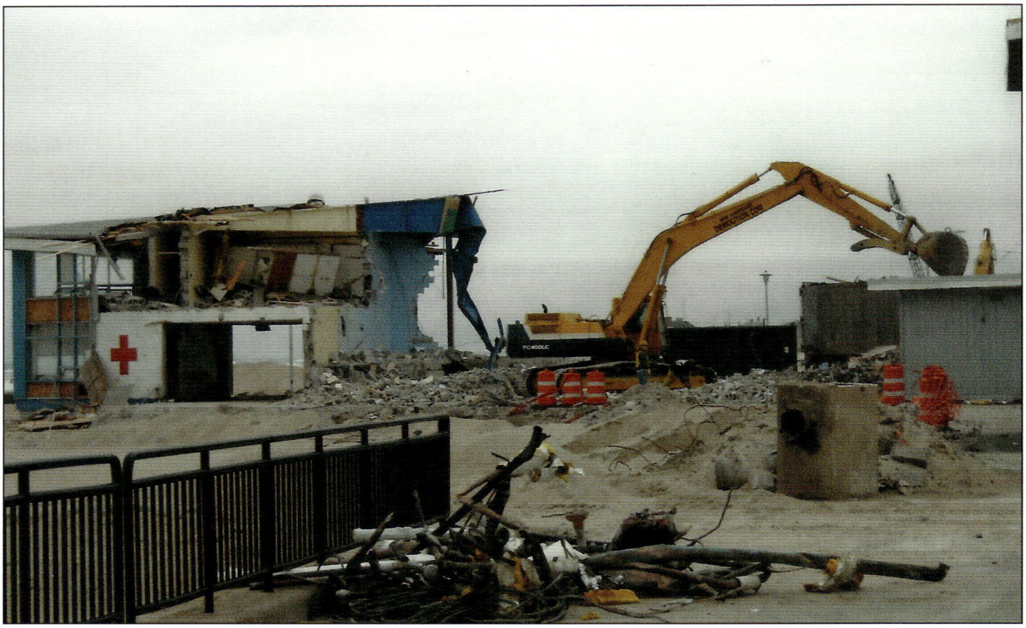

In October 2010, demolition of the old Seashell Complex began. The 1962 complex was beginning to show its age after nearly 50 years of wear and tear from storms, sand, and the salty sea air. According to an article by Patrick Cronin in the *Hampton Union*, people were sad to see the old Seashell torn down because it was a landmark. However, most people were glad that the beach facilities were being improved. (DRED.)

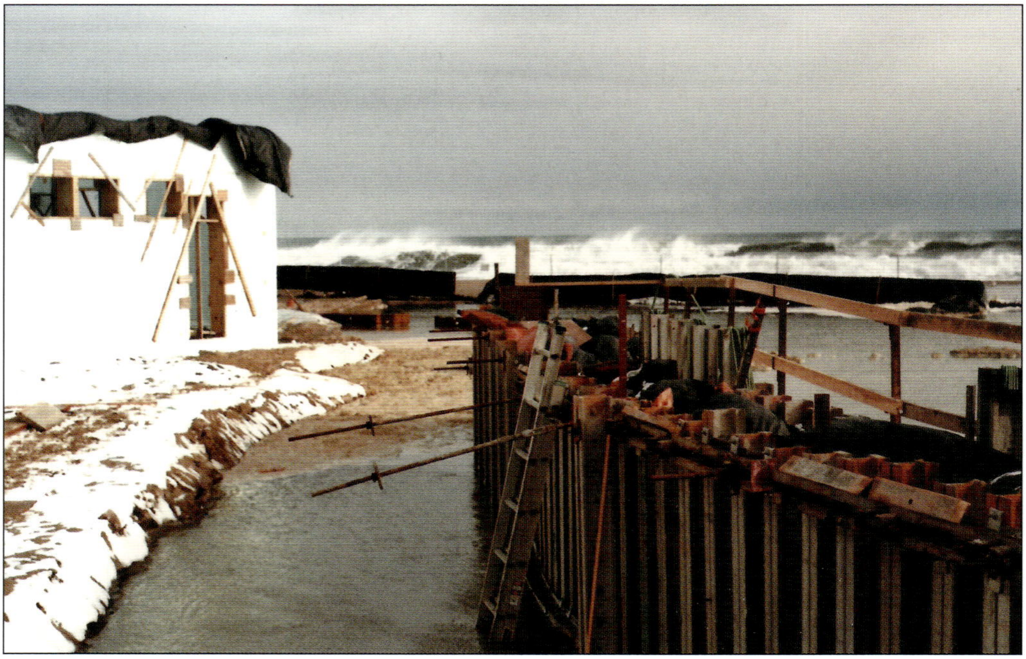

Even while construction was fully underway in December 2010, the seacoast's erratic weather still greatly affected Hampton Beach. During an incredibly high tide, the entire construction site flooded. The water would normally seep into the ground, but it was so cold that the ground was frozen solid and the water had nowhere to go. (DRED.)

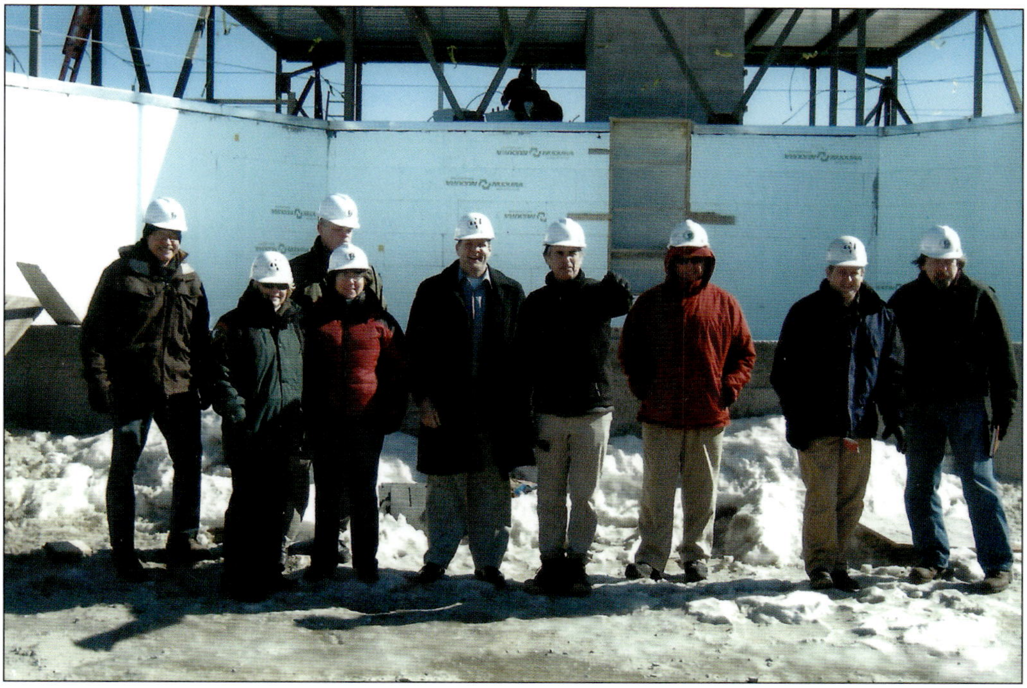

Taken in 2010, this picture shows many of the leaders of the Hampton Beach Redevelopment Project. Included are planners, architects, and construction workers. They are, from left to right, Tom Mansfield, Gail Wolek, Mike Housman, Johanna Lyons, Chris Sununu, Ward D'Elia, Roger Dionne, Chris Nikias, and Gary Bashline. This particular day was especially frigid, and everyone who had to sit on the girders recalls being absolutely miserable. (DRED.)

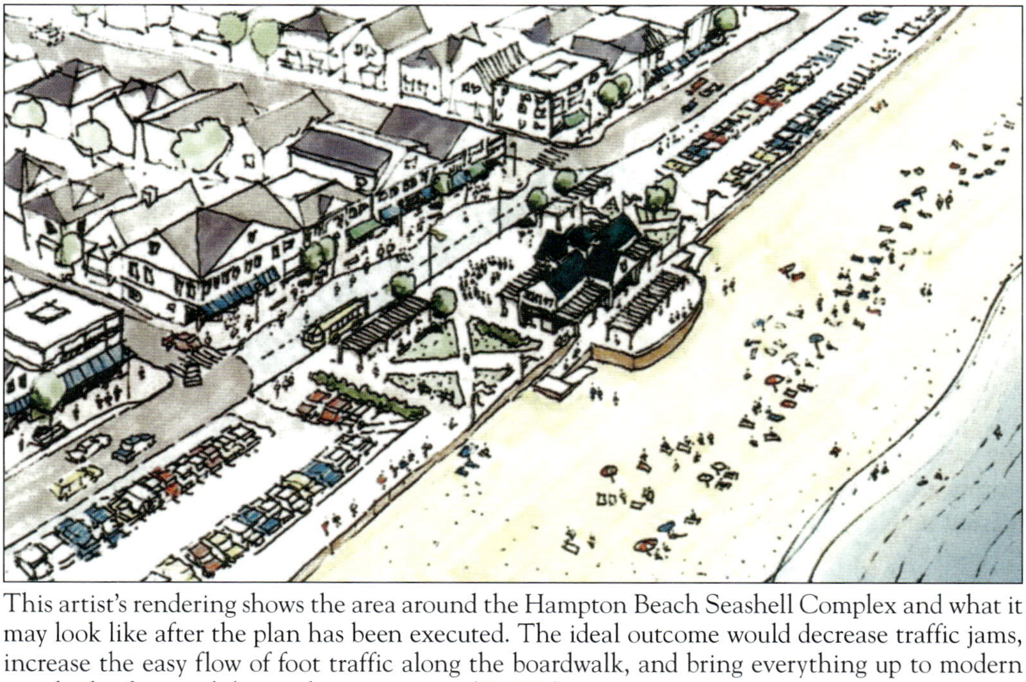

This artist's rendering shows the area around the Hampton Beach Seashell Complex and what it may look like after the plan has been executed. The ideal outcome would decrease traffic jams, increase the easy flow of foot traffic along the boardwalk, and bring everything up to modern standards of accessibility and convenience. (DRED.)

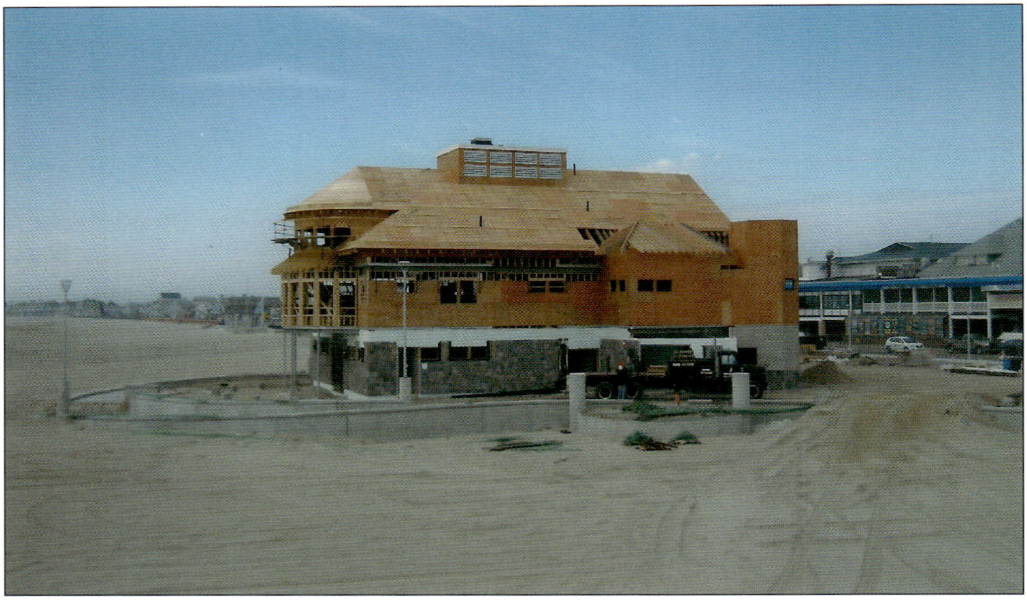

Construction for the new Seashell Complex began at the beginning of 2011. This picture, looking south from the watch station, gives an interesting perspective of the new complex. When complete, it will have an easy ramp system that allows for quick and simple transportation between sandy beach and the boardwalk. On the right of the building, facing the boardwalk, is the new Seashell stage. (DRED.)

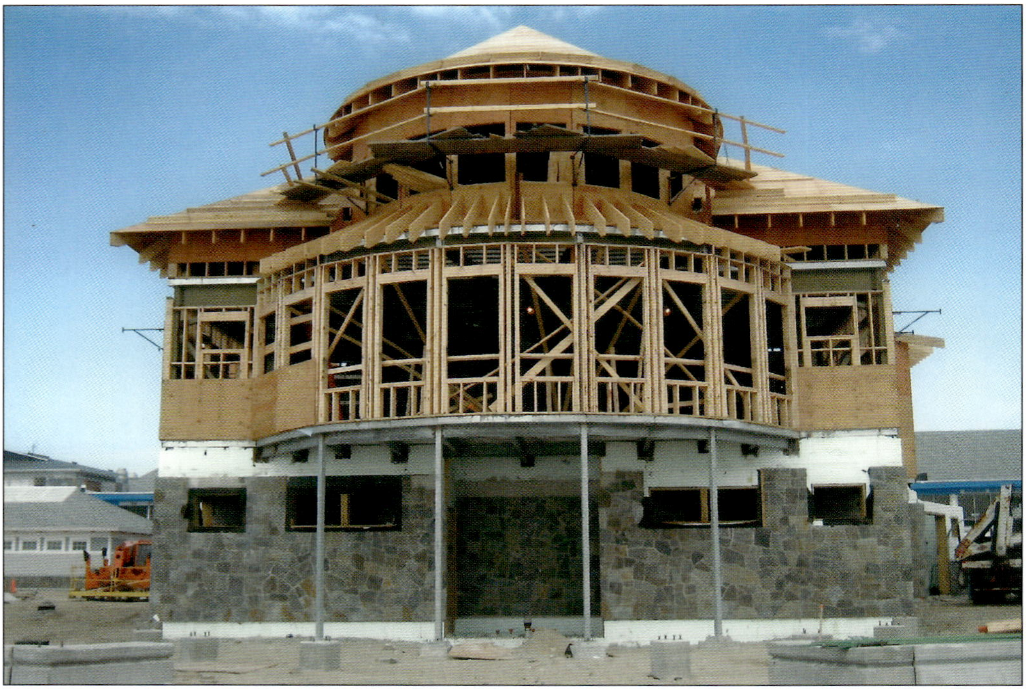

This picture of the new Seashell Complex under construction looks west into what will become the conference room. The room will have a circular wall of windows that will provide amazing views of the beach, as well as of the coast to the north and south of the beach center. The top floor will serve as the lifeguard office and can be used as a sort of watchtower. (DRED.)

Gordon Carlisle is a well-known local artist who specializes in creating indoor and outdoor murals. Here, he is working on a mural in the conference room in the new Seashell Complex in November 2011. This particular mural includes images of the beach, the marshes, the sand dunes, and many other scenes that represent different periods of Hampton Beach history. (DRED.)

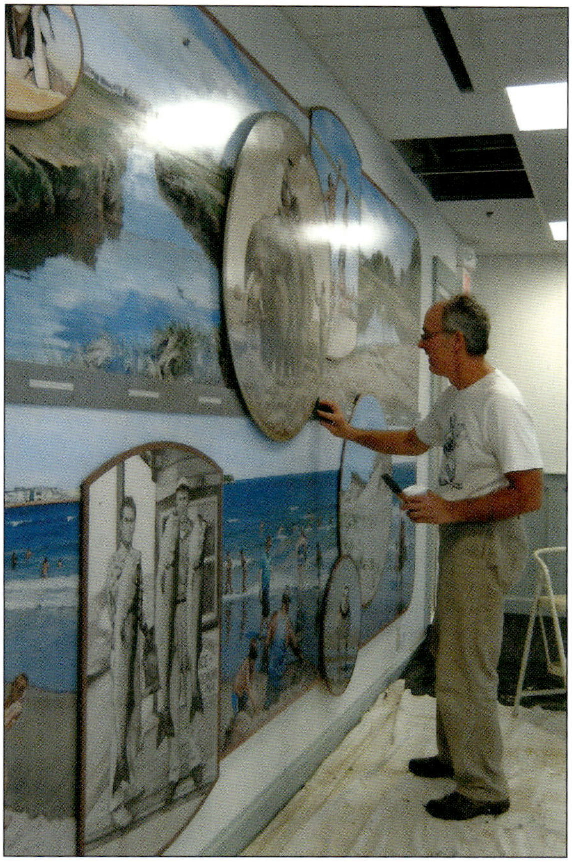

These fish sculptures were installed all along the boardwalk at Hampton Beach in November 2011. This particular statue is very near the playground. Standing around the fish sculpture are, from left to right, Thomas Berger, the artist; Tom George, a representative of DRED; and Randy Duquette, a representative of DRED in the Division of Parks and Recreation. (DRED.)

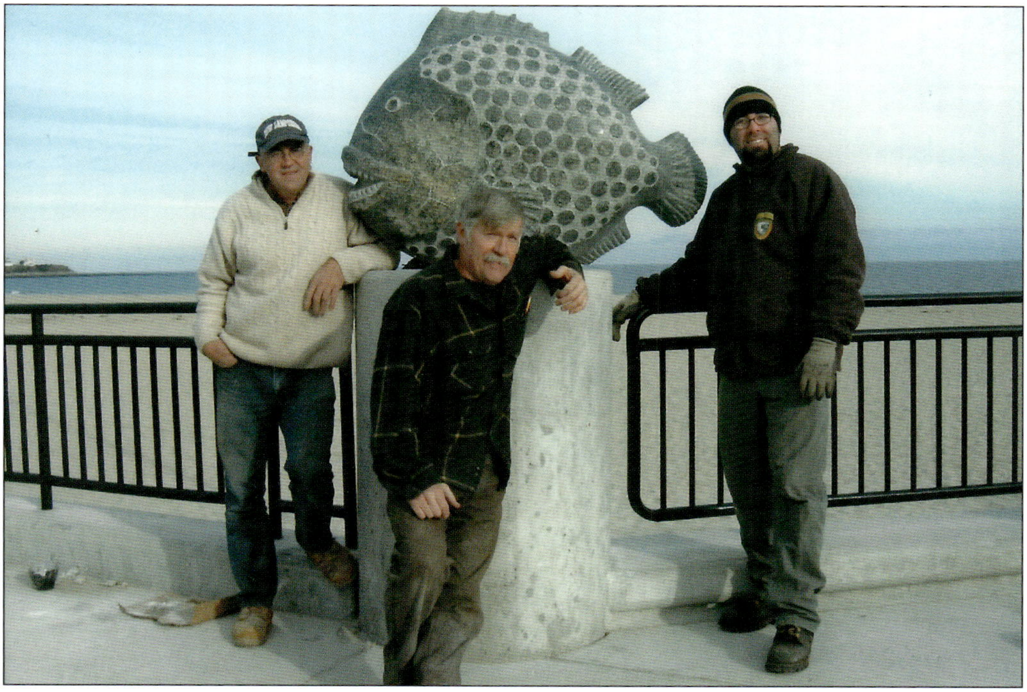

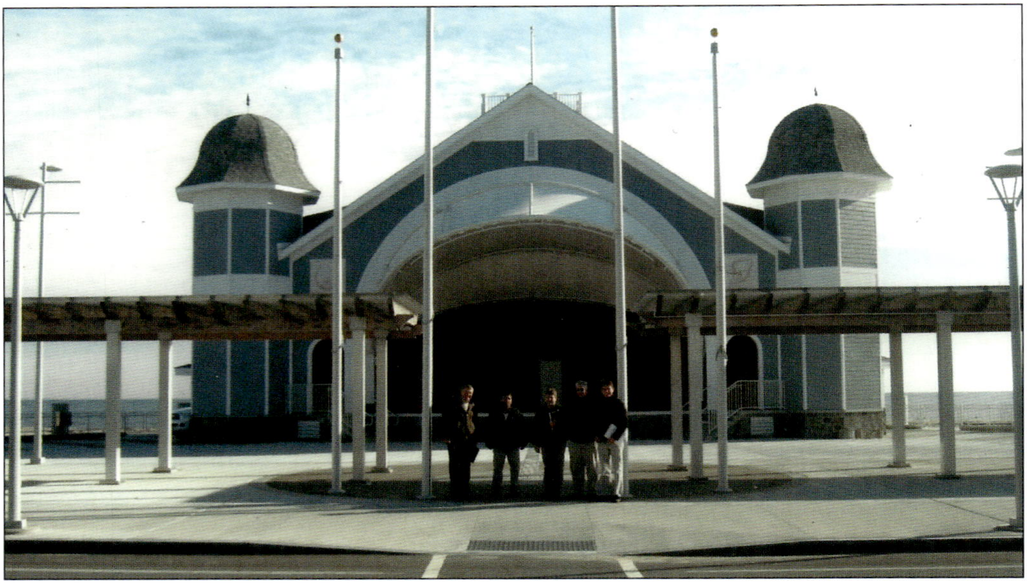

This view of the new Hampton Beach Seashell Complex looks directly at the Seashell stage and east toward the ocean. Like its predecessor, this stage is designed for open-air shows. The towers on either side of the stage were built with the bell-shaped roofs to pay tribute to the bandstand that was originally built on the site in 1901. Standing in front of the stage is part of the Hampton Beach Redevelopment Planning team. From left to right are Tom Mansfield of DRED, Bill Conte and Chris Nikias of Harvey Construction, Roger Dionne of Public Works, and Ward D'Elia of Samyn-D'Elia Architects. (DRED.)

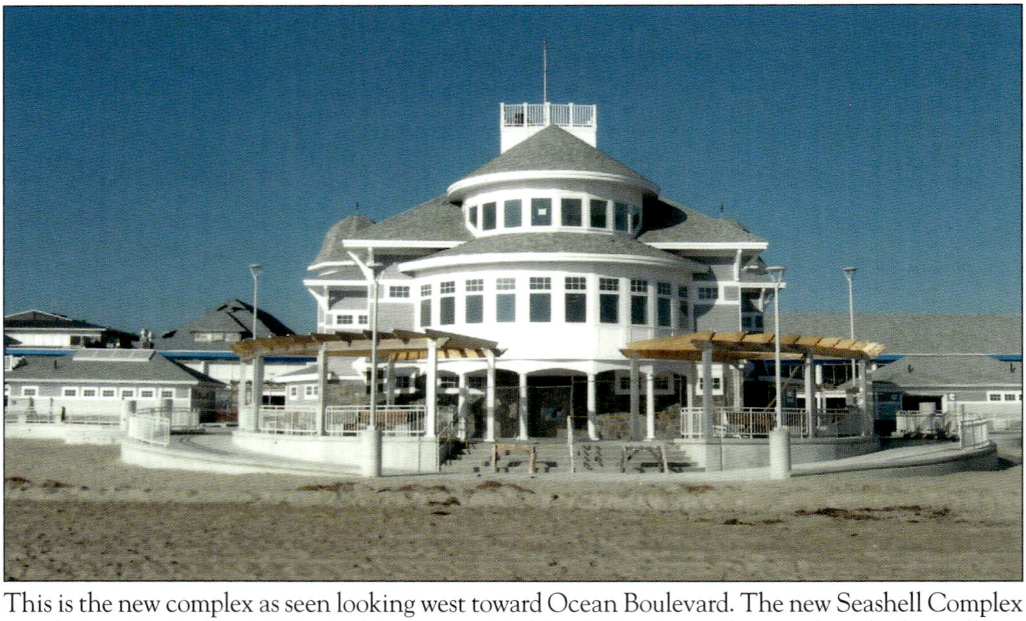

This is the new complex as seen looking west toward Ocean Boulevard. The new Seashell Complex was designed by Samyn-D'Elia Architects out of Ashland, New Hampshire, and was built on almost exactly the same footprint as the original, with the center stage and the pavilions on either side. The extensive ramp system shown here allows for easy access to and from the beach. The new Seashell Complex is just one small step in the Hampton Beach Area Master Plan to continue to improve the beach. (DRED.)

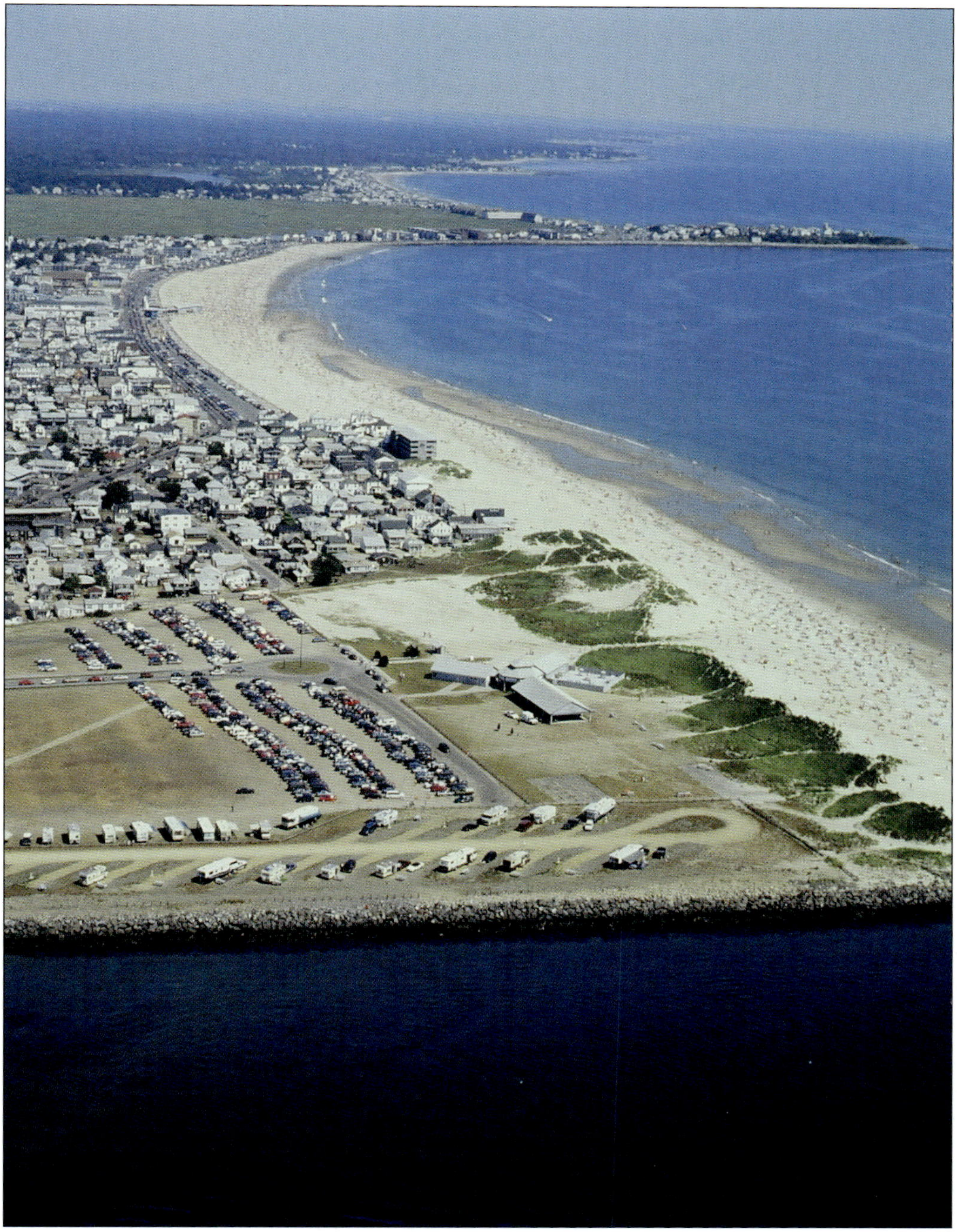

This aerial photograph of Hampton Beach shows the entire stretch—from south beach where the State Bathhouse used to stand all the way north to Great Boar's Head, which reaches out into the ocean. This picture affords an excellent view of Route 1A, also known as Ocean Boulevard. This road more or less follows the entirety of New Hampshire's 18 miles of coastline, and is one of the most beautiful drives in the state. In his 1843 poem "Hampton Beach," John Greenleaf Whittier reflected the feelings of all those who vacation at the beach: "Good by to pain and care! I take Mine ease to-day: Here where these sunny waters break, And ripples this keen breeze, I shake All burdens from the heart, all weary thoughts away." (HHS.)

Discover Thousands of Local History Books Featuring Millions of Vintage Images

Arcadia Publishing, the leading local history publisher in the United States, is committed to making history accessible and meaningful through publishing books that celebrate and preserve the heritage of America's people and places.

Find more books like this at
www.arcadiapublishing.com

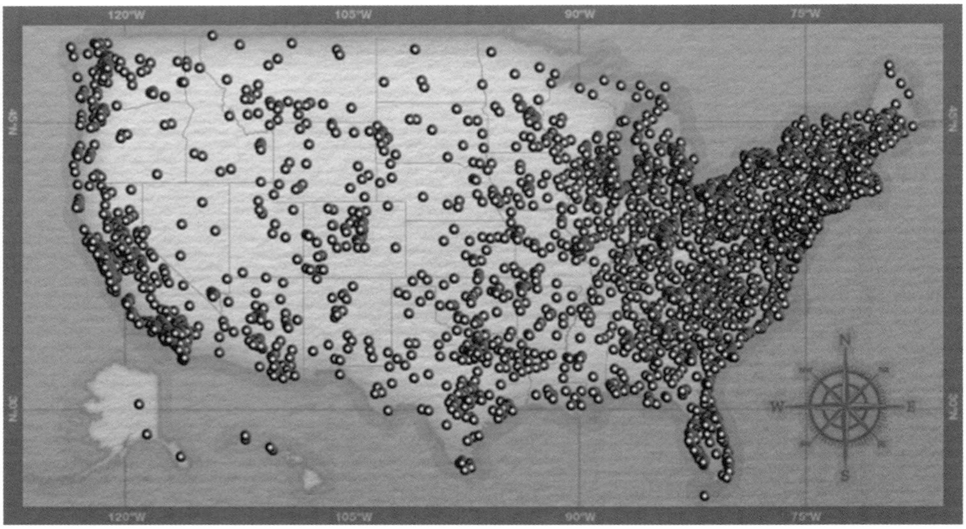

Search for your hometown history, your old stomping grounds, and even your favorite sports team.

Consistent with our mission to preserve history on a local level, this book was printed in South Carolina on American-made paper and manufactured entirely in the United States. Products carrying the accredited Forest Stewardship Council (FSC) label are printed on 100 percent FSC-certified paper.

MADE IN THE USA